GOD'S SPECIAL AGENTS

Modern missionary heroes
from the two-thirds world

BY JOHN LINDNER

GOD'S SPECIAL AGENTS

Copyright © 2003
Christian Aid Mission
First printing 2003

All Scripture quotations are quoted from the King

All rights reserved. No part of this book may be reproduced in any form, except for brief quotations in a review article, without permission from the author or publisher.

Published by:
Christian Aid Mission
1201 5th Street Ext.
Charlottesville, VA 22902
www.christianaid.org
info@christianaid.org

Cover design by John Lindner Jr.

ISBN 0-9741325-1-9
Library of Congress Control Number 2003093334

Printed in the USA by
Plus Publishing
St. Louis, Missouri

Contents

Foreword by Dr. Bob Finley 5

About the Author 7

Acknowledgements 9

1. Why the Fuss Over Indigenous Missions? .. 11
   A brief review of the rise and development of the indigenous missions movement and its implications for missions today

2. The Reluctant Preacher 19
   Alley Gonzalez and Agape Evangelistic Mission, Philippines

3. Warrior for the Lord 41
   Luis Alberto Guerrero and the Lord's Vineyard of Colombia

4. Carving a Stone Mountain 57
   P.M. Thomas and Himalaya Evangelical Mission (formerly Kashmir Evangelical Fellowship), India

5. The Galloping Horse of North India 75
   P.G. Vargis and the Indian Evangelical Team, India

6. Vision for Mission 93
   William Johnson and the Pakistan Gospel Assemblies

7. Pentecost Revisited 109
   Silas Owiti and Voice of Salvation in East Africa

8. Outfoxing the Witch Doctors 133
   Cebien Alexis and Army of Christ in Haiti

9. The Goldfish and the Whale 159
   Paul Pang and Schools for Christ, Hong Kong

10. The Sadhu's Legacy 175
    P.J. Thomas and Sharon Fellowship, India

11. Church Planter Extraordinaire 191
    Rizzy Montes and Living Rock Ministries in the Philippines

12. He Danced with Angels 205
    Subhang Sodemba and Himalaya Crusade, India

13. Undoing Goliath 227
    Vasily Boyechko and Good Samaritan Mission in Ukraine
    and former Soviet Union

14. Appendix: Letter to Gorbachev 267
    Letter from the Underground Churches of the Soviet
    Union to Mikhail Gorbachev

15. About Christian Aid 285

Foreword

by Dr. Bob Finley

For 50 years Christian Aid has been helping indigenous missions led by men of God who at great sacrifice have pioneered outreach in their own lands. Up until now their stories have been told only in snippets prudently published mostly in short newsletters and in the information-packed pages of our mission's magazine, *Christian Mission*.

At long last, John Lindner, for over 20 years editor of our magazine, has recorded the adventures, trials and victories of twelve of these anointed leaders to inform and challenge us all. Few Christians in North America understand the great struggle these pioneer mission leaders have led against hostile opposition, stark poverty, and missionary prejudice by tradition-bound Christians. As you read these pages you will be amazed at how much they accomplished with so little of this world's resources. You will also see what a difference some prudent help can make when utilized by consecrated servants of God directing the ministries they, themselves, pioneered.

As fascinating as the stories in this book are, they are not fiction. They tell real stories of real men who have reached the unreached, brought new life to thousands, planted churches where there were none, affected governments, and changed the course of history. These are modern missionary heroes. At the same time, they succeed not because they are super saints, but because they persevere with the natural gifts God gives to many of us and with the faith available to every believer.

This book should be read by every pastor, every missions executive, every missions committee member, and every Christian who wants to know how their mission resources can best be used to advance the cause of Christ today.

About the Author

John Lindner

For the last 24 years John Lindner has served on the missionary staff of Christian Aid as writer and editor of brochures, newsletters, news releases and our award-winning magazine, *Christian Mission.*

During the course of those years he has interviewed and interacted with hundreds of Christian leaders who visit Christian Aid in a continual procession. He also has made extensive trips overseas to see firsthand the works of God being carried on by indigenous evangelical ministries in Asia, Africa, Eastern Europe and Latin America.

Before coming to Christian Aid in 1979 he pastored churches for 17 years in Ohio and Michigan, and continues as an active elder in the Church of the Blue Ridge of Afton, Va. He combines the skill of a writer with the heart of a pastor and father.

He is married to the former Jo Ann Vaclavik of Jackson, Michigan. They have three daughters, Jeanne, Joyce and Jill, and a son, John Jr., who designed the book cover.

Acknowledgments

I thank God that He has given me the privilege of meeting so many of His Special Agents. My work at Christian Aid indeed has been a labor of love rewarded by the knowledge that my work helps bring awareness and support to these special saints of God.

This book began more than ten years ago and slowly took shape as opportunities enabled me to capture the life stories of overseas mission leaders. It seems especially appropriate to make them available on Christian Aid's 50th Anniversary year.

Though I take full responsibility for all copy, I want to thank Pat Pickering Zahry and Ann Witkower for their first and very helpful line edits of my manuscripts. I also thank my wife, Jo Ann, and my summer intern assistant, Sarah Carter, for their diligent proofing of my succeeding edits. I thank my son, John Lindner Jr., for his beautiful cover design, and John Scully for reproducing for this book the map first designed by my son for *Christian Mission* magazine. I thank the area directors of Christian Aid for assisting me in gathering overseas information, and the mission leaders themselves who took time out of their demanding schedules to share with me their life stories, and answer my repeated requests for more detail.

Even though these 12 are featured here, let not the reader assume that their stories are more interesting or their ministries more effective than those of others yet untold. These happened to be at the right place at the right time to give me their life stories. Yet they are only representative of a vast army of mission leaders of the two-thirds world who have equally interesting stories and effective ministries.

My prayer is that these stories will be used of God to generate much prayer and financial support for all these men of God.

Chapter 1

Why the Fuss Over Indigenous Missions?

A brief review of the rise and development of the indigenous missions movement and its implications for missions

According to Patrick Johnstone's *Operation World*, there were 84.5 million evangelicals in the world in 1960. By 2000 their number had grown to 420 million, an increase from 2.8% to 6.9% of the world's population.

What accounted for this phenomenal growth?

"The post-war surge of evangelical missions was an astonishing success story," he writes, "but most of the subsequent growth came from a new generation of indigenous evangelical movements around the world."[1]

What are "indigenous missions?" Definitions may vary. According to Dr. Bob Finley, founder and CEO of Christian Aid, indigenous missions are "native to the land." So by definition "indigenous" missionaries serve

---

[1] *Operation World, 2001, p. 5*

among their own people groups in their own countries. For example, a Nepali such as Prem Pradhan found the Lord away from home, went back to his homeland to preach the gospel among his own people, and the ripple effect started a hundred churches. Another Nepali, Resham Raj Poudel, a Hindu Brahmin priest, embraced Christ and began trekking the length and breadth of the land, personally preaching in 73 of the country's 75 districts. He subsequently organized a Bible corresponddence course since requested by more than 256,000 persons. By the end of 2002, 24,191 enrollees had completed the three-year instruction while thousands more were waiting for materials to be printed.

In practice, indigenous missionaries may actually be cross-cultural missionaries within their own country. For example, many mission leaders pioneering works in North India are Malayalays from Kerala. P.M. Thomas left a comfortable teaching position in Kerala to pioneer a work in Jammu-Kashmir in 1963. That work has planted hundreds of churches, and a dozen of its disciples have spun off other mission organizations that now have over 3000 missionaries on the field.

One of these, P.G. Vargis, a soldier from Kerala, accepted Christ while attending a gospel meeting in Thomas's church in Kashmir in 1971. The Lord lit his torch, and he soon left Thomas's ministry to start his own. Today the Indian Evangelical Team has over 2000 missionaries from and to people groups all across northern India.

Advantages of indigenous

Whether these "indigenous" missionaries are reaching members of their own or another people group within their country, several factors remain in their favor:

1. They are citizens in the country where they serve and their work can never be disrupted by the expiration or cancellation of visas. If wars or political instability

Why the Fuss Over Indigenous Missions?

develop, they stay on. They generally avoid the stigma of "foreigner."

2. Many already know the language of the target people group. Others are adept at learning a sister language. They already know the mores of the culture, having been brought up in it. The native missionary eats and drinks the local food, a practice that would wipe out the typical Caucasian missionary.

3. The native missionary essentially lives at the same economic level as the people among whom he ministers. His living allowance typically runs between $30 and $50 monthly, though some in urban areas may need more. He hardly ever takes a furlough, and doesn't have to buy airfare to and from America.

With these advantages and a high cost-effectiveness ratio, it is no wonder that over 130 mission agencies have arisen in the U.S. to advocate and assist indigenous missions. Some 30 exist in Canada. The Consultation on the Support of Indigenous Ministries, begun in 1996, is a "fellowship of evangelical organizations with a common interest in the support and development of Two-Thirds World ministries." They accomplish their mission through "networking, training, and publication—with emphasis on partnerships between North American and Two-Thirds World missions," according to a statement issued from COSIM's office in Atlanta.

Many of these 130 mission agencies are smaller "mom and pop" organizations that may have been thrilled to hear a Third-World missionary and decided to back his work. Three major organizations promoting the work of indigenous missions are Gospel for Asia in Carrollton, Texas; Partners International in Spokane, Washington, and Christian Aid in Charlottesville, Virginia. Like P.M. Thomas of India, Christian Aid has spawned a number of daughter agencies.

Other ministries emphasize training for leadership. For 40 years the Haggai Institute in Atlanta has been training indigenous Christian leaders. So far it has trained 44,000 alumni from 165 nations. The Overseas Council International started out as a Bible seminary in Seoul in 1974 and now offers 90 leadership training programs in over 50 countries.

Yet support of indigenous missions is not limited to groups founded for that purpose. Many traditional missionary-sending agencies now have departments that relate to and assist indigenous movements.

Wycliffe, for example, relates to as many as two-dozen National Bible Translation organizations. Two of these, Translators Association of the Philippines and Bible Translators Association of Papua New Guinea, are supported by Christian Aid. Through Wycliffe, indigenous translators are trained and facilitated to translate books of the Bible into some of the languages with fewer native speakers.

Pioneers, founded in 1979 to take the gospel to unreached peoples, sends aid to indigenous ministries as well as fields teams of missionaries from the U.S. and abroad. These teams work with indigenous mission groups. Sometimes team personnel join the national organization; at other times native workers join the mission teams.

The issue of dependency

One of the questions that has arisen over the support of indigenous missions is the matter of dependency. "Sending money to native missions will make them dependent on you," some say. In fact, the standard for indigenous works is that they be "self-supporting, self-governing, and self-propagating," a theme, incidentally, that was absconded by the Chinese Communists' Three-Self Patriotic Movement.

Those trying to get help for indigenous ministries wonder why sending $30 for a native missionary makes him more "dependent" on us than the American mis-

Why the Fuss Over Indigenous Missions?

sionary receiving $60,000 in annual support. It's not just the money, but the way it's handled.

Christian Aid, for example, never sends money to the specific missionaries "sponsored" through its ministry. Instead, it sends the funds to the headquarters of the indigenous mission with which the missionaries serve, which is also supported by Christians in their land. From the funds available, those leaders decide what missionaries get how much support. The missionaries are always under the supervision and discipline of the local mission board.

It's when these principles are violated that trouble develops. Agencies like Christian Aid, Partners International and Gospel for Asia serve a vital role in making sure the funds are sent in ways that enhance and do not disrupt the local work on the field. Accountability, responsibility and respect for local leadership must prevail.

Bakht Singh, a Sikh who came to Christ while a student in Canada, went back to his native India in 1933 to start a discipling and church-planting movement that has planted over 2000 churches. He is reported to have said, "We pray for God to supply our needs. When the money comes, we do not regard it as Indian money or foreign money, but simply as an answer to prayer. It is God's money."

The leader of a Pakistani Christian ministry recently pointed out that nearly every development in his country is funded with aid from foreign governments. These funds help build up his Muslim nation that then uses its strength to oppose Christians, who face discrimination on every front. "Why do Christians in the West question the validity of small amounts given to their brothers for improving their lot a little?" he asks.

He goes on to say that extreme Muslim groups have killed thousands of people in the name of Jihad. "They are being financed by foreign Islamic groups," he says.

"Cannot we counter that by helping native Christians preach the message of God's love?"

Self-supporting churches

To those who insist the local church in every land should be self-supporting, Christian Aid answers, "we agree."

But what about *missions*? Most American mission boards gladly receive funds from Christians anywhere in the world. Should not mission boards indigenous to the Two-Thirds World be entitled to do the same?

Yes, the local church may be able to pay the rent and provide a pittance for the pastor, but who's going to care for the widow and the orphan, help the desolate and destitute, reach out to the lost and fund church-planting efforts to unchurched villages? In the global community, that burden falls on us all.

The question is, does outside support really help, or does it get in the way? Examples have been given by others of how mishandled support has actually caused a stumbling block. When handled properly, however, support—whether from abroad or from within a country—is a vast enablement.

Foreign help—crutch or aid?

Our brother from Pakistan tells what support did for his ministry.

"When we began our ministry ten years ago, it was purely on 'national foundations.' We did what we could, but in five years we reached only one city and its surrounding areas. Then when you [Christian Aid] and others came along, we were able to reach all the areas of our region. This included 13 major cities and every small nook. This year we are going beyond our region."

Back in the 1980s, a ministry in Nigeria began reaching the then recently discovered Koma tribe. "Our missionaries spent most of their time farming their gardens and scraping together support for their

Why the Fuss Over Indigenous Missions?

families," the leader wrote. Then Christian Aid started sending support for their missionaries and they were able to devote full time to the Lord's work. Churches were planted and mission stations established.

P.G. Vargis, mentioned above, struggled for the first few years of ministry. He said, "From 1972 to 1974 our ministry consisted of only two workers. When Christian Aid started helping us we had 12. As support increased, the mission grew fast until it became the largest mission in India." From that point on it has surged forward exponentially, to over 2000 missionaries today who have planted more than 3500 churches across North India.

When Christian Aid asked the leader of Cornerstone Evangelistic Ministry in Kenya what difference its help made, he responded, "Before we used to travel on foot. Today we are using bicycles provided by Christian Aid."

That simple device may increase a missionary's area of outreach 25-fold. One African preacher, traveling by foot, was able to plant two churches in one year. Then he received a bicycle through Christian Aid. The next year he planted 15 churches! Such gifts don't create jealousy or dissention when implemented by the indigenous leadership.

300,000 indigenous missionaries

No one knows for sure how many indigenous missionaries there are. *Operation World* says there are 107,943 total missionaries working in or sent out from their own countries in Africa, Asia, Latin America and the Pacific regions.[2] The Third World Missions Association estimates there are 300,000 indigenous missionaries. K.P. Yohannan said several years ago that he thought there were 100,000 in India alone.

They are God's men and women looking to Him for empowerment and support. Jesus said, "Pray the Lord

---

[2] *Operation World, 2001, p. 747*

of the harvest that he will send forth laborers into his harvest" (Matthew 9:38). We should be willing to support the ones He chooses to send, regardless of where they are from.

In the following pages you will read the exciting stories of 12 of those He has already sent. And there's more where they came from.

This chapter originally appeared in World Christian *magazine and is republished here with kind permission of WINPress.*

Chapter 2

The Reluctant Preacher

The Story of Aley Gonzalez and Agape Evangelistic Mission in the Philippines

"Aieeee! Mother of God, help me! My baby! My baby!"

Helplessly, Marcela watched her two-year-old baby boy breathe its last struggling breath. Its eyes went askew. Then its tiny head turned aside as the little body went limp in her arms. Her wail could not recover death's prey.

Marcela placed the scrawny body on a little woven mat on the split-bamboo floor. They had no cushions. She tried to close its eyelids so she wouldn't have to look at the lifeless, diverging eyes, but they wouldn't stay shut. Fear cut through her grief as she looked toward two cots in the corner where her daughters, aged six and eight, struggled with the same life-sapping disease.

The year was 1930. The dreaded cholera was sweeping Mindanao Island, and no home in the tiny Filipino settlement of Pingaping was exempt from its curse. Of the seven children born into the Gonzalez family, four already died. Now little Aley had just breathed his last, and the two remaining daughters were growing worse by the minute. If they died, the Gonzalez household would end up childless.

Marcela and her husband, Tura, were exhausted from days of meager rations and sleepless nights. As dusk fell on the tiny Filipino village, Tura stepped out into the darkness to order a tiny casket made immediately. Authorities had ordered all bodies to be buried with 12 hours of death. That was the only way they could deal with the epidemic. Medicines were unavailable. The Gonzalez family and the other villagers were too poor to afford them, anyway.

Mysterious visitors

Early the next morning, the tiny casket was brought to the split-bamboo and palm-frond house and the frail body of little Aley was laid in it. Relatives and neighbors gathered to offer their inadequate condolences. Meanwhile, Aley's two sickly sisters got worse by the minute.

Suddenly there came a knock on the door.

Someone opened the door. There stood three youths.

"Hello. What do you want?"

"We would like to come in to pray with you and to sing a Christian hymn."

Immediately Marcela's back bristled. Protestants! They're the only ones who did that, Marcela thought. She wouldn't have them invade her privacy at a time like this.

"Let them come in," Tura said quietly. "It won't do any harm, and maybe it will do some good."

The Protestants stood in stark contrast to the family members. At a time of death they sang of hope and heaven. Their faces were radiant. They prayed for God to make Himself known to the family. Then, as quickly as they had come, they were gone.

Suddenly, little Aley turned his head and moved his misdirected eyes.

Aunt Flaviana cried, "He moved! He's alive!"

Marcela gasped, not knowing whether she dared pick up the fragile bundle. Then she snatched him into her arms and started dancing around the room, sobbing for joy. Neighbors heard the commotion and saw the tiny shed rocking and thought the two daughters had died, also.

Everyone in the room started chattering at once. The two sick daughters were momentarily forgotten in the joy of the revived son.

"My baby! My baby!" Marcela sobbed joyously. "God has given me back my baby!"

Suddenly they remembered the Protestants. Where had they come from? Where did they go?

"Quickly, let's find them," someone said

They ran outside and began asking their neighbors, "Did you see the Protestants? Early this morning three youths came to our house. They sang. They prayed. They quoted the Bible. Then they left. Did they come to your house? Did you see which way they went?"

No. No one had seen them. None had heard them.

There were only six houses in the hamlet. The strangers could hardly have come and gone undetected. Yet no one else had seen them.

"Are you sure they were Protestants?" one of the neighbors asked. "You know there is not a Protestant church for miles around."

"We don't know who they were," Tura replied. "But they were sent by God. Our little Aley is alive!"

Though children in neighboring homes continued to succumb to the deadly cholera, Aley's sisters recovered and gained weight on the family's subsistence diet. Aley recovered, but his eyes never completely straightened.

Complete salvation

When Aley was born, the town official had entered his name as Wire (pronounced "weary") in the town Register.

"I don't know where the name comes from or what it means," Aley said.

The local Roman Catholic priest objected to Wire's name. "It's not a Christian name," the priest protested. So he christened the infant Alejandro (Spanish for Alexander and pronounced *Aleyhándro*). He's been "Aley" ever since.

The miraculous recovery of their three children opened Marcela and Tura's hearts to the gospel. A few weeks later, on the way home from market, they passed a street meeting conducted by young people from the Congregational Church. They heard the same gospel songs the young people had sung in their little house that night. They stopped to see if they could recognize any of them. They couldn't, but as they listened to the gospel message, they gave their hearts to the Lord.

War-time trials

After this, they moved to Mainit, about six miles south of Pingaping, where Tura landed a job as town clerk. A year later, Naomi was born. Four years after this, Mamerta, who had survived the cholera epidemic, died at age 16. Their sorrow was tempered this time with the assurance that she was with the Lord Jesus.

1939 brought the outbreak of World War II, and the Philippines became a major theater. Aley used to watch the dogfights between the Japanese and American planes in the skies over Leyte Island. When Tura's job as clerk with a mining company ran out, he took up tilling the soil to put food on the table. That was when he decided to serve the Lord full time.

The Reluctant Preacher

Because of the war, Tura started preaching without official approval. After the war, the Presbyterian Conference accepted him, although his sixth-grade education qualified him for only the smallest churches, unable to provide adequate support.

"We were always hungry and never had decent clothes," Aley remembers.

Tura pastored a succession of five churches. Some were so remote he had to paddle his outrigger canoe half a day just to reach them. Aley says the largest offering he ever saw his father receive was seven cents.

Finally, Tura was assigned as pastor-treasurer at the National Heroes Institute, a high school run by Presbyterian missionaries in Malitbog, Leyte. Even there, the meager salary afforded by the enrollment of 100 impoverished students barely provided food for two weeks—though it usually had to stretch to four.

Aley often accompanied his father on his morning rounds going to parishioners' homes to beg a few morsels so that his family could have some semblance of breakfast. Grudgingly, the boy would follow his father to the garden plot behind a parishioner's house and help him dig up enough cassava roots to hopefully last a week.

High school days

When he reached high school age, Aley hired himself out to families in the area. He would watch their children and do laundry and chores in exchange for high school tuition. As Aley trudged the five miles to school each day, he had plenty of time to dream of the day when he would become a professional boxer and make lots of money.

Aley's eyes continued to give him trouble. The kids at school always made fun of him. "There goes google eyes," they would taunt. Aley's appearance made him the target of physical attacks. Perhaps to learn defense he took up boxing as a sport.

This made his mother furious. Having robbed death of her son in infancy, she wouldn't readily release him to a human opponent now.

"You'll get your block knocked off," she would say.

Once Marcela learned about a fight in advance. She marched into the village before the fight, unlaced Aley's gloves and stripped them from his hands.

"You're not fighting this fight," she declared. And that was that.

From then on, Aley never told his mother about his secretly arranged events. All of his 100 bouts were unofficial, and no decisions were rendered, though Aley felt the crowd often favored him as the winner.

Nicknamed "the Boxing Saint" because he was the son of a preacher, he sometimes boxed two fights in one day. Though he never flattened his opponents, some quit after a few rounds. At times he, too, saw stars, though he was never knocked out. Coming home with swollen cheeks or black eyes would provoke a good scolding from Mother and a tongue lashing from his high-school sweetheart, Constancia. But the thrill of boxing more than compensated for all his bruises, physical or verbal.

Prayer terror

One thing Aley couldn't stand was his father's prayers. His father rose at 4:30 every morning for prayer. After praying through the list of needs for the day, Tura would always pray, "And God, please make my son a preacher for You."

Aley shuddered. Not that he minded church work. He gladly assisted his father by handing out tracts and singing with the evangelistic team or the choir. He had even learned a few principles of piano playing while in high school. He didn't mind playing a supporting role,; he just didn't want to be on the front line. Being a preacher was not for him.

To Aley, ministry meant misery. His parents were always in ill health due to malnutrition. He'd had enough of starvation diets.

Painful persecution

Then there was persecution. Not just name calling. This was the rock-throwing, head-bashing kind.

Aley learned always to carry a piece of thick cardboard with him when he accompanied the evangelistic team. This was to shield him from stones thrown by the anti-Protestant Catholics and rabble rousers. Peace officers offered no protection.

Once a man sneaked up behind the preacher and crashed a guitar over his head.

Aley knew a preacher who had been stabbed 40 times. His cheeks were slashed, his chin chopped, and stab wounds were all over his body. Miraculously, he survived, though severely disfigured.

Aley wanted to avoid that kind of confrontation at all costs.

Then there was his speech impediment. He couldn't even pronounce his native Cebuano without a lisp.

"Daddy, do you think anyone would want to listen to a preacher who couldn't even speak his native tongue properly?" he asked.

This, compounded by severe stage fright, should have adequately disqualified him from ministerial candidacy, he thought.

Still, his godly father only prayed the more earnestly for his son's entrance into the ministry.

Agreeable compromise

Aley graduated from National Heroes Institute in 1949. When he announced he wanted to take up prize fighting, the downfallen face of his father chastised him.

Perhaps he could be a teacher instead.

That still wasn't Christian work.

Finally, he proposed a compromise.

"Daddy, I'm not cut out to be a preacher. Let me study sacred music. Then I can always help the preachers. But I don't want to be a preacher myself."

The compromise seemed acceptable. Aley did not mention that this was only a temporary ploy until he could eventually slip out of Christian work altogether. So off to a well-known Presbyterian school on Negros Island Aley went.

Aley soon learned, however, that the school founded by sincere missionaries had since strayed from the fundamentals. It no longer taught the foundational doctrines such as inerrancy of the Scriptures and the virgin birth. Members of the faculty denied the miracles of Jesus. They said Jesus didn't really feed 5,000 people with five loaves and two fishes; He just encouraged people to share what they had brought with them.

Moreover, Jesus wasn't coming again, they said. Didn't He say where two or three were gathered in His name, there He was in the midst of them? So Jesus was already here; how could He possibly come again?

Thus they dismissed or reinterpreted all the fundamental doctrines.

In addition, many of the students smoked, drank, and engaged in worldly activities, such as dancing. The school officials did nothing, not even when the non-Christian students complained. So Aley decided he would get all the music studies he could that first semester. Then, when the semester was over, he would go to Bethel Bible Institute near Manila. Two of his high school friends had enrolled there. He felt he could overlook its Pentecostal slant as long as it proclaimed the basic doctrines Aley held precious.

Culture shock

At Bethel, Aley went into culture shock at the first chapel service. The students raised their hands as though someone had stuck a gun in their backs. Everyone clapped their hands unashamedly. They sang and prayed loudly, and punctuated everything with loud shouts of "Hallelujah!" and "Amen."

Why did everything have to be loud? How could one pray seriously with all that noise? Some even dared rock to and fro with the music. Such demonstration, Aley's tradition told him, was fit only for the football stadium or boxing arena.

Some were dancing and jumping. Others were mumbling incoherent syllables. Suddenly, someone standing next to him fell with a thud to the concrete floor. Aley was sure the blow must have caused brain damage.

How could such confusion be honoring to the Lord? Each chapel service was more a nightmare than a blessing. Aley wished he were back at the other school. At least the people there knew how to do things decently and in order.

But there was no escape. The doors were locked at night, and he had no money for bus fare even if he could get out. At least he could show them his superior intellect. Making the honor roll elated him for a time.

His sense of achievement was short lived, however. Though he had graduated from high school and most of his classmates had less than an elementary school education, his "inferior" classmates could out-preach him on the streets. He used to hide behind them on the street corner so he would not be called upon to testify.

"Give me power to witness the way they do," Aley began to pray. In fact, he determined that if he did not experience a breakthrough, he would not proceed into the ministry. God seemed indifferent to his plight.

"All I got was a hoarse voice," he said.

Finally, one night in November, 1951, while praying for his classmates, the Lord filled him with Himself. His tongue was loosed and he began to praise God without restraint. He worried that he was disturbing his roommates, but they and the faculty members joined him in his midnight revival. After this experience, his speech impediment and his stage fright disappeared. At the next evangelistic outing, he surprised himself when he voluntarily stepped forward and boldly testified. When he graduated that spring, he was prepared to face the persecution he knew awaited him.

Teaching fellow

In June, 1952, Aley joined the faculty of Immanuel Bible Institute in Sogod, southern Leyte, and married Constancia that November. The next year the school moved to Cebu City and there Wire Aley, Jr. was born. Three years later, Aley was offered a position on the faculty of Bethel Bible Institute in Manila where he taught music and other subjects. In 1962, he was recalled to IBI to head up the music department. Through all these assignments, he was active in street evangelism and crusades.

Conducting these outings, he was once choked by a police officer, twice punched in the face, and many times stoned and threatened. Once while he was preaching, four drunks armed with bolo knives stormed the platform from behind. Amazingly, no one on the platform reacted, thus defusing a potentially bloody encounter.

Once he was manhandled by a crowd led by the barrio official in Agusan del Norte, and the mayor in Surigao del Norte led the police force to drive Aley out of his jurisdiction. Many times irate citizens banged empty cans to prevent an outdoor service from beginning while the police stood by entertained by the commotion.

"Persecution is a part of our lives and ministry," Aley says.

Ministerial misery

Aley's entrance into the ministry had given great joy and satisfaction to his father. Now the testimony of Aley's personal experience with God encouraged him all the more. Tura, who had been dismissed from the presbytery when his son entered the Pentecostal school, continued to pastor his two churches independently. About this time, Aley resigned his post at the Bible school and started doing pioneer island-to-island evangelism on Dinagat Island, southeast of Leyte.

During these years, the Lord blessed Aley and Constancia with two more boys and two girls. All of them have remained faithful to the Lord. Some take active roles in the ministry; others support it financially.

When Aley's father died malnourished and in poor health in 1966, Aley felt led of God to take over his work. The people renamed the church in San Jose "Gonzalez Memorial Assembly."

Working alone with no group backing him, Aley's family suffered from poverty as severely as his parents' family had suffered, especially after son Janley came along later that year and daughter Eufe in 1968. It was quite a feat feeding seven hungry youngsters, besides Constancia and himself.

Breakfast consisted of the coarsest of corn meal—the kind used to feed the roosters—mixed with the lowest-grade brown sugar that left a bitter aftertaste. Lunch and supper consisted of plain rice—no meat, only rarely a little fish, and a few vegetables. These meager rations were sometimes supplemented with boiled sweet potato or cassava root.

"For more than five years my family lived on this subsistence diet," Aley said.

"Many times I cried secretly when there was nothing substantial on the table. How painful it was to watch my hungry children expecting more when there was none. Many times I cried upon reaching the top of a mountain with barely enough strength to continue and then realize that I still had ten miles to go to reach my waiting congregation."

Miracles not enough

Aley used to think that if the Lord would just work an outstanding miracle in their midst, people would flock to God. His experience proved otherwise. God healed a man who was totally paralyzed and a child given up by the hospital to die of cancer. But apart from these two individuals and their families, Aley could not count a single new convert since taking over his father's work.

It was enough to make this boxing saint think about quitting. So after struggling for five years, Aley decided to take up piano tuning, a trade he had learned in college. Perhaps that way he could at least feed his hungry family.

While contemplating this change in profession, Aley bought some cheap fish at the market one day in 1969. When he unwrapped the package at home, he realized it was wrapped with a page from an American newspaper. A short article told about a small Christian boat ministry in Tampa, Florida, called Agape Mission. A photo showed a man identified as Captain Hanon Styles waving from the deck of a boat. Having no other information than the name, city and state, Aley wrote.

Long distance communication

Miraculously, he received an answer—16 months later! The first letter had taken eight months to arrive in Tampa after being postmarked in several states. The response, similarly, had traveled through several Philippine provinces before finding Aley in Cabadbaran.

"How much money do you need?" the letter asked.

"I don't need money. I just need your prayers," Aley wrote back.

After a couple more exchanges like this, the people in Tampa concluded Aley was legitimate, and sent him a check for $350. Only Aley didn't know it was money; he had never seen a check before.

"What is this?" he asked the postmaster.

"That's money," the postmaster said. "Take it to the bank and they will give you money for it."

Aley was so excited he ran home without buying a thing.

"What did you buy?" everyone asked when he walked in the door.

"Nothing," Aley said sheepishly. He went right back out to the local market and bought all the stuff he needed for the grandest feast they had had in years.

The letter began a relationship that brought some relief to Aley's destitute situation and became the key to keeping him in the ministry. As a follow-up, a Christian attorney, a postal clerk, a Tampa journalist, and noted Christian writer and editor, Alan West, visited Aley's Mindanao ministry. When they returned home, they sent medicines, clothing, and modest financial gifts from time to time.

Birth pangs

Later, Jamie Buckingham became acquainted with Aley's ministry, visited him in the Philippines, and invited the pugnacious preacher to visit America. The author didn't count on Aley's visit challenging his own lifestyle, and wrote about it in a *Logos Journal* editorial, "Please don't look in my closet," reprinted in 1978 by Logos International in the collection of editorials entitled *The Last Word*.

With the promise of at least occasional help, Aley organized his ministry in 1972 and named it, Agape Evangelistic Mission, in honor of the Tampa ministry. Now, at least part of the time, his family would have nutritious food to eat. And for the first time, Aley dared welcome another preacher to join him in the work.

Unfortunately, Aley learned too late that the man was a jealous minister desirous of taking over the work. The man split the main congregation, taking two-thirds of the members (two families), leaving Aley with only one family in the church.

It was a blessing in disguise. The man took the problem families. After they were gone, the remaining family experienced a genuine revival and began to pray and witness earnestly for the Lord. All the carpenters working on the mission house were converted. One of them, Andy de la Cruz, came to help with the ministry, and he proved to be genuine. Outstations began to grow. As the main congregation swelled, the elders took on the responsibility for ministering in those difficult places. Soon there were four preaching points and four churches.

The new workers were as tenacious as Aley. By 1981 Agape Evangelistic Mission consisted of 23 Filipino missionaries (four of them unmarried). These worked among 14 small congregations and a number of mission outreaches scattered on the mountainous seashores of northern Mindanao and southern Leyte islands.

New relationship

Steady help started coming when Christian Aid started sending help in 1983. One of the staff had met Aley at a house meeting in Ohio before coming to Christian Aid, and, after joining the staff, recommended Aley's ministry for help.

Commendations from fellow Filipino ministries as well as the Christian attorney in Florida vouched for Aley's sincerity. Financial records showed accountability. Christian Aid started sending $150 monthly in 1983, and increased it gradually over the years.

That regular support, minimal as it was, made a significant difference for Agape Evangelistic Mission. In addition to helping to meet the needs of Aley's family and missionaries, it meant that for the first time Aley could help others instead of looking for a handout himself.

Having lived among destitute people all his life, Aley's heart was especially sensitive to the needs of young people. He gladly shared his own support with any young person needing financial help to go to high school or Bible college. At one time he was feeding 33 young people around his table.

Two tiny hands

One day Aley was walking along the village dirt road and, passing a shack, he saw two tiny hands stuck through the bamboo slats. From within came a little girl's frail voice pleading, "Something to eat?"

Aley peeped in and saw two tiny tots shut in the house and a third, the youngest, tied to a post. All were sickly and malnourished. The shack itself was little better than a Filipino toilet. Its walls and floors were of discarded bamboo splits and the worn-out nipa roof obviously leaked everywhere.

Questioning the neighbors, Aley learned that the mother, Mrs. Soria, had been deserted by her husband. She peddled any item she could find to provide for her young family. She couldn't afford a babysitter, so she shut the youngsters in the hut while she was gone. Often the young mother went out without eating and sometimes fainted on the road for lack of nourishment.

Aley returned when the mother was home and obtained permission to take the children to his house for a meal.

"My heart bled as the famished children used both hands to stuff as much food as they could into their tiny mouths," Aley recalls.

The mother let the middle girl, Angelica, stay with the Gonzalezes. The oldest, Mary Jane, stayed with her mother to help take care of the youngest, Teresita. Christian Aid found sponsors who started sending $10 monthly for Mrs. Soria and each of her two other girls. Eventually, Aley was able to build a better shelter for the Soria family. With help sent from America, Aley bought new split bamboo walls, nipa roofing, and plywood floors. A Christian carpenter rebuilt the hut at no charge.

Support makes a difference

The regular support also made a vast difference for the workers. "Our congregations give the best they can, as I preach hard on giving," Aley says.

Offerings in a typical village church run from 10 to 25 pesos per week. At 25 pesos per dollar, village offerings top out at about $4 per month. Sometimes local believers bring some bananas, some cassava roots, some vegetables, or—in a seacoast village—a fish.

"This helps provide food for the local worker and his family, but it can hardly sustain him and provides nothing for ministry expenses such as literature or jeepney fare," Aley explains.

Shortly after he started receiving regular help in 1983, Aley wrote:

"Thank you for the support you sent for my needy workers. None of those whose congregations are able to sustain their workers will share in it; only those who are truly needy.

"Missionary Felicilda's place is so hard to reach that I plan to take him his support two months at a time. I plan to go there next week. He will be beside himself with joy when he receives it. And I will be even happier to see him so happy."

Roman Catholic resistance

Regular support and additional workers were a boon to the work, but stubborn local resistance persisted. In 1986 Aley decided to start a new work in Malitbog, a town across the bay from Lilo-an. It was a 45-minute boat ride and a three-hour road trip along the shoreline.

"This town is the bastion of the Spanish scion," Aley says. "Catholicism is strong and succeeded in driving out a Christian high school years back. It was in a neighboring town that I was choked while preaching a number of years ago. I know what to expect when I start the work."

Aley thought the best way to reach the village was by conducting a vacation Bible school. That should be harmless enough, he thought.

A public school official got wind of what was going on, however, and led the villagers in a verbal assault on the children attending the meetings and on their parents for allowing them to come. The parents, in reaction, pulled their children out of the VBS and whipped them. In the end, a few parents attended the closing ceremonies and four came forward for prayer. Today, one of Agape's missionaries shepherds a small flock there and he shares Christ with others who will listen.

Roman Catholicism in the Philippines is bitterly anti-Protestant. Roman Catholic bishops even published a pastoral letter throughout the nation's newspapers in 1989 accusing "fundamentalists" of being agents of the CIA.

In one area riddled with rebel fighting, some of the townsfolk actually poisoned the drinking water used by the local gospel worker's family. All of the family members drank of it. The older children noticed its peculiar odor and taste, but none of the family members suffered any ill effects. To the culprits who had been watching, expecting serious illness or even deaths, the incident became a testimony of God's glory and power.

Guerrilla warfare

The most life-threatening resistance, however, was the guerrilla warfare that raged in increasing intensity up until about 1990. Philippine government troops and New Peoples Army communist rebels clashed constantly in Aley's area. Any stranger was immediately suspected by both NPA rebels and government forces.

Once en route to Surigao City by motorcycle, Aley passed a government soldier hidden from view. The soldier didn't recognize Aley, a stranger, and took aim at him. Some civilians, seeing the soldier point the gun at

Aley, cried out, "That's the pastor from Cabadbaran!" The soldier lowered his gun.

A few weeks later there was an all-out war near one of Aley's outstations. Three government planes zoomed in, bombing a suspected rebel hideout. Missionary Rubio's congregation was scattered and the church was converted to an armory.

Because of the intense warfare, Aley moved his headquarters from the northern edge of Mindanao Island to southern Leyte. There he continued to pay weekly visits to the churches, one month concentrating on Leyte Island, the next month visiting those on Mindanao.

With the collapse of communism in the Soviet Union, the rebels' source of armaments dried up and the activity of the NPA greatly diminished. Having already established his new base of operations on Leyte Island, Aley divided the work with his son, Philip, in 1995. Philip now tends about 20 churches on Mindanao Island while Aley continues his church-planting ministry on Leyte.

Danger at sea

The physical mechanics of just getting to the churches would be enough to deter all but the most stalwart. In one place, he literally climbs up a rope hand over hand to reach the people who live at the top of the high embankment.

Once when Aley was going from one island to the next on an inter-island ferry, the boat he was on collided with another in the middle of the night. The impact was so severe that the other ship sank in five minutes. The ship Aley was on listed and panic ensued.

Aley looked out through pitch darkness to see where he could swim. Suddenly, his ship righted and he breathed a sigh of relief. The boat turned around and picked up those in the water. No one drowned.

Several times, the Lord providentially kept him from disaster. Once he wired his wife from Mindanao Island that he would be arriving home Monday on the inter-island ship, the *Casandra*. But when he got on the bus to go to the pier, he took the wrong bus and ended up on the other side of the island. The next day the *Casandra* sank.

Another time he was in Baugio north of Manila and wired Constancia that he would arrive home by ship via the *Don Mariano* in two days. Then, something made him change his mind and, despite his shortage of funds, he went to the airport and flew home. His wife was surprised to see him so soon. The next day, the *Don Mariano* also sank.

On land, the usual means of public transportation is the legendary Filipino jeepney—a covered Jeep stretched to seat 18 to 30 people. But passengers don't limit themselves to available seats. They stand in the aisles, grab bars on the outside, cling to the sides, sit on the roof, and stand on the rear running board.

"I don't mind hanging onto the sides of jeepneys," Aley says. "I'm just concerned about my workers in pioneer areas. They need my help, so I must visit their respective areas."

After being temporarily sidelined with a heart problem in 1989, he confessed, "I almost got killed hanging onto the side of a passenger jeep. I no longer have the strength to hold onto a jeepney."

Aley considered buying a jeepney, but the $10,000 cost for a new one was prohibitive for his modest ministry. He had a Toyota 3KH engine and paid a friend to put together a home-made jeepney using a Toyota cab and a pick-up rear end.

Pregnant possibilties

Despite being surrounded by enough problems to sink a battleship, or at least a ferryboat, Aley never loses sight of helping the individual.

One summer day, a teenage girl showed up at the Gonzalez house.

"Will you help me?" she pleaded. "I have no place to go."

Upon questioning her, Constancia learned that the girl, Amalia, was a 17-year-old drug addict and had been thrown out of her home by her parents. "I think we can make room for you," Constancia said, opening her home to her.

Constancia didn't know that the girl was pregnant, but in a short time, Amalia's bulging tummy revealed the truth. The boy responsible was notified, but turned his back on the unwanted problem. Amalia's parents also refused to have anything to do with her. Constancia provided the care and support Amalia needed during her pregnancy. This loving care led her to embrace the Lord Jesus as her personal Savior.

In due time, little Rhea Claire was born. Amalia's family still wouldn't let her back into their home because now she had been contaminated with the Gonzalezes' evangelical religion. Not being able to care for the child herself, Amalia made the Gonzalezes Rhea's legal guardians. Amalia, with Christ in her heart, then completed her high school education.

Because Aley and Constancia were there, this teenage girl and her infant daughter will have a better chance at life. So will the Soria family and countless others touched by this tenacious, pug-nosed preacher and the missionaries who serve with him.

"Not as one that beateth the air"

With his educated background, Aley could join the professional ranks. His Bachelor of Christian Education degree qualifies him to teach in a high school; his B.A. equips him to teach in a college, and his M.A. permits him to teach at the graduate level. Still, he gladly chooses the simple life and prefers ministering among those who have nothing in the rural villages.

It was a great blow to him when Constancia died of diabetes in 1993. But Aley and his team of committed workers joyfully carried on, helping whom they could and preaching to whomever would listen.

Aley never intended to remarry, but in 1998 he met Elsa Ombao, then 44 and principal of the Agape Academy in Cabadbaran. As they talked, Aley realized he had met her when she was a youngster. The Lord worked His magic and they were married on December 28, 1999.

Aley's children began to suggest that he might retire and enjoy his latter years, but he says, "No way. As long as I can still hike, I will go, and as long as I have a voice, I will preach."

Though aging physically, his spirit is renewed day by day. His vision: starting more evangelistic churches along the coastal towns and rural villages of southern Leyte in the Philippines. To ensure continued operation should he become physically incapable of carrying on, Aley merged his work in southern Leyte with that of his son, Philip, in Mindanao.

His persistence echoes Paul's spirit, "I, therefore, run, not as uncertainly; so fight I, not as one that beateth the air" (1 Corinthians 9:26).

And to think Aley almost bypassed the ministry for the empty fame of boxing. Today, he would never consider anything but serving the King of kings. His father would be proud of him.

Chapter 3

Warrior for the Lord

The Story of Luis Alberto Guerrero and the Lord's Vineyard of Colombia

Placido was "unconvertible."
Gersain was a thief.
Basilio was a fighter.
Sergio beat his wife.
Manuel's wife left him because he was drunk all the time.
Jose was very foul-mouthed.
Benito was a sorcerer.
Orlando was an assassin.

So was Inocencio.

And some were several of these.

Now they all serve the Lord Jesus Christ as members of a rugged band of preachers called "The Lord's Vineyard" in Colombia.

Working along with them are Elias, whose father was a pastor; Felix, who accepted the Lord when he was a child; and Polycarpo, an 18-year-old zealot.

Their "vineyard" is one of the roughest in the world: an area infested with drug lords chased by government military, with rightist paramilitary groups ready to defend their turf against all comers, and God help anyone who gets in the way.

This unlikely band of preachers began in an equally unorthodox location: a mental hospital.

At least that's where their leader, Luis Alberto Guerrero Ruiz, was staying when he found the Lord. His family name, Guerrero, means "warrior" in Spanish. But he was no warrior then; he was an incurable patient.

Mental patient

Born in 1938, Luis was the eldest of nine children. He had three brothers and five sisters. When he was 14, his father was killed by terrorists. Luis longed for the day he would be old enough to join the army. Then he could go and kill some terrorists and avenge his father's death.

His father had been employed by the government as a road maintenance worker and farmed a small plot of ground. After he was killed, the family moved to Bogotá to escape the terrorists. There his mother worked as a cleaning woman to feed her family.

When Luis turned 21, he joined the army. Three years later, he married Rita, "the girl next door." Fifteen days later he was stricken with epilepsy.

This was no ordinary epilepsy, where one passes out and then comes to again and resumes a somewhat normal life. Luis became aggressive, out of control.

Luis's fellow soldiers put up with his erratic behavior for two years. Then they placed him in a mental hospital for the next 21 months. None of the neurologists could identify the cause for his epilepsy, which had not bothered him as a youth. It just came on him sud-denly 15 days after he was married.

Gadara revisited

While Luis was in the sanitarium, his brother Saul and one of his cousins became Christians. They started going to an Assembly of God church in Bogotá where a Canadian missionary named David Wormer was in charge. They began reading the Bible and praying, and became convinced Jesus Christ could heal Luis.

So they came to the prison and obtained permission to take Luis to a service at the church.

After the message, they took Luis to the front of the meeting hall for prayer. When Wormer put his hands on Luis' head to pray, Luis felt as though worms were crawling through his body.

People converged around him. Everyone was praying fervently out loud. Luis tried to break loose and run away, but the believers held him fast. He tried to strike the pastor, but had no strength.

Surrounded by all these praying people, Luis felt as if the worms were exiting his body through his feet. Finally, Luis slumped to the floor.

In a moment he opened his eyes. His gaze was normal. The believers helped him to his feet.

"You need to accept Jesus Christ as your Savior," missionary Wormer said, and he carefully led Luis in the sinner's prayer.

As Luis confessed his need and asked Jesus Christ to be Lord of his life, he felt a warm peace envelope him.

"I'm whole! I'm cured!" he cried out.

His friends had carried him in totally deranged. Like the Gadarene demoniac, he left whole and in his right mind.

Soldier preacher

He did not return to the mental hospital. Instead, the very next day he went straight to the army post where he was assigned and started preaching.

Everyone noticed that Luis was in his right mind. His fellow soldiers had put up with this crazy man for two years, bearing with his abnormal speech and conduct. Now they saw him reading the Bible aloud and speaking normally.

The commander walked up to him. "Have you accepted Jesus Christ as your Savior?" he asked.

"Yes, I have," Luis declared.

"Good," he said. "Keep going to church!"

From that moment on the army headquarters became Luis's training ground. He kept going to the church in Bogotá, and everything he learned he came back and preached to his fellow soldiers. A number of them accepted the Lord through his preaching.

While he was allowed to preach to his fellow soldiers inside the camp, as a soldier he was not allowed to preach outside the camp. So Luis decided to take his accumulated leave (he had accumulated five months—one for every year he had been in the service), and went on a preaching tour on his own time.

He never went back. By the time he had used up his five months' leave, his five-year stint in the army was over. He applied for release and was honorably discharged in February, 1965.

While Luis was in the mental hospital, he was allowed to have home visits with his wife. Rita conceived and Flaminio was born January 2, 1964. Rita gave birth to another child, Luisa, on Christmas Day, and Ruth Anna came along in 1966.

Heeding the Lord's call to preach, Luis never looked back.

Violent opposition

"I was unstoppable," he declared in retrospect. "Everywhere I went I shared what the Lord had done in my life. I preached on the streets and from house to house. My wife enthusiastically joined me, because she saw the miracle of my transformed life."

When Luis went to Chaguani, a four-hour drive from Bogotá, the Roman Catholic priest didn't like his preaching and sent people to kill him. He was assaulted three times. One man shot at him with a shotgun, but the shots scattered around him; none of them touched him. Another man threw a machete at him; he missed and ran away, shaking. A third time they beat him. He was so sick afterwards the doctor prescribed 30 days' rest. Luis, however, kept on preaching.

One day he was walking down the street with four other people when five robbers assaulted him. One of the robbers pulled out a machete and struck a believer on the head. Luis could see the man's brains in the wound, but miraculously the man survived and lived to old age.

Another time robbers surrounded him and intended to kill him. Luis turned and ran, tripped on something and fell face forward into the mud. Suddenly he felt a giant hand lift him up over the treetops and set him down far away. When his feet touched the ground, he kept on running. Then he realized he was on the other side of Chaguani.

The first three women who confessed Christ as Savior in that town were raped. The men thought that raping them would cause them to deny their faith and bring the gospel into disrepute. But God gave them victory and the believers continued steadfast. That first church continues to this day, a congregation of about 80.

Divine assignment

After a while, Luis grew restless. His anointing was to be a missionary, not a pastor. Then one day Luis felt

God was speaking to him about going to remote Casanare Province, but he told no one about it. That night he went to a church in another neighborhood where Diogenes Villa from Miami was preaching. Luis and Diogenes had never met. Yet in the middle of the sermon, the preacher stepped down from the pulpit, walked over to where Luis was sitting, put his hand on his shoulder, and prophesied:

"My servant, because you were faithful and, like Daniel, didn't kneel before the beast, I will take you from this place to another place. It is a desert place, but I will make rivers of water flow out of it. Get up and go where I am sending you, because I have many people there that need to hear you. You will suffer a lot there. You will go through many dangers, but I will keep you under the shadow of My hand. Don't be afraid of what you are about to suffer, because in the way that I was with Joshua, so I will be with you. Go where I am sending you, because I need to do work there. I have many souls there."

Then the man went back to the pulpit and continued preaching right where he had left off.

To Luis, it was a signal gun. Within 15 days he assigned the church in Chaguani to another fellowship. To others, even his wife, he seemed like a crazy man again.

"Quick, let's pack and go," he told Rita. So they gathered their three children and few belongings, and hitched a ride in the back of a cattle truck. For two days they shared the back of that truck with cattle, goats, chickens, vegetables and various other things.

When they got to the town of Yopal, then just a small town, there was no church, no believers, nothing. Today it is the capital of Casanare Province with five evangelical churches in the area, all planted by the Guerreros.

Pioneer church planter

These didn't spring up overnight, however. It took days and years of long, arduous toil.

When Luis and Rita arrived in town, they didn't know a soul. They tried to make friends, but nobody trusted them. It's not easy to make friends in an area infested with terrorists. The townspeople thought they might be government spies and avoided them.

So Luis began preaching on the streets. The whole family accompanied him. They had no musical instruments, so Luis and Rita would begin by singing *a capella* while their children handed out tracts to bystanders. "To the townspeople we appeared as lunatics," Luis said later. At least everyone realized that he was a gospel preacher, and not a spy.

Luis did yard work for people, and hired himself out as a farm laborer. He would come home late in the afternoon, clean up, and then go preach on the street in the evening.

Rita washed clothes and cleaned houses. This gave her contacts with many women. In the evenings she joined her husband for ministry.

Slowly, through public preaching and private conversations, people began to trust Christ as their Savior and recognized Luis as a genuine missionary. After a year, a nucleus of blood-bought believers gathered to worship the Savior in the beauty of holiness, though it was not until 1968 that the gathering grew in size and maturity to organize as a church.

That accomplishment was not without pain, either. In 1967, Rita gave birth to her fourth child, Damaris. The baby contracted meningitis and, lacking medical services in this remote place, died. Then Rita became partially paralyzed with palsy. Finally, little Ruth Anna became sick with malaria and anemia. Luis had no choice but to ask another organization to take over the church so he could take his family back to Bogotá where they could get better health care.

Rita and Ruth did recover, and Rita gave birth to another daughter in 1968. They called her Damaris, in place of the child who died. With the family back on their feet, Luis headed back to Casanare Province in 1970. There Josué was born that same year.

Redeeming the rebels

Making Yopal his headquarters, Luis began making journeys into the surrounding countryside. Whoever he met got a gospel greeting, regardless of his political persuasion.

On one of his trips, he saw a house on the hillside and thought he would see who lived there.

A man came to the door with guns in his holsters. Luis told him he was a gospel preacher and had just stopped to bring friendly greetings. He pulled out his Bible, read a Scripture and gave some comment. The man just stared at him, so Luis bid *adieux*, and went on his way.

On his way back, he stopped by the house again. This time the man was more friendly and invited Luis in. Inside, he met the man's seven sons, all rebels, and the women they lived with—none of them was married. Luis held an instantaneous gospel service. Since they seemed receptive, Luis left a Bible and went his way.

Months later, Luis was passing that way again and stopped to visit the house. The head of the house said he had been very touched by what Luis had said on his previous visit, and would he please preach to them again. Luis preached, and every member of the household accepted Christ as their Savior. Luis then had the privilege of baptizing every one—and solemnizing their marriages.

Instead of a meeting place for revolutionaries that house became a gathering place where 40 born-again Christians worship the Lord.

Good horse sense

Luis takes most of his trips on horseback. His faithful horse, Messenger, knows exactly how to act. When Luis approaches a house and the people inside come out to see who it is, the horse butters them up by brushing up against their legs. If they invite Luis in, Luis dismounts, and when he enters the house, the horse follows!

One time, as Luis was traveling through the mountains on horseback, he heard a loud chopping sound in the distance. Luis dismounted, climbed up the mountain, and surprised a man who was chopping wood. Luis shared the gospel with the man, Sergio, who had never heard it before. There on the mountainside, in the middle of the forest, Sergio accepted Christ as his Savior. Today Sergio is one of Luis's faithful coworkers.

On another of these trips, Messenger developed a severe stomach sickness. He started staggering, gnashing his teeth and kicking. As Luis approached a certain house, he saw a lemon tree in the yard covered with lemons. He harvested an armful of lemons, squeezed the juice, prayed over it, and poured it down the horse's throat. Immediately, Messenger calmed down and recovered from his sickness.

"We've never seen a horse cured with lemon juice," the family members said.

"The Lord worked a miracle," Luis replied, and he preached the gospel to them. They all repented of their sins and accepted the Lord.

In his various treks into the countryside and surrounding villages those first 11 years, Luis planted 11 churches. Chiefly a pioneer missionary, he didn't know what to do with them once he planted them. He gave away six, including the first church in Yopal, to other organizations. In 1976 he decided to organize the remaining five into an association of churches he called

"The Lord's Vineyard" (no connection with the Vineyard movement in America).

Daring disciples

In his trips through the backwoods, Luis met and won many to the Lord, and some of them have joined him as fellow missionaries:

Benito was a sorcerer. He cast spells on women to take advantage of them. Luis shared the gospel with him. Benito repented, left his witchcraft practice, and now preaches the gospel.

Orlando was an assassin. He killed for hire, even for sport. Sometimes he would pick a fight with someone on the street. The last person that he killed was in police custody. Police were taking the man to jail; Orlando grabbed the man out of their hands, shot him dead on the spot, and then laid down his gun and surrendered to the police.

Inocencio also was an assassin. Luis met him on one of his gospel ventures and led him to the Lord. Now Inocencio also preaches the gospel. When he approaches guerrilla bands on the road, he fearlessly goes up to them and starts talking to them about Christ.

One of the Vineyard missionaries visited the jail and preached the gospel. He gave one of the prisoners, Orlando, a Gospel of John, and later a Bible. When Orlando got out of jail, he went to the church in Venturoso and gave his heart to the Lord. He was radiantly changed and became a preacher of the gospel.

Another Sergio was a drunkard and a wife-beater. Luis visited the home and preached the gospel. Sergio's wife accepted the Lord, but not Sergio. Later, through the prayers of God's people and his wife's virtuous life, he accepted the Lord. Sergio has labored for the Lord in three different regions.

Placido was "unconvertible." He hated the gospel. But the patient witness and prayers of his mother eventually softened his heart. He came to the Lord and fell in love with a girl in the church. They married and now are serving the Lord full time.

Sometimes these gospel preachers go out in teams, several believers from the local church joining them as prayer supporters. Once as a troop of eager believers pushed through the grassy savanna, a poisonous snake bit the leg of a mule on which one of them was riding. The mule, rider still astride, immediately fell over. The startled believers laid hands on the mule and prayed earnestly. The mule recovered and the troop went on.

Bogotá seminary

The work continued to grow. By 1987 Luis decided he needed to train some of the men eager to serve the Lord. So he took some of the men and moved back to Bogotá. They lived in his house while they attended a seminary in the city. After three years of sharing his house and provisions with these men, Luis realized that they were too comfortable in the city, and did not want to move back out to the boondocks. That was when Luis decided he would never again bring men from the country to the city for training. He would find another way to train the men.

Now Luis holds a weeklong training conference in four different regions every year, plus the annual convention at the central church. All the workers can attend one of these regional conferences, and most of them attend the annual convention. To provide food and travel allowances for 15 men to attend a regional conference costs about $750.

Friend from afar

It was about 1987 that Luis became acquainted with Christian Aid. A roaming field scout for Christian Aid, Fred Malir, heard about Luis and visited him in Bogotá. A working relationship was established, and Christian Aid found sponsors for some of Luis's workers, greatly helping the work. Luis put the money in a central treasury and doled out assistance to the neediest workers. Up until then most of them received the equivalent of less than $10 from the mostly cashless believers who attended their churches.

Occasionally one of these supporters also provided a bicycle for a worker. With no other means of transportation, it is not unusual for missionaries to take them on 100-mile journeys. At other times, a horse is necessary, sometimes, a boat.

Josué (not Luis' son) became a Christian through his parents and travels the river taking the gospel to many river towns. He has learned how to construct wooden boats. Obtaining a powerful outboard motor to counter the strong river currents is another matter. Such a motor costs $3000 and cannot be obtained without outside help.

Polycarpo works among the Tikuani tribe. Other Vineyard workers also labor among the Guahibo and Piapoco, each with its own, distinct language. When Luis first started going among them, they were impoverished, primitive and wore clothing made of tree leaves. Luis brought them used clothing and simple medicines. They appreciated his kindness and opened their hearts to him. Now many are believers.

Gruesome guerrillas

But the road today is not smoother, nor the way straighter. After 50 years, the army has not gained any victory over the drug cartels, and many believe government officials are paid off. Guerrilla bands and drug lords still control the countryside, while paramilitary groups are paid to protect those who have money.

The poor people are caught in the middle. Drug lords hire them as cheap laborers to work in their fields and manufacturing centers. Christians refuse to work for them, and so are even more despised and scrape by in even greater deprivation.

In one place, a terrorist stormed a small village and massacred men and women at random. Then he butchered them. After he left, survivors fished bloodied body parts—arms, legs, hands, heads and torsos—from shallow drinking wells, creeks and riverbeds.

The killer threatened the evangelical Christians living in the area, and all feared for their lives. Luis and his missionaries prayed fervently. Before the terrorist could carry out his wicked scheme, he was shot and similarly butchered by a paramilitary band.

In the midst of such gruesome terror, Luis and his band of faithful missionaries keep on preaching the gospel of peace to whomever they meet.

Religious rebels

At one of Luis' training seminars, a woman came and said she was sent by a guerrilla group. "We want someone to come and preach the gospel to us," she said.

The missionaries said nothing, suspecting this might be a trick.

"Let's pray," Luis said

The whole group went into earnest, vocal prayer.

After they had prayed an hour and the room quieted, Elias spoke up. "I feel the Lord wants me to go," he said.

He and his wife, Carmencita, and their two small children went to the place where the guerrillas lived.

"Why have you come here?" the leader demanded.

"A woman told us to come," Elias said.

"What are you here for?"

"We have come to preach the gospel."

"OK. You can preach, but we won't pay you."

Nine months later Elias and Carmencita were discipling 15 new believers in the ways of the Lord.

In another region, the terrorists told Pastor Edgar that if he did not leave, they would kill him. So Pastor Edgar left and stayed in another village a short distance away. The only people left in the town were the guerrilla terrorists and the local believers who were members of that church.

"We don't want any more pastors here," the terrorists said. "and if they set foot here, we will kill them."

God has an interesting way of turning tables on His enemies. One female member of the terrorist group became mentally disturbed, and then lost her mind. The terrorists were beside themselves. Finally they approached the believers and said, "Look, we want you to send for your pastor so he can pray for us. We won't harm him."

They sent someone to fetch the pastor, he prayed over the woman, and the Lord healed her. He was allowed to stay.

"This is not a war of man against man," Luis told me. "The Lord also is in the midst of the battle and He is fighting.

Faith overcomes fear

Luis still goes to army outposts and requests permission to preach, a request that is usually granted. In one place, 20 soldiers and one lieutenant raised their hands to receive the Lord Jesus Christ as their Savior.

"Humanly speaking, we are afraid," said Luis, "but our spirits exult in the authority God gives us to preach to these people and share the Word of God with them. Our hope is that some of them will ultimately turn away from their wickedness and commit their lives to the Lord. That's why we stay here and why we preach."

The battle is still raging, pastors in some places are being shot, congregations scattered, but Luis Guerrero is one warrior who won't quit.

Chapter 4

Carving a Stone Mountain

The story of P.M. Thomas and the Himalaya Evangelical Mission (formerly Kashmir Evangelical Fellowship)

Like a sculptor carving a face out of a stone mountain, P.M. Thomas keeps chipping away at the seemingly impregnable forces hardening people's minds and hearts against Christ in the mountains of Kashmir.

As with sculpturing stone, the work is slow and tedious. And like one who fashions faces out of marble, Thomas has seen forms of beauty and grace appear. But it is not without price.

The little prince

Thomas grew up in a comfortable Syrian Christian family in Kerala, a state in southern India. Syrian

Christians trace their ancestry to those who came to India with the apostle Thomas. They hold equal status in society with the Brahmins—Hinduism's highest caste.

Whereas most people eked out a living on a small plot of land, Thomas's family was wealthy. His Grandfather Puthenparambil Idicheriah owned and operated the first bus in the area. The prosperity of that business enabled Grandfather Idicheriah to put his eldest son, P.I. Thomas, through college. The son went on to earn an M.A. degree—the first person to earn a post-graduate degree from that village.

The second son, P.I. Mathai, married. When Mathai's first son was born, they named him Puthenparambil Mathai Thomas. This reflected respectively his ancestral name, the given name of his father, and the name of his uncle who, like so many others, was named after the First Century apostle.

Little Thomas ruled the family estate like a little prince. He never had a worry, never a lack. Anything he wanted, he received. As he grew into his young teen years, he joined a gang. They delighted in strewing a footpath with thorns and other mischief. Then the boys' interests turned to girls, and one day the gang leader was killed trying to steal a girl out of her home. Thomas might have been among them, except one day Someone changed his life.

In the autumn of 1944, while Hindus celebrated their harvest festival, Christians conducted a spiritual revival. Ranni Kochupadesi was the evangelist. As this Malayalam speaker laid out the claims of Christ to the hundreds gathered in Attakulam Marthoma Hall, people began to weep and cry out under a burden of sin. Many, convicted by the Holy Spirit, stood to confess their sins and receive Christ as their personal Savior.

Young Thomas, age 14, stood with them. As he accepted the Lord with tears, he felt the burden of sin lift. After the meeting, Thomas walked home feeling like he wasn't even touching the ground.

"I became a new boy," he said later.

Youthful missionary

A missionary spirit immediately gripped the teenager.

"From the very day I accepted Christ, I had a burden for perishing souls. It grew stronger day by day and I knew that some day I would be working as a missionary somewhere in northern India," he said.

He organized a prayer group among his high school friends, and soon 50 young people were meeting regularly to pray at Mallappally High School.

Many of them later went into noted Christian service. Saphir Athial became the principal of Union Biblical Seminary then at Yeotmal (today called Yavatmal). C. Chacko became the registrar at Allahabad Bible Seminary. M.N. Samuel and K.M. Chacko became pastors of significant churches. And Varghese Kattapuram went to Africa as a missionary.

Dream evaporates

But Thomas's dream of missionary service suddenly evaporated. In 1947 his grandfather's bus company went bankrupt, dashing his dreams of going on to college.

Ironically, standing in front of the Church Missionary Society College in Kottayam and watching his former classmates going to their classes only intensified Thomas's desire to continue his studies.

"Some day the Lord will help me pursue my studies," Thomas told himself.

The answer came in a strange way. Instead of studying, Thomas was invited to teach. The headmaster of the Punnaveli Primary School operated by the CMS was a good friend of the family. He invited Thomas to teach the children there. Knowing the economic plight of his family and seeing no way to pursue a missionary career at that time, Thomas accepted.

When he received his first monthly salary of 12 rupees (then about four dollars), he promptly turned it over to his father to help with the family expenses. In six months' time Thomas was promoted to the CMS English School at Punnaveli.

During the next seven years the missionary call intensified in Thomas's life. Being a Malayalam speaker, he knew he would have to master Hindi if he ever was to bring Christ to the people of northern India, so he took an eight-month leave of absence to learn Hindi.

While studying Hindi, he began evangelizing his fellow students, and conducted Bible study meetings in his rented quarters. Several young people were born again and formed a young people's musical team.

In 1953 he took off another year without pay to devote full time to speaking in the churches of southern India. The young preacher who had preached faith from the Bible wanted to see if a person could truly live by faith.

The year's experiment proved satisfactory to Thomas as an individual and he seriously began thinking of resigning his teaching to serve the Lord on the mission field. But with his whole family depending upon his steady income, how could he ever leave his secure teaching position. *Perhaps,* he thought, *he could teach until the term ended. Then he would at least get the 100 rupee bonus summer pay. That would help.*

Plan vetoed

The pressure intensified when Thomas attended a special conference of the All Kerala Christian Fellowship in Maramon. Augustine Salins was preaching about Jacob urging the people to get rid of all of their foreign gods and golden earrings (Genesis 35).

The Spirit of the Lord began to convict Thomas of his quest for financial security.

"Lord, I can understand why they had to put away their foreign gods, but why did they have to bury their golden earrings?" Thomas asked the Lord in his heart. "Is gold bad?"

Thomas was thinking of the 100-rupee vacation pay he would get when school started in the fall. All he had to do was postpone resigning three more months until the spring term ended, and then show up on the first day of school in the fall.

Thomas's plan did not impress the Lord. "What is innocent enough for others is not my will for you," came the still, small voice.

"But Lord, how shall I survive?" Thomas whispered.

Thomas felt led to open his Bible to 2 Chronicles 25:9. What he saw amazed him. King Amaziah of Judah had hired the army of Israel to help him fight against the Moabites. But a prophet of God told Amaziah not to let the army of an idolatrous nation go with Judah's army to battle. When Amaziah asked the man of God how he could recover the 100 talents that he had already paid to the army of Israel, the man of God answered, "The Lord is able to give thee much more than this."

"If the Lord could recompense 100 talents, He certainly can make up 100 rupees," Thomas concluded. He wrote his letter of resignation and submitted it without even discussing it with his parents. He knew if he discussed it with them first, they would do their best to persuade him otherwise.

Commitment and temptation

This single act of obedience set off a chain reaction among his family members. One of his younger sisters, Ammini, dedicated her life for full-time missionary work and enrolled in Bible school. Before completing her first year, she married the Rev. Kunjukutty Athialy, who became the first known Indian missionary to Nepal after Sadhu Sundar Singh. Immediately after their marriage, they left for Nepal. One by one, all of Thomas's brothers and sisters committed themselves to full-time missionary work.

Another instant reaction occurred: temptation appeared. Someone in the USA heard about Thomas and offered him a full scholarship at a theological school in Los Angeles.

In those days, going to America for theological training was almost like going to Paradise. "Seek ye first the kingdom of God and His righteousness and America and all its dollars shall be added unto thee," was the popular notion.

"Lord, what should I do?" Thomas cried out. Every morning for six weeks he walked down the street and spent the day in prayer and fasting until evening. As he agonized in spirit, he realized that many who had gone to America for training never returned for ministry.

A visible answer to Thomas's prayer came in the form of a letter from Union Biblical Seminary in Yavatmal. It said that Thomas could enroll in its B.D. program—a small miracle since he had never gone to college.

Reluctantly, Thomas wrote to the school in Los Angeles, thanking them but declining the offer. The Lord's ways are eternally satisfying, but are rarely self-gratifying.

The Lord was carving Himself a missionary.

Round-robin mission jaunt

During that first summer after resigning, rather than return home to his family in Kerala, Thomas decided to visit the mission field of northern India. One of his lecturers had given him ten rupees. With that he could purchase a train ticket all the way to Kanpur—if he went third class, standing part of the way in extremely crowded conditions. Dr. Abdul Haq, the converted Muslim associated with Dr. Billy Graham, was going to hold an eight-day evangelistic campaign there. Thomas secured a position as counselor in return for food and lodging.

After the campaign, Thomas didn't know where to go, had no place to stay and was without funds. Trying to make it easy for the Lord to answer his prayer, he prayed, "Lord, would You please supply me with a space about two feet by six feet under the veranda of some shop where I might sleep at night?"

The next day Mr. Cliff Robinson, the American director of Youth for Christ in India, asked him if he could preach at a Youth for Christ rally in Delhi. The featured speaker, a well-known bishop, had canceled at the last minute.

Excited, Thomas immediately agreed—forgetting that he didn't have a rupee in his pocket. How would he ever get to Delhi? Again the next morning, he mustered his faith and went to the train station, hoping that the Lord would provide him the few rupees necessary to purchase a third-class ticket to Delhi. When he arrived at the station, Cliff Robinson met him with a first-class ticket in hand.

When Thomas arrived in Delhi, a chauffeur-driven car brought him to a spacious bungalow where he had a bedroom all to himself. The room had two beds, and Thomas was so excited about the commodious accommodations that he slept in both beds each night!

From Delhi, Thomas went to Kashmir in the top of India and visited mission works in Srinagar and Udhampur. He returned to Yeotmal with two cents in his pocket. The timely provisions on this journey were proof again that the faith life was possible.

While enrolled in UBS, Thomas studied for his B.A. down the street at a Hindu university. In 1961 Thomas completed both B.A. and B.D. degrees *magna cum laude*. Now came the real test: Would the eagle leave its nest?

Comfort zone

Sometimes the Lord tests us with hardships. At other times He waits to see if we deliberately refuse the soft life.

An Anglican Bishop offered Thomas the principalship of the Christian Institute at Alleppey as a preliminary step toward ordination. It was a relatively large, three-storied institution and Thomas would be surrounded by Christian friends.

"I went back on my calling and accepted the assignment as a temporary measure," Thomas said later. While there, he received many speaking invitations, which all the more flattered his ego.

"I continued to preach the missionary message while not actually obeying it myself," Thomas admitted.

Then, on a speaking engagement in Trivandrum, he met Christy.

Missionary marriage

Often meeting an attractive young lady can sidetrack a young man from his avowed purpose. For Thomas, meeting Christy had the opposite effect. She was the only daughter of Kunjappy Upadesi, then one of the most outstanding evangelists in Kerala.

"Papa, please let me go as a missionary to northern India," she had often begged.

But every time Papa Upadesi had replied, "I will not send you out as a single girl. Get married first. Then you can go wherever you want."

In an arranged appointment, Father Upadesi escorted Thomas and Christy to a room with two chairs and said, "You can discuss what you want in here." And then left.

There were some awkward moments. Finally, Thomas said softly, "Don't look at the prestigious building where I am working, and don't look at my salaried position. I'm going to North India as a faith missionary. We may have to sleep under a tree, and there may be no food to eat. Will you be willing to come with me for such a life of sacrifice?"

Thomas waited apprehensively for Christy's response. Her reply astonished him.

"I have had many marriage proposals," she said, "all from men in secure positions. But I have been waiting for a man to ask me that particular question. I will be happy to go with you."

They were married in 1962. The next year they sent out a typed prayer letter to their closest friends informing them that they were leaving for Kashmir on November 1. On that day they said good-bye to friends in Kerala and boarded the train at Trivandrum. They had with them only a handful of belongings and their infant son, Santhosh.

As the train stopped again at Tiruvalla and Kottyam, more friends wished them well—and pressed into their hands warm clothing and blankets. Thomas and Christy had never experienced a Kashmir winter.

In those days, there was no direct train from Kerala to Kashmir. The Thomases had to change trains in Madras and Delhi. They also stopped to visit friends in Yeotmal along the way. Sixteen days after they left home, their train pulled into Pathankot on the southern edge of the state. They boarded a bus for the three-hour road trip to Jammu, the winter capital, and then transferred to another bus for the remaining two-and-a-half-hour leg of the journey. Exhausted, they finally pulled into Udhampur at four o'clock in the afternoon. It was winter, and there wasn't a church within 100,000 square miles.

One-room outpost

Udhampur had long been a mission station of Worldwide Evangelization Crusade. They had won some converts, and small groups gathered here and there for prayer, but no church buildings had been constructed. Now the few remaining foreign missionaries were leaving. WEC missionaries Mr. and Mrs. Tom Cain knew about the Thomases' coming and had located a small brick hut for their living quarters. Because it was on a main highway and near the bus station, the rent was high—30 rupees (at that time $5) a month.

The two missionaries from Kerala found Kashmir unbelievably cold. The house had no heat, and no rug covered its dried mud floor. Thomas found two discarded planks to use as cots, and some newspaper for a mattress. They slept with all their clothes on. Thomas had sent some goods on ahead, but they had not arrived yet, and their baggage was lost.

A few days later, Thomas received a check for 150 rupees from K.V. Cherian, the founder of the All Kerala Christian Fellowship. Thomas took it to the bank, which received it and said he could have his money as soon as the check went through the system. The Cains heard about it, and advanced Thomas the 150 rupees until the check cleared.

That enabled the Thomases to rent a little house built originally for refugees. It wasn't any warmer, but it had a cement floor that was cleaner and its concrete block walls offered greater security.

A month later a second check arrived. The third month another. Thomas deposited all with the same bank, but still received no cash. By this time, the Cains had advanced Thomas 450 rupees. In the fourth month all the checks were returned with the message, "We have no dealings with the State Bank of Travancore." The local bank in remote Kashmir simply was not able to complete the transaction with the small bank in Kerala, some 2,500 miles away. After this, the Cherians sent their gifts by postal money order.

About this time, the Cains bid a final *adieu*. Thomas and Christy were on their own.

Lonely journeys

Work in these cold months was slow. Only four other people crowded into their one-room hut for their first Sunday service. The preacher who had spoken at grand conventions in the South presented the Word just as earnestly to these few. He was sure that if he preached the Word faithfully, it would not return void (Isaiah 55:11).

Sympathetic army personnel gave Thomas an old army tent to hold meetings at the nearby refugee camp. He also rented a building up town for Sunday services.

During the week Thomas traveled many miles handing out tracts and sharing Christ one-on-one. If he had money, he took the bus. Often he walked because that was the only way to reach a village.

This was Hindu territory with a strong contingent of Muslims. Not all wanted to hear about Christ. Some turned him cruelly away and would not contaminate their drinking cups by offering him, a Christian, a drink of water. Many nights Christy wondered if her husband would return. How welcome his footsteps sounded.

As Thomas gently hammered home the gospel, the hardness of some of these mountain folks softened. By the following September seven persons had accepted Christ and were ready for baptism. The next April five more were baptized.

The success of his efforts irritated his landlord.

"We need our own meeting place," Thomas announced.

Marvelous provision

Thomas began to pray earnestly for funds with which to buy a small piece of land. Instead of receiving more, however, the gifts diminished. Sometimes there wasn't even enough to buy food, and Christy and Thomas fasted to the Lord.

One day Thomas felt the Lord tell him, "Wherever the soles of your feet shall tread shall be yours."

Thomas and Christy and the handful of believers walked around Udhampur stepping on some of the best pieces of property available.

As a last resort, and with little faith that it would do any good, Thomas and his little flock appealed to the civil authorities for a piece of land.

"We don't even have a place of burial," Thomas told them.

Hindus owned large tracts of sacred land throughout the region, and Muslims owned similar properties. The authorities looked upon Thomas's request as an opportunity to demonstrate that the government was truly a secular (non-Hindu) state. To the little flock's amazement and exuberance, authorities gave them three-quarters of an acre on National Highway Number One free and clear! They only required that any building be at least 50 feet from the roadway.

It was a hilly piece of property that lay below road level. The believers started leveling it with their shovels and baskets. Christians among the army personnel stationed at Udhampur brought in some power equipment and helped.

It wasn't long before the believers had constructed a mud hut nine feet wide, 11 feet long and six feet high. The preacher didn't realize the importance of foundations, so the walls sat on the ground. Thomas packed up his tent and few belongings, nailed a wooden cross on the front of the mud building and moved in.

Thomas and his family (which now included daughter Grace, born June 6, 1965) ate and slept there. On Sundays they moved their few belongings (a wooden trunk and a single bed—no chairs) into the yard and conducted church in their mud hut.

Motor home

But it was a miserable accommodation. The roof leaked so badly that one day during a heavy rain the family came home and found their cooking utensils, Bibles and clothes floating in the water.

"Lord, where shall we go?" they cried as they bailed out their soggy structure.

The next day, a team from Operation Mobilization stopped and asked if they could park their malfunctioning truck on their land. Thomas gladly consented. For the next few weeks they enjoyed a luxurious bedroom with battery-powered lights until the monsoon season was over.

The one-room hut could hardly accommodate 15 people squatting on the floor. Immediately, Thomas made plans to build a 14-by-24-foot addition out of brick.

Obstinate opposition

The two-dozen believers had barely completed the foundation when a clerk from the court walked up to Thomas and handed him a stay of construction.

"I can't accept this, because I do not read Urdu," Thomas said, knowing full well what it was. Urdu was the official language of the state of Kashmir.

"You will have to bring me a copy in English," Thomas said. English was the official language of the federal government acceptable in all states.

As soon as the clerk left, Thomas and his crew grabbed the tent and started putting it up over the foundation. By the time the official returned two hours later, the lower footage of the walls were completely encased in the old army tent.

Then, like Nehemiah of old, Thomas realized he would have to work by stealth. Defying the stay order, Thomas and his crew worked at night. They slept in the mornings, and went out for ministry in the afternoons and evenings. They had little money and often they performed the exhausting labor on empty stomachs.

"Every brick has its own testimony," Thomas says.

But with the tent completely surrounding the walls, passersby did not notice the walls going up one row of brick at a time—not even when the walls literally began raising the roof.

Still the stay orders kept coming—a total of six—each one from a different office, each with a different objection.

"We dreaded to see a khaki uniform coming our way because we knew it would be a court courier with another stay order," Thomas said. "It was a miracle they didn't use police action against us."

Through stealth, perseverance and prayer, the little brick meeting hall was completed. But when men came to put on the roof, they discovered that one end of the building was one-and-a-half feet wider than the other! It didn't matter to Thomas that the building lacked a foundation. He and his family were glad to move into it and vacate the dank mud hut.

However, they had to move their belongings—a wooden chest and table—out into the yard every Sunday so the church could meet there. And they faced another problem: the congregation was growing and the hall that was commodious for 24 was now crowded with 50. So by faith Thomas ordered 50,000 bricks brought in and planned a new two-story structure 30 feet by 60 feet.

Holy hullabaloo

This time Thomas poured a foundation—so good that engineers later said it would support three stories. That was when the trouble really started. When the size of the new structure became obvious, the members of the local *Aryasamaj*, a nationalistic Hindu society, stirred up vehement opposition. They wrote defaming articles in the local newspaper, and led a noisy protest through the city streets.

"It will defile our holy temple," the protesters argued.

"The holy river will be desecrated."

"The gods will vent their anger against us."

Local shops closed. Public rallies denounced the Christians. Many who had been friendly with Thomas suddenly stood against him. Even the deputy commissioner, the highest official in the district, sided with the opposers.

Again stay orders started coming, and again Thomas proceeded with the construction.

Then one of the members of the Muslim minority wrote a letter to the chief minister saying they supported Thomas. When some of the educated Hindus heard about it, they similarly came to Thomas privately and expressed their sympathy for his endeavor.

Higher authority

That night Thomas read Ecclesiastes 5:8—"If you see the oppression of the poor, and the violent perversion of justice and righteousness in a province, do not marvel at the matter; for high official watches over high official, and higher officials are over them."

That did it. Thomas and a few believers went to Srinagar to meet with the chief minister of the state.

"We have been worshipping in Udhampur for over one-and-a-half years. We ask that you enforce the provision of the Constitution of India that guarantees freedom of religion," Thomas told them.

To their relief and amazement, the chief minister stayed all proceedings against the land and building.

Upon returning home, Thomas's joy was quashed by a telegram stating that his elder sister, Mary, had died. It was the first death of a close family member in Thomas's family. But he couldn't go to the funeral. It would take five days by train, even if he had had the money.

Quietly, Thomas and Christy held their own memorial service in their little house.

Mortal blow?

By 1971, the ground floor of the new building had been completed. Plans called for adding a second floor and then a permanent roof. But Thomas didn't have funds for that. So he got permission to cut some trees for timber and gather some bamboo and grass from the forest and construct a temporary thatch roof.

The temporary roof was completed just in time for Thomas's annual convention. The completed ground floor would be used as a meeting hall, and Thomas and Christy and their two children could use the brick addition to the mud hut as their living quarters. At last Thomas would have a place he could use for study and prayer, and not have to move all of his things out every Sunday.

Then the sledge-hammer blow hit. Enemies of the gospel had managed to get the local government to post an eviction notice on the building. It said the property had been reallocated for a tuberculosis clinic and Thomas was ordered to demolish his own church and vacate the premises. If he failed to do so, the local government would do it for him and charge him for the expenses.

That night Thomas stood in the meeting room ready to begin a four-day convention. He was holding the eviction notice in his hand when he suddenly slumped to the floor with severe chest pain, sweating and vomiting. Friends rushed him to the hospital where doctors said he had suffered a heart attack. Fear struck the little flock as they began to think that maybe the big bad wolves were going to win after all.

Two days after his admittance to the hospital, Thomas penned a letter to Indira Gandhi, then in her first term as prime minister. He never dreamed she would ever read it, but it was something he felt he needed to do.

A few days later, Thomas saw Christ stand beside his bed and pray for him. Within days, Thomas walked out of the hospital a healed man.

When he returned home, he learned that Christy had mailed a form letter telling of recent events to all their friends and contacts. Now a pile of checks, money orders and bank drafts lay on the table.

"I kind of wished this heart attack had come a little sooner," Thomas mused.

To his further surprise, Thomas started receiving calls from high government officials. First, the chief secretary, Mr. Mangath Rai, called, and then the chief minister of the state, Mr. Sadique. Both assured him he would have no more trouble. The deputy commissioner who had so vehemently opposed Thomas was suspended pending corruption charges and later died of a heart attack.

The work multiplies

From that point onward, the Kashmir Evangelical Fellowship, as Thomas's work was then called, experienced a move of the Spirit of God. It soon spread to members of the civil service and to army personnel.

A boy who had run away from home five years earlier suddenly returned after three days of fasting and prayer. The whole family of high-caste Hindus trusted in Christ alone.

A young noncommissioned officer from the army came to Thomas for counsel. Though he and his wife had been married for seven years, they had no child. The Thomases prayed for them. The woman gave birth to a son the next year and eventually had four more children. The officer, P.G. Vargis, accepted the Lord, resigned his commission and became a full-time missionary. Several months later he started his own ministry, which subsequently moved to Punjab and has since spread throughout northern India.[1]

A young captain, A.M. Samuel, began attending Thomas's services with his wife. After a year and a half, he resigned his job and started another ministry near

---

[1] See chapter five, "The Galloping Horse of North India."

Udhampur. Today he leads an effective ministry with about 30 missionaries reaching across northwestern India with scores of churches and hundreds of believers.

Sosamma was a high-ranking army nurse and easily would have become a colonel had she stayed in the military. When she resigned her commission to serve the Lord, she relinquished a higher salary than the others. Her sacrifice and commitment greatly elevated the ministry in the eyes of the people. She married Thomas's brother, P.M. Philip, and worked for the ministry a number of years.

A young Tibetan resigned his position as a postgraduate lecturer in a government college and went to work full time with P.M. Thomas. Mr. Elijah Gergan obtained his M.Div. and M.Th. in Korea and went to serve at Ladakh, a most difficult area lying between 9,000 and 13,000 feet altitude.

A young man with the General Reserve Engineer Force suffered a peptic ulcer for seven years. During one of the meetings when miracles were being manifest, P.M. Joseph laid hands on his own body and prayed. His complete healing astounded everybody including himself. Like the others, he also left his engineering post, began serving the Lord full time, and has since started five churches near Jammu.

Another army man, T.C. Chacko, had grown cold toward the Lord. After attending Thomas's meetings, his faith revived. Like the Vargises, he and his wife had not had children, either. Thomas prayed for them and a year later his wife gave birth to twins. Chacko has since started another missionary work now centered in the state of Himachal Pradesh.

Altogether, the ministry of Kashmir Evangelical Fellowship has spawned about a dozen other ministries, which collectively have over 3000 missionaries serving the Lord in northern India.

Crisis from within

Of course not all of this growth was easy, and many of the separations were painful at the time. The worst crisis occurred in 1988—just when KEF was getting ready to celebrate its silver anniversary. While Thomas was on a speaking tour in Kerala, he was smitten with prostate problems and had to have surgery. While he was incapacitated, two of his brothers tried to take control of the ministry and drafted most of the senior missionaries into their scheme. Only Thomas, his wife, his son, and two other workers remained.

Thomas was later exonerated of all accusations, but the work was decimated. A compromise was reached that enabled each of the workers involved in the conspiracy to keep the mission station they had worked. For a while, they formed their own organization that was supported with outside help for a year. But the organization soon disintegrated. Those who conspire against others rarely get along well with themselves.

"Not two of them are left working with each other today," Thomas says.

Thomas philosophizes, "Such problems only occur where there is life and growth. There are fewer problems where work is stagnant. We have also learned that problems draw us closer to the center of God's will. Through problems, we learn better how to serve Him."

God vindicated Thomas in other ways. Even the Hindus who opposed the construction of the church on the basis that it might defile their holy bathing sites later had to post a notice that the river was no longer safe for sacred bathing. The waste from several hospitals, including the tuberculosis hospital that was supposed to replace the church, now pollutes the river.

Beginning again

After the crisis of 1988, God blessed KEF with all new personnel who carried the Word of God throughout the Himalaya region of North India. Believers from Nepal and Bhutan also joined the work and took the gospel back to their own resistant countries.

As the work spread beyond Kashmir, Thomas began looking for a more central headquarters location. In 1995 he found a place in Gorakhpur in Uttar Pradesh. He relocated there and renamed the work Himalaya Evangelical Mission because it then was reaching the entire Himalaya range of India, Nepal and Bhutan.

HEM has a 20,000-square-foot headquarters complex in Udhampur with classrooms, assembly halls and accommodations. In Gorakhpur it has a central church and headquarters. It conducts an English-language school for children in Kashmir, another in the local dialect, and a missionary training institute at Gorakhpur.

Thomas and his associates carry out relief work among some of the thousands of refugees along the Pakistan-Kashmir border and provide medical services, including two eye clinics.

HEM now has more than 200 missionaries holding forth the word of Life in ten states of North India, Nepal and Bhutan. These include 25 missionaries working in Kashmir with Thomas's son, Santhosh. Together they have planted over 100 churches. In addition, the nine churches KEF missionaries planted in Kashmir before the crisis continue to maintain fellowship with them.

The whole is quite a leap forward from the original four persons who joined him for his first Sunday service in the one-room hut.

Indeed, the now silver-haired missionary has fashioned quite a shrine for the Lord in these Himalaya Hills. The temple is made not from marble, but from living stones—human lives redeemed through the grace of Christ. An outward glance may show the cracks of human nature and weathered effects of years of adversity. But if you could look inside as the Lord does, you would see something grander than the Taj Mahal—hearts made holy by the blood of the Lamb.

Chapter 5

The Galloping Horse of North India

The Story of P.G. Vargis and the Indian Evangelical Team

The young, noncommissioned army officer looked out on the beauty of the distant Himalaya Mountains.

Having given his life to Christ only three months earlier, P.G. Vargis had taken his holiday leave to visit the Kashmir town of Katra. Each year, some 600,000 Hindu pilgrims swelled this town of 5,000 and painstakingly climbed the 11-mile trail to the shrine of the Hindu goddess Kali. Then they slowly descended again, exhausted, and their hearts were just as empty as when they went up.

Vargis had brought along some gospel tracts and had handed them out. *I can show some of them the true way to salvation,* he thought. *If I had an adequate supply of literature, I could reach 200,000 people a year.*

Now on this New Year's Day, 1972, with his supply exhausted, he sat watching the low-hanging winter sun sink behind the Kashmiri hills.

As the nearer valleys darkened from the shadows, little cooking fires began to appear on the hillsides. Suddenly, a realization jolted his reverie. Each fire represented a family—human beings, all living in ignorance of Christ.

"Who will tell them about Me?" the Lord Jesus spoke quietly to his heart.

Vargis fidgeted. His life was beginning to come together. A few more years in the army and he could retire with pension. Meanwhile, he could witness on base, and preach while on leave. He was already using a tithe of his wages to buy and distribute gospel literature. Wasn't that enough?

The shadows deepened, and each firelight brightened by contrast.

"Help us," they seemed to plead.

He felt the Lord was telling him to quit his army post and serve Him as a full-time faith missionary.

"I have no education," Vargis argued within himself. "I have no training, no backing. I wouldn't know what to do."

"I will be with you," the Lord assured him.

It was nearly night now. As far as Vargis could see, little lights dotted the hillsides. Each flicker represented a mother, father and children, all dwelling in spiritual darkness.

"Will they perish forever because you don't go to them?"

Vargis agonized in his spirit. He knew there was only one acceptable answer.

"O.K., Lord, I'll do it."

Later, he wrote of the event in his diary, "Though my bones may lie in some unknown valley in Kashmir, though my wife may become a widow in her twenties and my son an orphan in his childhood, nothing will turn me back. I will go ahead with my Savior, who called me and anointed me to evangelize the unreached."

The commitment was made. Carrying it out would not be easy.

Revived from death

Vargis was born into a high-caste Syrian Orthodox home on April 13, 1942. A strange sickness struck the newborn and within a few days his grandmother pronounced him dead. Since the child had not been christened, he could not even be buried in the church cemetery.

Ammu, his distraught mother wailed loudly but her mother rebuked her. "Don't carry on like that or you'll bring more trouble on yourself," she said. She then put the cold, lifeless body on a banana leaf and gently slid it under Ammu's cot. *Maybe putting the infant out of sight would help relieve Ammu's grief,* she thought, while they waited for the oldest brother and a servant to dig a tiny grave in the backyard.

After everyone else had left the room, Ammu knelt beside the bed and cried quietly so no one could hear her. Her dear husband was working in another town miles away. If a runner were sent, and her husband returned immediately, three days would be the soonest he could arrive. The body would not keep that long in the heat of summer.

Suddenly, through tear-blurred eyes Ammu thought she saw a little finger move ever so slightly. She stared in disbelief, hoping against hope. It moved again.

"He's alive!" she screamed.

She carefully pulled the tiny body out from under the bed and cradled him in her arms. Gradually, the infant revived. The family was grateful to God, and christened the child Geevarghese, Malayalam for Gregarios, a popular saint among Syrian Orthodox followers. The name was later shortened to Vargis, which is translated into English as "George."

God clearly had a claim on Vargis' life. Conveying that claim to Vargis' consciousness and that of his family was another matter. Vargis had been redeemed from death to bring a new quality of life to many. But no one understood that then. It was many years before Vargis realized it himself.

Disillusioned with religion

Vargis grew up with a seemingly unquenchable thirst driving his life. As a youth, he agreed to ordination as a priest's assistant. The first time he entered the holy place reserved only for priests, a holy awe overcame him—until he noticed the casual air of the priests behind the sacred curtain. They bickered and joked and became angry with each other. They weren't any more holy than he was, Vargis concluded. That ended his romance with the Syrian Orthodox Church.

In his college days, Vargis studied mesmerism and black magic and worshipped Hindu gods. He began drinking and smoking and seeing worldly movies. Still, nothing satisfied the thirst that was in him.

A Hindu holy man once advised him, "There is a vacuum in the heart of every person. If you fill this vacuum with God, you will not have to smoke, or drink, or do vile things."

That made sense. But how did one find God?

Yoga didn't help.

Maybe if he visited the Kali goddess in Calcutta, she would bless him.

After traveling to the site, Vargis stared up at the statue of the four-armed woman wearing a garland of male heads and a skirt of severed arms. In one hand she held a freshly amputated head still dripping blood into a basin held by another hand. A third hand held a sword dripping blood, while her fourth hand held the devil's trident. A long tongue protruded past her chin.

"How could such a blood-thirsty idol bless anyone?" he wondered, and turned away.

Ultimately, Vargis dropped out of college, did odd jobs for a couple of years, and then joined the army. He became a cynic of every religion, and loved to stand on his footlocker and give "sermons" mocking the Christians' beliefs. He drank alcohol from morning till night and smoked 130 cigarettes a day.

But he was miserable. One day he decided to go and bathe in the River Ganges. Maybe that would deliver him from his bad habits.

Hindus not only prized bathing in the holy river, they believed dying beside it brought special blessings in the after life. After death, professional cremators are hired to burn the body and return the ashes to the family.

When Vargis looked into the river, what he saw repulsed him. Not only was the river terribly polluted with sewage from upstream cities, in the filth floated several half-burned bodies jettisoned by cremators who had hurried their job. As he stared in dismay, he saw bodies of several babies sacrificed to the river bobbing in the brine. Vargis could not bring himself to step into the desecrated stream. He turned away utterly disillusioned.

Suicide option

Though he had led a corrupt life while in the army as well as at college, back home he was still considered a reputable young man. His father was wealthy and highly respected in the village. Ultimately, his father arranged a marriage with the daughter of another respected family, and on July 24, 1967, Lilly and Vargis were married. Lilly was a devout member of the Mar Thoma Church (named after the apostle Thomas) which had come out of the Syrian Orthodox Church as a result of a spiritual awakening in the nineteenth century. By this time, however, the revival had waned.

Meanwhile, Vargis' torment of soul continued. He got into trouble and feared he might be court-martialed, so one day in Delhi decided to end his life. He wrote and mailed letters to his sister and his cousin. He didn't bother to write his wife.

As he stood on the verandah ready to pop a handful of sleeping pills into his mouth, he suddenly wondered what he would face after death. Was the Christian teaching right? Was there a real heaven? Hell? God? He didn't think so. But if they were real, he knew where he would end up.

Or maybe the Hindus were right: There is only one chance in 100,000 to escape the torment of continual rebirth. For just one sin, the Hindu scriptures taught, one must be fried in a copper pan without oil for 1000 years—multiplied by the number of hairs on the body of a cow. In either case, he couldn't take the chance. He was too distraught to live, and too afraid to die.

The military officers in charge of his case showed him kindness—they gave him time to straighten things out. During this time he went to the library to read the biography of Mahatma Gandhi. It mentioned that Gandhi received strength to become a good person by reading the Sermon on the Mount in Matthew 5-7.

So Vargis began reading the Bible. The gospels, Psalms and Proverbs were like soothing oil to his aching heart. When he read Isaiah or Jeremiah, he stood condemned. He quit reading the Bible, though he still respected it.

In June of 1970, he requested and received transfer to Udhampur, a town of about 10,000 located in the foothills of the Himalaya Mountains of Kashmir in the northern reaches of India. After visiting his wife, he departed for his new assignment, while Lilly remained in Kerala where she continued—and completed—her teacher's training.

Soon after his arrival in Udhampur, Vargis received word that Lilly was pregnant. A few months later, he received another notice that she had miscarried. Vargis wrote his brother-in-law to send Lilly to him as soon as she was well enough to travel by train. Lilly arrived in Udhampur in March 1971.

Life-changing encounter

In late September, an evangelist and former Muslim, Jordan Khan, spoke at the Protestant church in the town. Lilly, who was now expecting again, asked Vargis to go with her. When Vargis refused, Lilly began to cry. Then, remembering her doctor's advice, "Keep her happy to avoid another miscarriage," he decided to go with her.

The second night Lilly was not feeling well and urged Vargis to attend without her. He went again, reluctantly, to please his wife.

That night Khan preached on Revelation 3:20, "If any man hear my voice and open the door, I will come in and will sup with him and he with me." Then the evangelist said: "If you confess your sins to Jesus and invite Him into your life, He will forgive you, and will give you a new heart."

That was what Vargis wanted. But as the service ended, he remembered the one time he had confessed to a Roman Catholic priest. *It's all a hoax,* he concluded, and slipped out a side door to avoid the preacher.

An army captain driving an army truck offered to give him and a few others a ride back to the barracks. Vargis gladly clamored on board with the rest. On the way, the Holy Spirit began to convict him. Suddenly he remembered Jordan Khan saying, "When Jesus comes in and 'sups' with you, He stays with you through the night (death). Then, in the (resurrection) morning, you rise to be with Him forever."

Vargis seemed to hear Jesus speaking to him, "I will give you a new heart." Right there in the truck, Vargis confessed his sins and asked the Lord Jesus into his life. He began to quietly praise the Lord. What joy and peace flooded his heart.

"Vargis," a human voice suddenly spoke. "We're at your place."

He opened his eyes. He was the only passenger left in the vehicle and the captain was asking him to get out. He went into his room and recorded the date, October 1, 1971.

Vargis and Lilly were on a honeymoon all over again. "I married her in 1967, but I didn't fall in love with her until after I was saved," he admits.

And he was on a honeymoon with the Lord, too. He told everyone he met about the Lord Jesus and what He had done for him. He began using a tithe of his income to purchase gospel tracts and booklets and gave them to people at the bus stop, in the army base, on the street, and everywhere he went.

During the year-end holidays, he went to Katra to hand out gospel tracts to pilgrims visiting the Hindu shrine. That was when God spoke to him about becoming a full-time faith missionary.

Once that decision was made, he immediately felt peace. Only he did not yet realize what it would require.

On January 19, Lilly gave birth to a baby boy. They named him Aby, after the Biblical Abraham.

Obedience in baptism

Soon after that, he felt the Lord speak to him inwardly: "You must be baptized with water."

Startled, he searched the Scriptures to learn what this meant.

"You've been talking to the Pentecostals!" his wife charged.

"No, Lilly, the Lord spoke to me," he answered.

Together, they read Acts 2. When those who heard Peter's sermon said, "Brethren, what shall we do?" Peter replied, "Repent and be baptized, every one of you in the name of Jesus Christ for the remission of sins, and you will receive the gift of the Holy Spirit."

For Vargis, the matter was settled.

"Don't force me," Lilly warned. She was still angry.

Up until then, the Protestant church in Udhampur led by P.M. Thomas had baptized converts from Hinduism, but never before had it immersed anyone who had been sprinkled as an infant.

Vargis arranged to be baptized in March following a Sunday morning English service, and to have Aby dedicated during the afternoon Hindi service. The night before the events were to occur, the Lord spoke to Lilly's heart as well. So on March 12, 1972, Vargis and Lilly were baptized, along with several others.

Five chapattis

By July, Vargis still had not resigned from the army and the prospect of stepping out by faith as a missionary scared him. Those who served with Brother Thomas lived by faith. There was no guarantee of support. *How will I ever be able to feed Lilly and Aby if I resign from the army?* he thought. He got on his knees before the Lord.

"If I fed 5,000 with five chapattis, how many chapattis do I need to feed you, your wife and son for one year?" the Lord asked him. (A chapatti is a pancake-like Indian bread, similar to a tortilla, made of wheat flour.)

Vargis began to calculate: If five chapattis provided 5,000 meals, then one chapatti would provide 1,000 meals. He concluded that one-and-a-quarter of the Lord's chapattis would provide all the food he, Lilly and Aby would need for the next year. A simple thing for the Lord to do!

Yet they needed not only living expenses, but ministry funds as well. While in prayer, Vargis sensed the Lord's counsel: "Son, when the apostle Thomas came to India, which American mission was there to send him a check every month? Which church was sending his monthly support?"

The apostle could hardly have gotten even a letter. There was not a single Christian in India to greet him when he arrived. Then Vargis remembered the verse,

"Jesus Christ, the same yesterday, today and forever" (Hebrews 13:8).

If He sustained the apostle Thomas, He can sustain me, Vargis concluded.

So Vargis determined to trust the Lord completely for his needs. He would give away all his possessions except a few clothes and head for Katra, the Hindu pilgrimage site in Jammu-Kashmir. Yet, could he, Lilly and Aby survive in that hostile environment?

Presenting the plan to his wife's family was another major obstacle. All were nominal church members, except one brother. He was a firm believer, but he didn't go along with Vargis' "fanatical" ways. So when Vargis was about to leave from the family home in southern India for Katra, he desperately sought some reassurance from the Lord that he was doing the right thing. After all, no one in the family encouraged him.

The galloping horse

Sunday morning he prayed about which church to attend, and felt led to go to a small, gospel-preaching church about three miles away. He felt he would receive some "word from the Lord" there.

The silver-haired pastor allowed Vargis to give his testimony to the congregation. Afterwards, the pastor stood to give the benediction, and then hesitated.

"Beloved ones," he said, "I was waiting to know if anyone else has a prophecy from the Lord, other than the one I received this morning."

No one responded.

"While I was praying this morning, I suddenly had a vision. I saw a war horse galloping across many frontiers, and nobody could stop it or bind it. It went all over North India, and still it kept going on to further territories."

Turning to young Vargis, the pastor said, "Young man, don't look back. The Lord is with you. GO!"

Vargis felt as if he had been shot from a canon.

The Galloping Horse of North India

He was discharged from the army, and the next day Thomas placed all his cash resources as a thank-offering to the Lord in the Udhampur church, and the small band of believers there dedicated him and Lilly to the Lord's service.

No room for Christians

Arriving there at 10 in the morning on October 30, 1972, he immediately began to inquire about rooms.

"Yes, we have rooms. What is your religion?"

"I am a Christian."

"Sorry, we have no rooms for Christians here."

Similar refusals continued repeatedly until three o'clock in the afternoon. By this time Vargis was tired and beginning to doubt. He stopped at the side of the road and prayed, "Lord, if you have a room for me here, please show me where it is."

"Sir," a voice shouted from the other side of the road. "Do you need a room?"

"Yes, I do," Vargis replied, dumbfounded.

"Then come with me," a young man said.

The young man took him to a tea shop and ordered a glass of hot milk. "You are like my older brother," he said. "Here, drink this. I'll go find you a room."

In about 15 minutes the young man came running. "Come," he said. "I give you two choices. You can choose."

The first building had only a plain room and a kitchen. The second one was a beautiful house with courtyard. Vargis told the owner he would rent one room with an add-on kitchen of about 6' by 4'. He was elated.

Lilly and Aby joined him seven days later. The next day, Vargis and his family began distributing tracts.

Learning Hindustani

Though Vargis' mother tongue was Malayalam and he spoke English and Hindi fluently, he realized he would have to learn Hindustani (a form of Hindi that includes Persian and Arabic words that today is called

Urdu), the language common to this northern region, to communicate to the townsfolk. He cried and prayed and struggled. Soon he was speaking Hindustani quite well.

Then Vargis and Lilly started literacy and hygiene classes for about 24 children. These were children of the "untouchables" who stood daily begging from the pilgrims. Every day, the Vargises selected two of the children to have lunch with them. They tenderly washed the children, anointed their heads with oil (a daily practice in sun-scorched India), and allowed them to eat with them. The children could hardly believe this was happening to "outcasts."

Follow-up visits to the homes further endeared the Vargises to the parents. After only five months of patient endeavor, 18 persons had accepted Christ and were ready for baptism. By Vargis's first anniversary in that place, he had baptized 78 new converts. Such results for North India were unheard of.

Mountain mama

One day while visiting door-to-door, Vargis and Lilly met a woman from the mountains who took keen interest in their message. She learned where Vargis and Lilly were going and every day showed up in the houses they visited. Finally, she accepted the Lord and confessed her faith publicly. She implored them to visit her village in the mountains.

The trip would be too rough for Lilly and Aby, so two Christian men went with Vargis. The woman's house was on the fourth mountain past the end of the bus line, a 30-mile journey over very rugged terrain. Water was available at only two places in the 30 miles.

The first time Vargis visited there, the people were overjoyed to have someone from the outside world visit them, and they were warmly received.

The second time he visited them, and he almost lost his life.

The woman, a widow, had eight children: four grown men and four daughters. The young men misunderstood his motives and planned to kill him. The woman, Hannah, came to him privately the next morning and told him to flee for his life. As Vargis grabbed his bag, he noticed the oldest boy sharpening his ax.

Vargis did not run, for he did not want to attract attention, but he walked as fast as he could until he was outside the village. Then he ran like crazy. Winded, he finally stopped to rest briefly and take a drink of water. Then he realized he had left without filling his canteen. Seventeen miles of mountain terrain lay between him and the next water. As he looked back, he saw the young men descending the mountain he had fled. There was no turning back.

Suddenly a hen fluttered along the path by an egg she had laid. *Surely, a house must be nearby,* he thought. He found the house below his path and bargained with the householder for a flask of water and six eggs. Then he was off. He reached the bus stop before his pursuers and arrived home safely.

Change of heart

About a week later the oldest son arrived at his house.

"Padre Sahib [Sir], we are sorry that you left our village so quickly. My mother asked me to come and fetch you again for four days of meetings."

"I am glad you want me to return," Vargis replied, "but I cannot come just now. Go on home and I will come after some weeks." Vargis had no intention of going.

But the young man persisted. He came to the Bible study that night. *Pretended spirituality*, Vargis thought.

The young man came back the next night, and the next.

Finally, after several days, the Lord seemed to be saying, "Go with him." Vargis went.

It was dusk when he reached the village and the people greeted him warmly. A meeting was called and a little fire kindled, since it was now dark. Vargis feared to close his eyes to pray. *As soon as I close my eyes,* he thought, *they will kill me.*

Nevertheless he shut his eyes and began to pray. Immediately, he heard voices and opened his eyes. It seemed as though everyone present was praying out loud.

"What happened?" Vargis asked.

"Padre Sahib, after you left so hastily the last time you were here, I felt so bad, I immediately began to pray for you," Hannah said. "After a long while, my sons returned. My oldest son came to me and said, 'Mama, I'm sorry.' And he started to cry. Then he accepted the Lord. After a while my next son came. Soon, all my children came to me and they all accepted the Lord. Other people in the village have believed with us. Now we are here to learn from you."

Vargis was overjoyed. Before he left he baptized 18 new Christians.

Beginning again

Up until this point, Vargis had been serving the Lord under the leadership of P.M. Thomas of Kashmir Evangelical Fellowship. Vargis now felt the Lord was telling him to separate and work independently. Thomas released him, and the two men continue as friends and supporters of each other's ministry to this day.

The work in Katra grew. Other men began to join Vargis and his wife. In mid-1973, Sankru Abraham, the first indigenous worker from Jammu-Kashmir, came to Katra to work with Vargis, and in October, P.M. Joseph joined him.

Vargis told each of these men: "I have no money. But I promise you this: If I get only one chapatti, I will share it with you equally." They understood.

Soon they had three mission outposts in the mountains surrounding Katra. So in July, 1974, they named their work Kashmir Evangelical Team.

The work continued to spread, and in 1976 they opened their first mission outpost outside Jammu and

Kashmir in the state of Punjab. Accordingly, they renamed their ministry Indian Evangelical Team to reflect the expanded outreach. The Lord was working to enlarge Vargis's vision to include all of North India.

The team forged ahead, motivated by C.T. Studd's words, "Let us gamble our lives for Christ! If we perish, we perish." They chose as their slogan, "Reaching the lost at any cost." Many times they proved these words by risking their lives to share Christ.

Vargis's brother, Josh, joined him in the work in 1974. Mathew George, a graduate of Bharat Bible College, came in 1975. Vikram Jeet arrived in 1979.

Jeet for Jesus

Jeet had been a disciple of a powerful Hindu guru, Satya sai Baba, known for his seemingly magical powers of extra-sensory perception, psycho-kinetics, and an ability to make objects appear and disappear.

Sai Baba gave Jeet power and riches, but at age 21 Jeet had no inner peace. One day, one of Vargis's co-workers gave him a gospel tract. Later, he arranged to meet with Vargis secretly at night, as he was too afraid to meet him openly. He accepted the Lord and eventually became a missionary.

One day as he was witnessing in a Hindu village, an angry mob attacked him, tore off his clothes, beat him with clubs, and dragged him naked through the streets. Jeet survived, strengthened in his determination to serve the Lord.

Another missionary was attacked by robbers while returning from a meeting. They beat him with a rod and a bicycle chain. When he saw the glint of a sword aimed at him, he broke away and ran with all his strength. His wristwatch was crushed, his bicycle stolen, and his Bible lost. But he escaped with his life, knowing that the Lord was his Deliverer.

It seems every team member can relate at least one similar experience.

Missionary magnet

The work expanded beyond Kashmir and in 1980 Vargis moved his headquarters to Pathankot, a city of 70,000 located at the juncture of three northern states: Kashmir, Punjab and Himachal Pradesh. A Bible school and headquarters building was completed there in 1981. The new headquarters was so impressive, it caused a prominent pastor from Chandigarh to remark, "You know, Vargis, ever since the British and foreign missionaries left, no one has built a work like this!"

Yet that was only a beginning. The hardship and challenge seemed to draw workers like a magnet. The team had grown from Vargis and Lilly in 1972 to six workers operating seven churches and three mission stations in 1975. A mission station, according to Vargis, is not a mere outpost; it is the field operations center for a full-time missionary overseeing several churches or outposts.

By 1980, the team was operating with 41 workers in three states. Workers had planted 41 churches and were operating 28 mission stations.

Five years later the team had 304 missionaries on the field overseeing the work of as many churches and 143 mission stations. These were found in nine states of northern India and hundreds of tribal people were coming to the Lord in Maharashtra and Orissa states. The expanded vision and work prompted Vargis to move IET's national headquarters to Delhi in 1986.

By January, 1997 the Indian Evangelical Team had more than 1,020 missionaries operating out of 720 mission stations in 14 states. That year they baptized 2,648 new believers and by then had planted more than 600 organized congregations, though only 70 of them had their own buildings.

Goal breaker

Vargis believes in attempting great things for God. "Let's wipe out the list of unreached peoples in 20 years," he said at a convention of tribal Christians in Orissa state in 1996. "Let's make it very difficult for people of our region to go to hell. Let's make sure none of them escapes hearing the gospel at least once!"

He set a goal of having 2,000 churches by 2000 and met that goal early. By December 31, 1999, IET missionaries had planted 2,254 pioneer churches in India, Nepal and Bhutan.

So Vargis set himself a new goal: 7,777 churches by 2010. He based that goal on Joshua 6:4 where he read of seven priests, seven trumpets, seven days, and seven times around the city.

Already by the end of 2002 IET's more than 2000 missionaries had planted 3,533 church groups that gathered around 200,000 believers across northern India. And this does not include any churches that left IET to become independent or join other organizations.

With that track record, Vargis will probably meet his goal. Move over, Himalaya Mountains, here comes a galloping horse.

Chapter 6

Vision for Mission

The story of William Johnson and the Pakistan Gospel Assemblies

"Come out of her you foul and unclean spirit!"

All eyes in the courtyard were on the middle-aged preacher dressed in Punjabi pants and shirt as he laid his hands on this frail wisp of a woman.

About 50 friends and relatives were gathered in the Din family courtyard to hear this man preach and to pray for Jamal Din's wife.

Nawab Bibi had been tormented by demons for 25 years. Often she believed they were attacking her, and thrashed about to beat them off. Eventually she lost her ability to speak and communicated by writing notes.

Finally her right side became paralyzed, making her a prisoner of her mute body. She was like a living corpse.

Two kerosene lamps barely lit the scene. The preacher was determined.

"Come out of her in the name of Jesus Christ!" the preacher shouted.

The woman's eyes went askew. Strange sounds came from her mouth. The preacher looked boldly into her eyes. He was not afraid.

Suddenly the woman went limp and everyone gasped. Was she dead, they suspected.

Then the woman recovered some consciousness and began to speak coherent words. Softly at first. Then she began to praise the Lord in a loud voice. When she lifted her right hand, the crowd burst into a cacophony of excitement.

"Thank God!" some shouted. The whole courtyard was abuzz. They had never seen anyone delivered from demons like this.

William the messenger

If it hadn't been for William, they would not have witnessed the miracle.

"Come visit your mother before she dies," Jamal had telegraphed his stepson, William, working in Karachi.

When William arrived home, he saw that his mother was in pathetic straits. She couldn't talk, couldn't move. She just lay there on the bed. Her shallow pants of breath gave them reason to believe she might not live long.

Then a school teacher friend mentioned an itinerant preacher who was visiting the next village. In a last-ditch effort, William went to fetch him.

"Go home, young man," the preacher said after hearing William's story. "I will pray and seek God's will. If I come, I will send messengers to let you know."

Later that same day two men who had received healing through the preacher's ministry arrived at the family home to announce that the preacher was coming. Quickly William went house to house, inviting neighbors and relatives to a gospel meeting at his house. That's what brought them here.

William's mother had been married earlier to Sardar Masih, and both were members of the Anglican church. In 1946, Sardar passed away suddenly, leaving his wife with three young children and expecting a fourth. William, the oldest at age five, was sent off to a Presbyterian boarding school, since the nearest primary school was in the next village. Later, his two younger brothers, Munawar and Anwar, and sister, Jamila, were sent there, also.

Two years later, his mother married a school teacher named Jamal Din. Though of traditional church backgrounds, neither was prepared for her long sickness, nor for the deliverance that followed.

The powerful exorcism made a tremendous impact on everyone present. William, Jamila, Nawab Bibi and Jamal all placed their personal trust in the Lord Jesus Christ that day, as did many others present. Today some 50 believers gather in the church birthed suddenly that day.

Munawar, William's younger brother, was not there. As soon as he could, William returned to Karachi and told his brother the good news.

"You have to go see Mother," he said.

When Munawar returned home, he found a new woman managing the house. His mother was bright and lively. She visited homes during the day telling people of the miracle the Lord had done for her, and leading many to personal faith in Christ. Then she began to teach the illiterate to read. Whenever Munawar awakened during the night, he found his mother praying to the Lord. He later made a commitment to the Lord. Every day church was conducted in the house. The Din home had become a revival center.

A changed William

Back in Karachi William worked for the government at the Ministry of Commerce involved in importing and exporting goods and drew a good wage. He sought out a lively gospel-preaching church and began tithing his income, which he had never done before. He testified, preached and prayed for the sick in meetings like the preacher did. He was thrilled as many times he saw instant answers to his prayers.

William's original surname, Masih, means "Christ," and is a label most families of traditional Christian background in Pakistan carry. He longed to have a name unique to himself and to his future family. He thought of the disciple John who leaned on Jesus' breast at the Last Supper, who called himself "the one whom Jesus loved."

I will be like the son of love, William thought to himself, and changed his name to Johnson.

In December 1962 he married a young woman named Nasim from the nearby town of Baddomalih. They eventually had four children: Simon, Hbadassah, Aqsa, and Salem.

In the next few years following his mother's conversion, Johnson began to spend time in fasting and prayer in an earnest desire to get closer to God. God increased his anointing.

One time he walked into a meeting, raised his hands and said simply, "Let us pray."

Immediately demons began to cry out. Before the preaching, before the praise time, Johnson began to cast out the demons.

One woman arrived at the meeting late. She stepped across the threshold, but immediately drew back and sat outside the door looking in.

"Why did you sit out here?" Johnson asked her after the meeting.

"When I stepped across the threshold, I felt a jolt of power, like an electric shock. I was afraid, so I stayed out here," she said.

Prayer was not just a routine, but a growing practice with Johnson. It was during one of his times of prayer in 1969 that he had an unexpected vision. He saw himself standing before a large crowd preaching the gospel, and people were responding. Suddenly, to the left of the crowd a wall stretched out, and on the far side of the wall, another crowd was gathered. Johnson turned sideways and saw another man speaking the exact same words he was preaching. The vision mystified him. He knew it had to do with his preaching the gospel. But it was five years before he learned its meaning.

Spirit-led journey

Johnson resigned his government job in 1971 so he could serve the Lord full time.

He first returned to his home area of Gujranwala and began to minister like the itinerant preacher who had prayed for his mother. He went house to house sharing his faith and offering to pray for any special needs.

Next he went to Baddomalih, his wife's home town, and began preaching in the surrounding villages. People repented and placed their faith in Christ as their personal Savior. His wife's parents donated land and on it a small church was built. In later years, a boarding school was added.

Still, the meaning of the original vision eluded him. One day as he was praying, what God said to Abraham impressed him: "Get thee out of thy country...unto a land that I will show thee" (Genesis 12:1). He began to tell members of his family that he was going to Europe.

"What country?" they asked.

"God will show me on the way," he replied. Two months later he departed for Istanbul, Turkey.

After arriving in Istanbul, he began walking up and down the train platform praying. As he passed a wall map of Europe, his eyes focused on Rotterdam. "Go to Holland," seemed to be the message.

So he bought a ticket to Holland. But while changing trains in Milan, he seemed to get a new message: "Go to Germany."

By this time Johnson had little money left and was reluctant to act on this new impulse. Still, the impression persisted and he reluctantly purchased a ticket to Frankfurt.

Once there he tried in vain to find a cheap place to sleep. After spending the whole night wandering the streets, he learned about a Bible school in nearby Erzhausen. It was Sunday, so Johnson took the train to the town about 15 miles south of Frankfurt and arrived just as worship was beginning. Upon learning that he was from Pakistan, the pastor asked him to share his testimony in the morning service. The people liked what they heard and asked him to speak in the evening meeting. They even gave him a small offering.

"Where are you staying?" one of them asked.

"Nowhere," Johnson answered.

"Then you must stay here," they insisted. So for the next ten days, Johnson stayed in the Bible school dormitory next door.

The vision explained

Much of these days and nights Johnson devoted to prayer. One day just before dawn, after spending the whole night in prayer, a glorious light entered his room and a voice said, "I am your Shepherd who brought you here and who opens doors for you." Then the strange vision of the two crowds divided by the wall repeated itself.

This time Johnson asked some questions.

"What are the two crowds? Who is the other preacher?"

This time the interpretation was given. The first crowd represented those who would be reached by Johnson and gospel preachers trained by him. As Johnson saw the man repeating his message to the second crowd, he saw a tape recorder running on the table. He knew this second crowd represented the spread of the gospel through gospel tools, such as the cassette tapes and videos, which could repeat his message word for word to hitherto unreached peoples. Johnson had never seen a tape recorder before coming to Germany. He saw one for the first time among the students at the Bible school next door.

Later that morning as Johnson was finishing his breakfast, a woman about the age his mother would have been came in and sat down at the table with him. "Will you accompany me to a missionary conference?" she asked. Johnson agreed.

On the train going there he determined in his heart that he would not ask any person for money, but that if anyone voluntarily offered to help support his vision, he would accept it as being from the Lord.

Holland at last

During an afternoon tea break, a man walked up to him.

"Hi. I'm William Boswell from Holland," the man said, and explained that he was interested in supporting missions on various fields.

"Where are you from?" Boswell asked.

"Pakistan," Johnson responded.

"Where's that?" Boswell asked.

"Near India," Johnson answered, who was beginning to suspect that this man might be chosen of God to play a role in fulfilling his vision.

Soon they were joined by one of the organizers of the conference.

"Would you be willing to share about your work in Pakistan for about ten minutes?" the man asked.

After some coaxing, Johnson agreed, even though he had no idea what he would say. When the meeting began, he took his seat in the middle of the audience hoping he would be ignored.

Johnson was the fourth man called to the platform. At first, he didn't respond.

"Isn't your name Johnson?" the person sitting next to him asked.

"Yes," Johnson said.

"Then go up there," the man said. "They want you to speak."

On the way up, the Lord impressed upon him to share about his vision. As he spoke, the man from Holland seemed especially blessed.

After the conference, Boswell approached him again.

"Would you be interested in coming to Holland and sharing your vision with some of my fellow believers?" the man asked.

Johnson said he would.

Boswell was surprised to learn that Johnson already had his ticket.

Johnson spent two weeks in Holland. He learned that Mr. Boswell was a coordinator for a large number of Bible-believing Christians who were concerned about carrying out the Great Commission, and were willing to do it through support of indigenous Christian leaders like him. Boswell said that from the missionary offerings given by the people, he would send support to his work in Pakistan. Johnson returned home in July 1974 rejoicing. A new chapter in his ministry was beginning.

A new vision

While praying one day shortly after his return, he had another vision. In it a ribbon stretched in front of him displaying the words "Pakistan Gospel Assemblies." He knew immediately that that was what he should call his work. He next moved to Lahore, then a city of about two million, and took steps to register his new ministry with the authorities.

With a modest amount of support coming from abroad, he now had a means to support other full-time workers. His wife's brother, Sadiq, was the first to join him. Together they conducted evangelistic crusades and God began to move in marvelous ways.

Between 1974 and 1984, the work grew rapidly. The financial support increased to $1,000, then to $3,000, and several times to as much as $5,000 monthly. The work thrived. By 1984, Johnson had 50 co-workers and had established 300 congregations. He daily thanked God for his friends in Holland who made it possible. It was a decade of glorious progress.

Towards the end of the decade, however, the funds began to decline. One day Johnson opened a letter from Boswell and in it he read that the ministry in Holland was having difficulties and it would not be possible to send further funds.

Johnson was dismayed. His work soon suffered. As workers went without food and clothing, some of them left Pakistan Gospel Assemblies to join other works. Congregations dwindled; sometimes whole churches switched affiliation. Those next two years were the most difficult Johnson had ever experienced.

New sources of help

About that time he was contacted by a ministry in Virginia that assisted indigenous works like his. The letter was inquiring about ministries in Pakistan, and stated further that if he was ever in the U.S., the staff would like to meet him and get to know more about his ministry. In due course of time, Johnson borrowed the money for plane fare and visited Christian Aid.

There mission leaders listened to his story. They asked questions. Took down references. They made no guarantees, but said they would do what they could. They gave him a small check—for $150.

He made other contacts. One group said it would help construct several needed church buildings. Another group of churches said they couldn't help his churches, but would support needy children. Others said they would help in another manner.

With this encouragement, Johnson returned to Pakistan. Then he met another hindrance.

Vision for training

Most of the churches in Pakistan are of Roman Catholic, Orthodox and traditional Protestant denominations. Their leaders were highly educated and disdained this faith preacher who didn't have academic training.

So Johnson went to work to acquire the kind of credentials that would stand up to the scrutiny of other church leaders.

He visited Vision International University in San Diego and took a copy of their course books back to Pakistan. He not only studied them, but taught them and translated them into Urdu. As he personally completed courses, he earned first a Master of Theological Studies and later a Ph.D. from the university. Third World Ministerial Divinity College in Nigeria had already awarded him a D.D. in 1985.

Armed with credentials that his peers could respect, he began his own Vision Bible College in 1992, using his course books translated into Urdu as his curriculum. Later he added the words "and Seminary" to the school's name to make it clear to authorities that he was training religious leaders, not would-be revolutionaries.

In this residency training program, Johnson trains about 40 men a year for the gospel ministry. They then go out as church planters in areas where there is no gospel witness. Some are assigned to churches that have no pastor. Their training consists of two weeks of classroom instruction followed by two weeks of field work. Those who take the one-year course receive a Certificate of Biblical Studies. Those who complete two years of instruction earn an Associate of Biblical Studies. Those finishing three years of work receive a Diploma of Ministry. A Bachelor of Theology degree is awarded graduates of the four-year program.

A third vision

The opening of Vision Bible College dovetailed with another visionary experience. One day while at prayer in 1991, God lifted Johnson up in the spirit and showed him 50,000 places in Pakistan that didn't have a gospel witness.

"How many of these are you willing to reach?" God asked him.

"Lord, that's too many for me. Why not involve other missions to get the job done? You know that I am already doing something."

"Don't talk to Me about other ministries," God answered. "I want to know how many *you* are willing to be responsible for. Whatever you decide, I will help you do."

In the vision, Johnson prayerfully considered the request and then said, "I'll take ten percent. I'll be responsible for starting churches in 5,000 places."

The encounter left Johnson both exhilarated and overwhelmed. How would he accomplish this seemingly impossible task?

As he prayed about the matter, he concluded his strategy would be threefold: worship, evangelism and teaching.

A Christian chiropractor in San Antonio donated a tent that would hold 5,000 people. Having kept up his import-export license from his government job, Johnson acquired the keyboard and sound system necessary to hold evangelistic meetings attended by crowds that size.

Evangelistic teams

Then he began putting together a 15-member evanelistic team. Ten to 12 members would travel with him to a specific crusade. They did everything: sang, played musical instruments, ran the P.A. system, put up and took down the tent, and did house-to-house visitation, counseling and prayer. Johnson quickly learned that people were attracted to strong music and praise, so he makes sure he has adequate instruments and sound system on hand.

The team members usually go to a certain area where Pakistan Gospel Assemblies already has a worker who has primed the pump for a crusade. In Pakistan, a solidly Muslim nation, persons of historical Christian background usually live in a segmented section of the community. Many of the residents are simply followers of a Christian tradition—they don't know Christ personally. When a Pakistani pioneer missionary goes to a new area, he begins by going house to house through the Christian sector.

"I am a man of God," he says. "May I pray for you?"

Sometimes specific needs are disclosed.

After going through the community once, he learns which homes are open to the gospel and makes return visits where he knows he will be welcomed. Then he begins holding Bible studies in a few homes.

Villages often are one to two miles apart, so one missionary can work in five to ten villages.

Crusade time

After conducting Bible studies in homes of friendly families for a while, he begins to talk about having a crusade. By this time, several local people have placed their personal trust in Jesus Christ as Savior, and have opened up a widening circle of family and friends with whom they want to share their faith.

Finally, the crusade team arrives for three to five days of meetings. People come nightly from five or six villages. By the time the crusade is over, a small congregation of believers is been formed in each one—all tended by the one missionary now become pastor. The congregations continue to mature under his leadership while they reach out further to the unreached villagers in their area.

Johnson always sought to conduct evangelistic meetings whenever he had opportunity, but began the crusade ministry in earnest in 1992. By 1995 his teams were conducting 20 crusades a year. In 1996 they conducted 40.

A five-day crusade in Lahore was attended by 15,000 individuals. About 2,000 of them came forward to place their personal faith in the Lord Jesus Christ.

Punctuated by miracles

Crusades are sometimes marked by outstanding healings. At a one-day meeting attended by about 250 people in October, 1996, a man brought his daughter for prayer.

"Here is my daughter," he said. "She is dumb. Pray for her!"

Johnson was agitated. He felt the man was testing him. If he refused to pray, he would lose face. If he prayed and nothing happened, no one in that place would ever listen to a Christian preacher again.

Johnson began by praying for a few others whose needs were not so easy to visibly detect. Then he came to the woman.

"Open your mouth," he said.

The woman opened her mouth. Johnson reached in, touched her tongue, and began to pray.

Instantly the woman began to speak.

Immediately people began to say, "We want to become Christians! We never saw anything like this before!" Some 70 people took Christ as their Savior that day.

Beware the Muslims

In a Muslim land—the word Pakistan means "Holy Land" in Urdu, the language of South Asian Muslims—evangelism is not always easy, or without consequences. To conduct a crusade requires two permits: one to gather, and another to use a loudspeaker.

Once a group of Muslims came forward in the middle of the message and demanded, "You have to turn off the loudspeaker."

"Why?" Johnson said. "I have a permit."

"It is the time for [Muslim] prayer," they answered. "We have to be able to hear the mullah from the mosque. You cannot run your loudspeaker during our prayer time."

Johnson makes sure he doesn't offend the Muslims.

The worst thing that can happen to a Christian is to be accused of blasphemy by a Muslim. Pakistan's anti-blasphemy law enacted in 1991 gives a mandatory death sentence to anyone convicted of blaspheming against the prophet Mohammed or the Qur'an. And according to Sharia (Islamic) law, the testimony of a non-Muslim is worth only half as much as the testimony of a Muslim. Christians have been condemned to death on the basis of a Muslim testimony without any physical evidence being presented against them. So the very act of accusation is condemnatory.

Acquitted of blasphemy

When Gul Masih, a Presbyterian layman, was acquitted on appeal of blasphemy charges after sitting on death row for three years, mosques in his home town announced, "A blasphemer has been acquitted." He had to flee the country to save his life.

In similar manner, a 13-year-old boy was accused of writing blasphemies against Mohammed on a mosque wall in 1993. As he, two co-defendants and a family friend were descending the courthouse steps, Muslim extremists drove by on a motorcycle and opened fire, killing one of the defendants. Even though witnesses said the boy was illiterate, and no evidence was presented showing the alleged graffiti, the boy and a 44-year-old man were found guilty. The two were later acquitted on appeal, but had to leave the country to spare their lives.

Despite these dangers, Johnson believes that Pakistan is wide open for the gospel, especially when preached by trained Pakistanis who understand the cultural mores of their society.

Renewed vision

In one village, 150 people comprising 26 families came to Christ in a gospel crusade and were baptized. They had come from a lifeless institutional church background and finding Christ as their personal Savior thrilled them. One of the families donated a piece of land. Another man said, "I have some money. I can loan you $3,000 to build a church." So a new congregation was formed and constructed its own meeting hall.

Not all congregations are so blessed. By the beginning of 2003 Pakistan Gospel Assemblies had grown to 2000 churches with about 100,000 members. Only 110 of these had their own buildings; the rest met in houses. Each five house churches could come together for Sunday worship in a meeting hall that can be built for $5,000. It then would also be used as a training center for local workers, a literacy center, and an elementary school for children.

The lack of buildings didn't stop Johnson from reconsidering the vision. Ten years after he first had the vision of 50,000 places without a gospel church, he began prayerfully to reconsider his answer to the Lord. Finally he said, "Lord, I repent. I will go for all 50,000 of those places."

Johnson has since raised up 10 gospel teams. Each team is able to conduct 10 crusades a year, and each crusade will reach about five villages. From the harvest of souls, a house church will be formed in each village—not bad for a total cost of $1,000 per crusade.

In addition, each gospel team member needs $50 per month support. With an average of 12 members per team plus funds for crusades, the annual budget for each team would be about $17,500 per year. That modest investment will result in 50 house churches per team per year, which averages about $344 per church.

The whole effort would gain 500 churches per year. In ten years, with adequate resources, the teams could plant 5,000 churches.

Johnson has coupled this with a plan for raising up indigenous leaders. He is developing 25 video Bible schools in various locations throughout the country. Teachers are trained, teaching videos are being produced, and lesson materials will be printed as soon as the necessary funds are obtained. When fully operational, the schools will be capable of training 500 local church workers per year. It costs about $50 per month to train each new worker.

A church planter likewise needs $50 support per month. A gospel kit to help train and equip a new missionary also runs $600 per year. Each kit includes teaching materials, a bicycle, portable musical instruments and a sound system. So equipped, such a worker with full support will plant five house churches per year.

"The harvest is plentiful, but the laborers are few," Johnson quotes Jesus, referring to the opportunity in Pakistan. The resources there are few, also. The churches can maintain their own local pastors, but to train and send out new workers requires resources beyond their means. However, with outside help, the vision could be fulfilled rapidly.

"We have the men, the talent and the will to get the job done," Johnson said. "All we need is the support, and we can plant those 50,000 churches."

He certainly has the vision for mission.

Chapter 7

Pentecost Revisited

The story of Silas Owiti and the Voice of Salvation and Healing Movement in East Africa

"You must be saved! You must be born again!" The preachers on the platform—one preaching and the other interpreting into one of the local dialects—were practically screaming.

"Jesus Christ died for your sins. If you accept Him as your Savior, He will take you to heaven. You can be sure of that."

Fanny Owiti had never heard a message like that.

"Where are these guys from?" she asked some bystanders.

She learned that the black preachers had been converted by some other African missionaries who, in turn, had been set on fire for God from the crusade conducted by Nicholas Bhengu.

Born 1909, Bhengu spent a semester at Prairie Bible Institute in Three Hills, Alberta, Canada. While there, he attended the school's annual missionary convention. When they called for volunteers for the mission field, Bhengu went forward and said he wanted to be a missionary to his own Zulu people in South Africa. This was too radical for the Canadian Christians at that time couldn't think of supporting an *African* as a missionary to Africa. To their traditional way of thinking, missions meant sending Canadians.

However, at that same missionary convention Bhengu met Ben Coleman, a retired Canadian railroad worker. Ben listened to Bhengu as he shared his burden to reach his own people for Christ. To him, supporting a black man, a Zulu, who already knew the language and culture of the people needing to be reached, made sense. He promised Bhengu he would send some help.

The first big crusade

In 1950 Coleman sent Bhengu a gift of $1,000. With that largess Bhengu printed and distributed posters, constructed a stage, acquired a large P.A. system, and purchased a tent that would seat 5,000. It was the first well-publicized, fully equipped crusade those black people had ever known. The first night 10,000 people showed up and 5,000 surged forward to accept Christ. Bhengu converted the tent into a prayer tent.

The meetings went on for days, and then weeks. People repented of their sins. Many turned in guns and weapons. Others received miraculous healings. Crime came to a standstill. Police were astounded. The phenomenon was written up in *Time* magazine.

News of the move of God spread to neighboring countries. People came from afar, received the glad tidings, and went back aflame to their own lands and preached the empowered gospel to others, who preached it to still others.

The crowds soon grew to 50,000 nightly. The meetings went on for six months with an aggregate attendance of well over 10 million. It is estimated that over 10,000 churches sprang from those meetings. Those fiery preachers Winnie was listening to were fruits of that movement.

The more Fanny listened, the more her heart was touched. *Oh, I want to be saved,* she groaned within herself, *but first I must tell Silas.* Being a dutiful African wife, Fanny knew she should clear any major decision with her husband before proceeding.

Silas had been raised in a Christian tradition that did not preach personal salvation. Though as a youth he belonged to the Africa Inland Church, he applied to Maseno High School, a mission school run by Anglicans. When he placed 11th out of 2,000 on his entrance exam, the officials wanted to admit him, but the school admitted only Anglicans. Learning that Silas had never been baptized, the officials said if he would submit to Anglican baptism, they would accept him. Silas complied.

While there, faith had been intellectually taught but never personally caught. After graduating he rejoined his denominational church, and got a job with the government. For the last two years he had been chief inspector of all building materials. He now had no time for God. He was too busy making a good living.

"Silas," Fanny approached her husband. "I heard some preachers on the way home tonight. They preached *salvation.* Oh, Silas, I want to be saved so bad. Is that all right with you?"

"Yes, that's all right with me," Silas answered shrewdly. "But if you get *saved,* be sure to pack your bags and leave, because I won't live with some fanatical woman."

Fanny was undeterred. Knowing that going contrary to her husband's wishes would bring great strife to their family (she was expecting their first child), she decided to bring the matter before God.

"Oh, God, You know how much I want to get saved. I love You, but Silas does not love You. He said if I get saved, I will have to leave him. But I don't want to leave him, because I love him. So will You please go and save Silas first? After that, You can come back and save me, also."

Silas heard his wife pray this prayer every morning. Inwardly he groaned. *She's reporting me to God. Well, at least she hasn't disobeyed me.*

Pentecost revisited

Silas and Fanny had a two-room house, a bedroom and a sitting room. The kitchen was outside. One evening they were sitting in their bedroom having a cup of tea when they heard someone praying in the living room.

"Who's praying in the living room?" Silas asked, as he got up to investigate.

When he peeked through the doorway, he saw no one. But then it sounded like the same voice came from outside the house.

Silas opened the door and stepped outside. Then the voice sounded like it was coming from down the street. Whoever it was, was speaking in proper Oxford English.

"Who's that speaking such educated English?" Silas asked.

"That's Washington Owiti," Fanny said.

"It can't be Washington," Silas answered. "I know him. He's my cousin. He's illiterate. He doesn't know English. He speaks only Luo."

"That's him," Fanny insisted. "The preachers said that after you get born again, God fills you with the Holy Spirit and the Holy Spirit can lead you to speak in any language He gives you."

"Really?"

"Yes, that's right."

"Well, if God can make an illiterate relative speak in flawless English, then you can go ahead and get saved. I don't mind letting a God like that into our house."

The next morning, Silas had a plan of his own. He left work early and went to see the relative he had heard speaking the night before.

"I heard someone in this house speaking flawless English last night," Silas said.

"Is that right?" Washington asked in Luo.

"Yes, I heard him myself. Did you have some educated people in your house last night?"

"No," Washington said, "we just had a prayer meeting with some believers. But during the course of the meeting, the Spirit took over and I began to speak in other tongues; I don't know what language it was."

"Well, would you please do that again, while I am here watching you?" Silas asked.

"Well, I can't tell the Spirit what to do," Washington said.

"You going to have another meeting tonight?"

"We plan to."

"Good. I'll come."

Silas went to the meeting that night, while Fanny stayed home and prayed.

After some singing, this uneducated cousin began to preach. This was no intellectual discourse like Silas so often had heard in school. It seemed like God took over the man's voice and was speaking directly to him.

At the end of the message, Washington said, "Everybody bow your head and close your eyes while we pray."

If I close my eyes, I won't see what's happening, Silas thought. He kept his eyes open. If this illiterate man was going to speak in English again, he wanted to both hear and *see* it happen.

This time Washington's wife, Monica, began to sing a beautiful English hymn.

She's even more illiterate than her husband, Silas said to himself. *She can't even read and write Luo!*

Amazingly, the hymn she sang was one Silas had sung in mission school. It was number 259 in *The Golden Bells Song Book*:

"Lord I hear of showers of blessings
    Thou art scattering full and free;
Showers the thirsty land refreshing;
    Let some drops now fall on me,
Even me, even me,
    Let some drops now fall on me."

The sweetness of this illiterate Luo woman singing this beautiful English hymn broke down every barrier in Silas' heart. *God is surely in their midst,* Silas thought as tears ran down his cheeks. If an invitation had been given, he would have been saved that night.

"Do you want to come again?" Washington asked after the meeting concluded.

"Yes," Silas answered. "When is your next meeting?"

"We have a meeting in the church tomorrow night," Washington said.

"I think I'll be there," Silas said.

Salvation arrives

"How was the meeting?" Fanny asked when Silas came home.

"Fanny, it's exactly as you said it would be. God is in their midst. I want us to go to the meeting together tomorrow night."

Silas and Fanny did go. To Silas, the man preached like he had come from heaven yesterday. When the invitation was given, Silas struggled within.

"Don't go forward in front of these people," a voice whispered. "Wait until you are by yourself or go off in the jungle by yourself. Then you can get saved just as well."

At the same time, Silas seemed to hear a more noble voice speaking to him, "Silas, today is your day. If you don't get saved today, the words that you heard tonight will condemn you in heaven."

As the congregation sang the closing song in Luo, Silas began to weep. He had never wept in church before. As his tears fell, he saw them as human beings with red, yellow, white, blue and green shirts moving toward the altar to be saved.

The voice within spoke again, "Rise, stand up and join the crowd. Go forward to be saved." He obeyed the voice and went forward, only when he got to the front, he realized that he was the only one there.

As he looked up he saw a flash of light. Then he saw Jesus on the cross, and the blood was streaming from His side and dripping on Silas's head. It seemed cold, penetrating to the core of his being, and as it did so, it cleansed every sin and then vaporized. He tried to confess his sins, but fell to the ground with heavy weeping. When he got up, Fanny had joined him. They both accepted Jesus Christ as their Savior that night.

Preaching fury

Experiencing salvation was like a bomb going off inside him. He remembered a friend that he had misled and went to him and told him that he was saved.

"Oh, Silas, do you mean to say that you can be saved in this day and age? It isn't possible!"

Silas said, "I have met Jesus Christ. You wait and see."

From that moment on, Silas preached and testified every moment he got.

He even gave his testimony in front of the Anglican Church he and Fanny were supposed to be members of.

The pastor became very angry.

"I don't want you witnessing that kind of gospel to members of our church," he said. "We are educated people and we don't go for that born-again stuff. If you don't stop preaching that nonsense, I will excommunicate you from the church."

Silas couldn't help himself. He felt so good about his salvation, he couldn't keep from telling others about it. He preached in the market places, on the street corners, everywhere he could gain an opportunity. Soon he gathered a number of converts and began conducting Sunday morning worship services.

His theme was: You must be born again, filled with the Holy Spirit, and God will do miracles. People flocked to hear this message, new to their ears.

Under police surveillance

This was 1954 and the Mau Maus were terrorizing the British for control of Kenya. Some American missionaries became jealous of Silas's results and reported him to the British Colonial Government. The police suspected that Silas's meetings were just a front for some back door Mau Mau activity.

They hauled him down to the police station many times for questioning. Each time, after thorough interrogation, they found nothing warranting arrest and let him go. Still, a policeman attended every service and recorded every hymn and testimony. Later, police scrutinized all his notes looking for some hint of a secret Mau Mau connection.

One day the police officer attending the meeting held in the shade of a large, spreading tree came under conviction. As Silas preached the Word, he fell to the ground and began weeping and confessing his sins, getting his crisp, clean uniform all dirty. After a while, the officer got up, brushed himself off, declared his faith in Christ, and took Holy Communion with the congregation.

He returned to the station and told the police commissioner, "This is the best group of Christians I have ever met. They have only two faults: They sing their choruses over and over again too many times, and when they pray, they pray too loud and cry like babies."

Despite these shortcomings, the police who had staked out Silas's meetings saw nothing harmful in his ministry. "He needs to have his church officially registered with the government," they concluded. "Then he will no longer be under suspicion."

They invited Silas down to the police station and explained to him how to register his church. As a result, on May 16, 1956, Voice of Salvation and Healing Church was one of the first indigenous church movements registered in British Kenya.

As the spirit of revival continued, Silas and his growing band of preachers preached in the market places, in high schools, in colleges. They held conventions, inviting the multitudes to come and hear the Word of God. Newly saved church members contributed bags of corn, beans and what they had to feed those who came. The Word of God spread throughout Kenya's Nyanza Province, Rift Valley Province, Western Province, Coast Province, and Central Province. People responded to the salvation message by the hundreds.

Beyond the borders

The Spirit of God was not bound to Kenya. The politicians who drew the borders of the countries did not align them according to the habitats of the people groups. The Luo people lived in neighboring Uganda and Tanzania, as well as in Kenya. So Silas and his team of preachers crossed into neighboring Tanzania and Uganda preaching the gospel to people of their own tribe, and to all who would listen.

They walked almost everywhere they went, because in those days they had no financial resources. They were rich in spirit, but poor in this world's goods.

One day Silas and his team walked 30 miles and were exhausted. When they finally reached their destination, they found a whole crowd of people hungry to hear the gospel of salvation. Silas was led to a small room where there was a cot. He fell into the bed exhausted. Ten minutes later he was back on his feet, ready to preach.

Despite his weariness, Silas preached with a great anointing, and many came forward to receive Christ as Savior. One of those who accepted Christ that day was Benson Anjejo. He later became one of Voice of Salvation's most powerful preachers in Tanzania. Many joined him, and the move of God was off in a powerful way in Tanzania.

Visited by Idi Amin

Next God led Silas and his team into Uganda. They preached in Kampala, the capital, and in Jinja, Uganda's second largest city. From there they went to Entebbe, Aoima, and around Lake Albert bordering Congo. Silas preached in many stadiums and hundreds came to know Christ.

That move of God was threatened in 1971 when Idi Amin overthrew President Obote. Then followed the darkest period in Uganda's history when thousands of people were killed and hundreds of churches burned.

One day, Idi Amin attended an Independence Day celebration in Nairobi, Kenya, and was scheduled to have lunch in Kisumu, Silas' home town. At the same time, Silas was chairing an evangelistic crusade with well-known American evangelist, T.L. Osborn. As Amin's small plane flew over Kisumu, Amin spotted the large crowd gathered. Presuming they had gathered to welcome him, Amin promptly ordered his plane to land on the school soccer field instead of at the airport where officials were waiting to meet him.

Silas walked forward, met Amin, took him by the hands, led him up on the platform, and offered him an opportunity to greet the crowd, which he was well pleased to do.

Soon after his encounter with Idi Amin, Silas decided to go to Uganda and appeal to Amin personally not to harm the Voice of Salvation churches. Silas was greeted like a State visitor when he arrived at the Presidential Palace. He had opportunity to talk with the Minister of Religion, and Voice of Salvation churches were never banned in Uganda.

In fact, the minister urged Silas to start preaching on Uganda's radio and television network to bring the gospel to the people of Uganda. Silas thanked him for the invitation and said he would see what he could do.

As he left the palace, he passed a regiment of soldiers who all lowered their guns and aimed them directly at him. "Lord deliver me," Silas whispered as he walked out with the guns pointing at his back. Not one shot was fired.

After that the work of God in Uganda continued to grow, and continues to grow even to this day. The government of Uganda gave Silas a piece of land on which to build his Uganda mission station. By this time, Silas's lowly band of fiery missionaries had grown to about 200. This was in addition to those who were pastors of local assemblies.

David's mighty men

These 200 were like David's mighty men. They were powerful preachers who could go anywhere on a moment's notice. Everywhere they preached, people's hearts were gripped with the need of repentance and scores came forward to receive Christ with tears. Everywhere they preached, a church was planted.

These new churches were truly birthed by the Holy Spirit. The process is simple. A missionary takes with him someone who recently experienced a miracle or dramatic answer to prayer. They go to a place where there is no church. The church member gives his testimony and the missionary preaches a Word-based message. Several converts result.

Or someone comes sick to one of Silas's crusades, is prayed for and is healed. He or she is asked to stay for several days of discipling and prayer. Then a preacher goes with the person to his or her village. The new believer gives his or her testimony, and the missionary preaches the gospel and gathers the converts.

In either case, Silas then sends a church planter to disciple the new converts and win still more to the Lord. The missionary watches to see who exercises leadership and appoints an elder and other officers. Finally a senior pastor visits the group several days and observes the people in action. If he approves, he ordains the elder as pastor. He then returns to his church and the church planter moves on to another location.

Encounter with a leopard

These missionaries face difficulties and sometimes grave dangers in their travel. One time, James Odero and Pascal Maliyamungu[1] went on foot to catch a bus after a meeting in Tanzania. When they got to the bus station, they learned the bus had already left. It was early in the day so they decided to start walking and find a place to sleep when night came. As evening approached, they were nowhere near a village, and spotted an abandoned house in the jungle. They went in and lay down, exhausted, and quickly fell asleep.

They did not realize in the near darkness that a mother leopard had given birth in that same hut. About midnight the mother leopard returned to feed her young. When the leopard saw the men sleeping there, she sat down right in the door and looked at them. When the young kittens saw their mother, they made a noise, and the two missionaries awoke to a frightening situation.

"O Lord Jesus, give peace between us and the leopard," they whispered. The men remained as quiet and motionless as possible. The leopard stared at them for what seemed an hour. Finally, the leopard must

---

[1] Maliyamungu menas "God's property" in Luo.

have concluded that the humans were not a threat, walked across the hut, and lay down to feed her young. Still, the men dared not move. Finally, as morning broke, the men saw that the leopard was sleeping with her young and crept silently out of the hut, thanking the God of Daniel for sparing their lives.

Having to walk to and from meetings is not only inconvenient, it places missionaries at risk of the elements, wild animals and thugs. If the missionaries had a vehicle, a motorcycle, or even a bicycle, they could avoid many delays and dangers.

Buying a bicycle in Kenya is like buying a car in America. The cost of a bicycle, about $150, is more than the common laborer makes in three months.

Help is on the way

About 1980 Silas came in contact with Christian Aid. A staff member visited him in Kenya, and after that small amounts of help began to flow regularly to the developing ministry. Christian Aid found sponsors to send monthly support for missionaries while others sent regular amounts to assist destitute children cared for in the Owiti home. Some sent gifts to purchase bicycles for missionaries.

Sometimes larger amounts were collected to help purchase a car or replace an engine. Silas thanked God for the gifts sent by his friends in America and Canada, joined from time to time with help from Scandinavia and elsewhere. These gifts helped provide equipment and facilities not possible without them. Yet if outside help ceased, the work would still continue, though not as extensively.

As the movement gained momentum, the ministry also grew in depth. Crusades provided the cutting-edge of evangelism. Most unchurched people were reluctant to enter a church, but out of curiosity they would stop by an outdoor evangelistic meeting—attracted by the vibrant music and testimonies.

To rent a tent and equipment, truck it to a town, set it up, and feed and accommodate 20 workers for a week , and sometimes part of the crowd, costs about $3,000. Some 3,000 to 5,000 attend each night for a week, and typically 200 to 300 people accept Christ. The price for such results is small, but often stretches the Voice of Salvation resources to the limit.

Many open doors

In addition to the crusades held in various towns, cities and provinces, Silas began to conduct three-day training seminars in various districts for pastors, elders, Sunday school teachers and youth workers. Many attend these who cannot attend the annual convention.

Annual conventions are held at Onjiko High School in Kisumu, Silas's hometown and where Voice of Salvation is headquartered. Up to 5,000 people attend. To feed such a crowd (the obligation of the host) Silas's crew needs to find $10,000 to buy 15 fatted oxen, hundreds of pounds of corn flour, sugar and other foodstuffs, besides paying rent for the school. The people give sacrificially but outside help is usually needed and welcomed.

Unlike in the U.S. where prayer, preaching and the Bible are forbidden, Kenyan high schools and colleges welcomed Silas's Biblical solutions to sex and drug problems. He began holding youth conventions every April and August when the schools were on holiday.

Education for children through elementary grades is available, but they still have to buy uniforms, books and supplies. High school, however, is for the chosen few who are both brilliant and can pay the fees. Some of the brightest children in Voice of Salvation churches lost one or both parents, or their parents were simply too poor to pay the fees. Recognizing that these youths were potential leaders of their country, Silas found enough money to pay the school fees for the most promising of these young scholars. He took up to a dozen to live in his own house. Another 40 to 50 live with other Christian families and attend high schools and colleges in Nairobi, Kisumu and elsewhere.

The fruit of such a program is easy to see. Several have passed their high school exams and gone to complete their degrees at the University of Nairobi. One girl passed her exams with such a high score she was the only student from her province invited to go on to college. Several have gone on to professional positions in business and government.

Silas and Fanny understood that not everyone is cut out for academics. Christian Aid helped some children get vocational training in motor mechanics, tailoring and carpentry. The training enabled them to pass government exams and qualifies them for jobs that will enable them to meet the needs of their families and support Christian work.

Fateful dream

By 1984 Voice of Salvation's fiery missionaries had planted about 600 churches scattered across East Africa. Then, just as the work was being firmly established, a tragedy almost destroyed it.

Silas and Fanny had traveled to the nation's capital for special meetings the first weekend in December, 1984. During those meetings, Fanny felt a special anointing. On December 3, the night before they were to return to Kisumu, she had a strange dream, and told Silas about it the next morning.

"I dreamed I was walking through a vast land all alone. Suddenly I saw a man standing on top of a hill, dressed in white. 'Come with me,' he said, 'I want to show you something wonderful.'

"I followed the man a long distance until there suddenly appeared another man, beautiful in his countenance and dressed in a gold robe. It was impossible to look into His eyes, but I knew it was the Lord Jesus.

"He said the same thing, 'Follow Me, and I will show you something wonderful.'

"We reached the top of a high mountain, and looked over the other side. I saw a lush green valley with a rainbow of flowers and very nice houses nestled among them. I've seen beautiful cities all over the world, but none of them begins to compare with the beauty and splendor of the one I saw in the dream.

"'Because of your dedicated service to Me, I will make you ruler over that city,' the Lord said. Suddenly He disappeared and I woke up."

Then she turned to her eldest daughter, Edie, and said, "If anything happens to me, make sure you take the wedding ring from my finger. That is your inheritance as the eldest daughter."

Then Silas and Fanny got into a car purchased with Christian Aid's help and headed home to Kisumu. On the way, an oncoming truck smashed into the car head-on. Fanny died instantly. Silas's legs and arms were all broken; two arms and one leg were paralyzed. Silas feared he would never walk or preach again.

For two months Silas was pushed around in a wheelchair. He was despondent. In frustration he cried out from his innermost being: "God, if You don't need my services down here any more, then take me to heaven to be with You, or else raise me from this wheelchair to serve You again." As he finished his prayer, he felt healing rush into his anklebones, and he knew he was healed.

The next day he told the doctors to remove the casts from his legs, and they did. Silas got up from the wheel chair and walked across the room unaided.

"Hallelujah!" he shouted. "God has healed me! I'm going to preach again!"

And preach he did. Soon he began running and jumping and preaching and praising God. No African preacher worth his salt ever stood still behind a pulpit!

Miracles continue

Silas had never gone to a seminary that taught him the days of miracles were past. So he expected miracles to occur in his ministry just as they did in the New Testament times. In fact, while he was still in the wheelchair, an officer in the Kenya government asked him to pray for his wife, who had lost her mind. Silas was taken to their house in the wheelchair. He preached a short message and then prayed for her. Even as he prayed, he saw the haziness in her eyes lift and her countenance change.

"Come have breakfast with us tomorrow morning," the man said.

"I'll be glad to come," Silas answered.

When the wife walked into the room the next morning she was her normal self.

At another time friends pushed a paralyzed teen-age boy to a crusade meeting on a bicycle. The boy could stand, but couldn't walk. After the message, Silas took the boy by the hands and prayed for him. The boy began taking small steps backward. Then the boy started walking forward, gaining momentum. Then Silas let go, and the boy walked faster while the crowd cheered. When Silas saw the boy again six months later, he was completely normal.

Probably the greatest miracle in Silas's ministry occurred while he was conducting a crusade in Norway in 1976. Elmer and Margaretta Eklund in Sweden had seen fliers announcing the crusade. Margaretta had been paralyzed for three years. A disease had left her incurable and the doctor had removed part of the spinal cord. When they learned about the meetings, Elmer drove his wife to the meetings. When Silas saw her crumpled in her wheelchair, he thought she looked like a withered little bird in a cage.

After a vibrant faith message, Silas prayed for her personally. She startled everyone by getting up out of the wheelchair and walking unaided. A mighty chorus of praise went up from the congregation. They visited Silas's ministry in Kenya three years later and have been supporters of Silas's ministry ever since.

Another miracle

Silas was introduced to Scandanavia by Ake Söderlund. He and his wife had been missionaries in Kenya during the early years of Silas's ministry. His wife contracted typhoid fever in 1960 and lay dying in the European Hospital in Kisumu. Ake knew Silas personally, and came to him and asked him to come and pray for his wife personally.

"You know I can't do that," Silas replied. "They will not let an African enter the European hospital."

"I know that," Ake answered, "and I don't know how you will get in, but you *must* come."

On the way to the hospital, Silas prayed specifically that the doctor would leave the room.

When they arrived at the hospital, Silas told Ake, "You go first and see if the way is clear."

When Ake got to the room, the doctor was there. Suddenly the doctor decided he needed his four o'clock tea. The hospital did not serve four-o'clock tea, so the doctor left the hospital for his refreshment.

"The doctor is gone," Ake came and told Silas. "Come quickly."

Silas went to the room, laid his hand on her forehead, and prayed very fervently but very quietly. He rebuked the spirit of typhoid, told it to leave, and then went back out to the car.

"Ake, you stay here and talk with the doctor when he returns."

When the doctor returned, Ake asked him to examine his wife.

"I just did that before I left," he replied. Then, after a pause, "but since you ask, I'll do it again—just for you."

He checked her eyes, her mouth; checked her breathing and heart with his stethoscope.

"I don't understand this," the doctor said. "There's absolutely nothing wrong with her. She can be discharged."

Outside, they told Silas, "We are going on a furlough to Finland. Will you join us?"

"Well, if I have a way to get there, I'll most gladly join you," Silas answered grinning.

The Söderlunds left, and a little while later a roundtrip ticket arrived in the mail. That was how Silas became so well acquainted with the Söderlunds.

Married again

After the death of Fannie, Silas was content to live the rest of his life a widower, but the elders began to pressure him to consider marriage.

"Brother Silas, you need to get married," they said.

"No. Never. I'm not going to get married. I can't. Not now."

Yet the elders persisted. Over and over again they advised him what he already knew: No African preacher could be respected around women unless he were married.

"Leave me alone," Silas said. "I need to hear from God."

What God couldn't say through the elders as a group, He began to say through one elder at a time. First, an elder 40 miles away came and told him that it was God's will that he should marry again.

"Do you know a young lady I should marry?" Silas asked, testing him.

"Yes, I do," the elder said. "Her name is Winnie. She is a vibrant Christian woman and an enthusiastic preacher."

Silas remembered Winnie. Her mother was dying of high blood pressure and Silas went and prayed for her. The woman was healed; Winnie witnessed the miracle and gave her heart to God.

She caught the fire of God and was sensitive to the Spirit of God. After completing high school, she graduated from Burkura Agricultural College with high scores. She had just been hired as an agricultural extension officer.

"Hmmm. I'll think about it," Silas said.

Soon after that a senior minister from a church 500 miles away came to Silas and counseled him, "You should marry Winnie."

Altogether four men came from four different places near and far and advised him exactly the same.

"God must be telling me something," Silas surmised.

So he called Winnie on the phone and asked her to come and talk with him. When she arrived he shared with her what the elders had said.

"I have to pray about it," she said. So she fasted and prayed several days. In the course of those days God came to her in a vision at night and reminded her that she had prayed several years earlier that she wanted to marry a preacher because she, also, loved to preach. In the vision Silas appeared before her and God said, "Here is a preacher." She was convinced.

Silas and Winnie were married on October 5, 1985. About 5,000 people attended the wedding, one of the biggest ever conducted in Kenya. The service was conducted in Voice of Salvation's crusade tent, which had been donated by Silas's good friends, T.L. and Daisy Osborne. The Rev. Ake Söderlund from Finland performed the ceremony.

Soon God added to their family in another way. In 1986, Winnie gave birth to a son. Predictably, they named him T.L. Osborne Owiti.

A large family

Winnie not only became Silas's wife; she doubled his effectiveness. Together they preached crusades, trained elders and church workers, held regional conferences, and conducted youth rallies. Both spoke to students at

Kewatta University, Moi University, Egerton University and the University of Nairobi.

Winnie championed youth crusades and women's ministries. She was elected Chairwoman of the International Women's Conference of East Africa. She organized the Voice of Salvation office, obtained funds to expand the headquarters, and built an orphanage. Across the entrance to the headquarters she had a sign erected, "Ministering love to a hurting world."

Winnie had a heart to help some of Kenya's many needy children—those who had lost one or both parents, or whose parents were too poor to feed and clothe them, let alone send them to school. Her first children's home housing 48 children had to close in 1990 due to lack of finances. Everything was rented, and when income fell off, they couldn't pay the bills.

In 1993 Silas and Winnie came to the United States and with help from Christian Aid gathered funds to build a children's home of their own. Ebenezer Orphans' Home—now called Ebenezer Life Center—immediately took in 60 boys and girls. Even though the accommodations were better than the children had ever lived in, the financially stretched ministry had to make them even better to comply with government regulations.

Next they started a kindergarten with 19 preschool children. The next year they had 30 children, and then 120 children. The children were eligible for public school when they reached age 7, but the authorities said they could not accommodate such an influx of new students.

"You should build your own school," they told Silas.

So Voice of Salvation opened its own school in 1997 with 67 children in grades 4-7. Each year the classes grew larger and the number of classes increased. When the children graduate from elementary school, they attend public high school. After that comes college.

"How do we send all these children to college?" Silas asked. "That's my biggest challenge now."

Training future workers

Silas feels it is more important that a man have the anointing of the Spirit and the call of God on his heart than a Bible school education. Yet he realizes the need for training. So he and Winnie conduct preacher's conferences from year to year and from region to region. Silas, Winnie and their veteran preachers teach salvation, healing, the work of the Holy Spirit, faith for miracles, tithing, holy living, love, obedience, dedication, commitment and evangelism.

The missionaries and local church workers get refreshed and then go back to their places and apply what they have heard. Voice of Salvation pays for food, accommodations and sometimes transportation, since very few of the preachers have cars, and not all have bicycles. Total cost of a typical conference attended by 500 workers runs about $6,000.

Through the combined efforts of Silas and Winnie and these fired-up preachers, the work continues to grow. When the accident occurred, Voice of Salvation had about 600 churches. A year later it had 700 churches. By 1993 it had 850 churches in Kenya, 120 in Tanzania and 60 in Uganda. Some of the churches started in Tanzania and Uganda joined other organizations. Even so, by 2000 it had 1000 churches in Kenya, 50 in Tanzania and 30 in Uganda.

Only about 20 of these churches are prosperous enough to support the mission beyond their local areas. Most have mud-walled buildings with thatched roofs. A few still meet under trees or in brush shelters Silas calls "bamboo cathedrals." Believers are willing to donate labor to build, but their tithes are insufficient to buy building materials. They barely support the local pastor. A building for 100 people with mud-brick walls, clay floor and corrugated metal roof can be constructed for $1,500. The roof alone costs half that amount.

Even as this chapter was being finalized, news came that the Owiti house burned to the ground. It housed not only the Owitis, but was a gathering place for workers and families and a temporary residence for visiting missionaries, a few widows and staff workers. What will they do now? Like the fabled Phoenix, they will rise from the ashes and fight the fire of adversity with the fire of Pentecost.

Chapter 8

Outfoxing the Witch Doctors

The story of Cebien Alexis and the Army of Christ in Haiti

"**L**et's go see if the witch doctors have any power," Cebien Alexis said to his friends, Tony, William and Prevail.

The three were pastors taking catch-up training at Emmaus Bible College in Cap-Haitien where 25-year-old Cebien also was enrolled.

"OK," they answered, game for an adventure.

They walked a ways to where Cebien knew a witch doctor hung out.

"Good morning, Father Carlos," Cebien enjoined.

"We've come to see if you can do something for us."

"What can I do for you?" the witch doctor asked, pleased that his services were being solicited.

"I'm from the Northwest, and someone wants to kill me and take my job. Can you help me?"

"What's your name?"

"I'm John the Baptist," Cebien said. His friends kept a straight face.

"John the Baptist?"

"Yes."

"Today is a good day for John the Baptist," Carlos said. "Everything will be okay for you. I can see that."

Well, he isn't seeing too well, Cebien thought to himself. *He doesn't know I'm not John the Baptist!*

"You have a business?" Carlos asked

"Yes, I have a business. I am in the market place. I sell just about everything."

"I see that. I see that," Carlos agreed, thinking that here was someone with money. "I'll take care of everything. You have some money?"

"Well, I brought some goats to offer for sacrifice," Cebien replied, "but I left them at a crossroads a ways back. It's about a half-hour walk from here."

"Why don't you go get them?" the witch doctor suggested. "Do you need someone to get them for you?"

"No, I can get them myself," Cebien said.

So he and his friends left, not to return. Cebien had made his point with his friends.

Haiti was founded on Voodoo, and it is widely practiced throughout the island nation. Though some witch doctors pack a sinister power, many just go through the motions to make a living.

"If you know God wants you to be a preacher," Cebien said to his comrades, "you don't need to be afraid of witch doctors. Just go up to them, tap them on the shoulder, and speak in a straightforward manner. Speak as a man of power, and they will fear you."

Such boldness and spunk characterize this church planter, educator, church architect, building contractor, mechanical entrepreneur, welfare administrator, father to hundreds of orphans, medical doctor and phytotherapy expert. He utilizes all these gifts to serve the King of kings and Lord of lords.

Born in England

Cebien was born in Mellingway, England, on August 20, 1944. His father, Armand, had worked for the electric company in Haiti and was a skilled lineman. Because he knew English, he was recruited by the British to do electrical line work in England. While there, a son was born to them. They called him Cebien, which in Creole means "it is good."

Cebien didn't stay there long. When he was two years old, the family moved back to Haiti. Four years later his mother, Julia, died, and Armand married another woman. She died in a car accident in 1956, and so Armand married a third wife, Germaine. Through that union, John, Ivon, Sonia and Aniece were born. None of this seriously affected the way Cebien was treated as a child.

Being born in England, Cebien's Haitian citizenship was at risk. So one day Armand took his son to Port-au-Prince and had his birth certificate "fixed." From then on, Cebien was a genuine Haitian citizen, of which he remains proud.

Then in 1959, a year before he finished high school, something happened that affected his family relationship and changed his life forever. He met the Lord Jesus Christ.

Salvation by missionary

An American missionary was conducting meetings in Haiti. Cebien heard the American was giving out candy at his vacation Bible school and went to get some.

Cebien was used to seeing white people in Haiti, but they all had spoken French. This man spoke unintelligibly. *He probably has a speech impediment*, Cebien thought. He didn't know the man was speaking English.

Cebien could understand the interpreter but not the missionary, so he stepped closer to hear better. He still couldn't understand a word. *The man probably doesn't have a tongue,* Cebien concluded.

At the end of the meeting, the missionary gave out coconut cookies. Cebien ate his with a grin.

"You gonna be here tomorrow?" he asked the missionary through the interpreter.

Assured he would be, Cebien came back the next day. And the next.

In the end, Cebien invited the Lord Jesus Christ into his heart and went home gleefully to tell his father of his wonderful salvation.

"You're an adult now," his Roman Catholic father shrewdly observed. "You have made your own decision to become a Protestant. Since you are an adult, you will have to live like an adult. From now on, you are on your own."

So at age 15, Cebien found himself homeless—a fact that makes him compassionate to Haiti's thousands of homeless street children even today.

Cebien found his way over to his Aunt Rose. She took him in, let him sleep there and gave him meals.

Preparation for life

One day his older cousin, Antonio, saw him walking along the street.

"Why aren't you in school?" Antonio asked.

"Because my father doesn't send me," Cebien replied

"Why doesn't your father send you?"

Cebien explained what had happened. Antonio had already become a Christian and was attending the Seventh Day Adventist Church. He had a good position with the government, so money was not a problem. Antonio bought Cebien shoes, clothes and books and enrolled him in a Roman Catholic boarding school, paying his way in full. Cebien graduated from Centre d'Apprentisage of St. Martin in 1964.

Next Cebien enrolled in a local government community college called Lycée Toussaint Louverture (Toussaint Louverture College). For the next seven years he gave himself to biology, physiology, anatomy, and other courses necessary to pursue a medical career.

Haiti's educational system allows advanced students to study independently without attending the classes. So during Cebien's last two years at Lycée Toussaint, he studied courses at Emmaus Bible College in Cap-Haitien, returning to Port-au-Prince by bus on Fridays to get his Lycée Toussaint assignments.

At the Bible school he not only learned the fundamentals of preaching, Biblical exegesis and exposition, Bible history, church history and theology, he also learned practical skills such as carpentry, block laying, shoemaking, barbering, architecture and drafting. The fathers of the school wanted to make sure their graduates could make a living and not just preach.

In addition to the acquired skills, Cebien exhibited a natural inclination in music. He learned to play the accordion, harmonica, guitar and chord organ and was able to lead choirs in eight-part harmony.

Cebien graduated from Emmaus Bible College in 1970 and immediately enrolled in a correspondence course with Emmaus Theological Seminary in Switzerland (no relationship between the two schools).

Upon graduating from Lycée Toussaint in 1971, he went to Switzerland for three months to complete his theology course and take his final exam. He then was invited to study phytotherapy (the medicinal qualities of plants) at the Institute of Phytotherapy in the Ivory Coast under the direction of Jean-Luc McKenzie. Cebien's paternal grandparents were herbal doctors, so Cebien had a natural interest and a head start in the subject. Cebien studied several months there and then returned to Haiti. Over the next several years he continued to study phytotherapy by correspondence. He returned to the Ivory Coast twice more for brief periods and finished his degree in 1979.

Through these studies he learned that plants have healing qualities without the bad side effects of drugs. This knowledge enabled Cebien to open a medical clinic near Cap-Haitien.

Native evangelist

At the same time, all this Bible training did not make him a preacher; it just sharpened his skills.

He had started holding street meetings immediately after he was converted. He'd borrow a microphone and a slide projector from the church, set it up on a street corner or empty lot, start singing some songs and show some slides to attract a crowd. When enough bystanders had gathered, he would preach to them.

During this time he learned from experience how to share his testimony, teach the Word, bring people to Christ, follow them up, baptize them, and conduct Bible studies. While he was going to school he was the vice-president of the Sunday school and taught a class every Sunday. So by the time he graduated from Bible college, he had evangelism and church work down pat.

After he graduated from Emmaus Bible College, the Oriental Missionary Society invited him to pastor one of its churches. They gave him a bicycle and offered him the then fat sum of $40 per month when most pastors did well to receive $10 or $20 monthly. Today those sums would be equivalent to five or six times as much.

Cebien served in that manner for about a year, and then resigned.

"You're crazy to resign," OMS people told him.

"Okay," Cebien replied, "but I want to be independent."

They took back their bicycle, and Cebien set off on his own.

Faith provision

Cebien practiced faith and positive confession in practical ways.

One day Cebien didn't have any food, so he was walking over to the OMS compound where he at least could get some free ice to suck on. On the way, he passed a woman selling avocados. Normally an avocado sold for about one or two cents. But this was an exceptionally huge avocado, and the woman was asking six cents.

That was an outrageous price. But Cebien devised a plan.

"I don't have any money on me now," Cebien told her, "but let me have that avocado now, and when I come back, I will give you 40 cents."

The woman believed him, and Cebien went his way munching on the avocado. It was more than he could eat, so he shared it with some of his friends.

He got his ice and on the way back spotted $11 lying in the street. He picked it up and gave the woman $1.

The first church

Now as an independent faith missionary he went to Ile Adam, literally Adam's Isle, with only $12 in his pocket. It's not really an island, but an inland area near Cap-Haitien surrounded by a lot of water.

He found an empty building that had been used for grinding rice. It was a dirty and junky place. The roof leaked and the walls were beginning to lean. The owner offered to rent it to him—$6 for the *year*! Cebien grabbed it up as a bargain, and the owner was happy he could rent it for so much.

At two o'clock Wednesday afternoon, Cebien went to work clearing out the debris and sweeping the floor. He obtained some lumber and constructed some simple benches.

"What are you doing?" passersby would ask.

"I'm going to have a gospel meeting tonight," Cebien would answer. "Come and see."

By 6:30 Cebien was ready for his first meeting.

A small crowd of about 25 people showed up. That night, a young married woman accepted Christ.

The next day, three other people came to Christ. Every night someone confessed Christ. By Sunday, 11 newly saved people came to the church service. A church nucleus had been formed in five days. Cebien began holding Sunday services on May 16, 1971. Before the year ended, 100 people were meeting regularly for worship. This was a milestone. The Baptists from America had spent 26 years there without establishing a church.

First big crusade

The people in Ile Adam were good people, but they had no jobs. They would bring Cebien a mango or something now and then, but they didn't have real money to give him. So that summer he went to Port-au-Prince to conduct a 40-day crusade. *People there have better jobs*, he thought. *They will be able to support me better.*

The crusade was a spiritual success. For 40 nights Cebien sang and preached his heart out. Over 1,050 people responded to his winsome ways and message. But his financial support came from a totally unexpected source.

While he was there, a Christian businessman who had known Cebien's family for years sent him a check for $165 from Nassau. With that bonanza, Cebien bought a bicycle for $34 and other supplies and headed back to Ile Adam.

Providential provision

One Sunday morning after he had returned, he preached hard and long. After the people left he was very hungry, but had no food to eat and began to scold God.

"God, here I am preaching my heart out. I am doing my job. But You're not doing Your job. If You don't give me food to eat, I'm not going to preach tonight."

With that, the exhausted preacher lay down on a cot in his little house and fell into a deep sleep.

When he awoke, he smelled food. He looked, and a plateful of deliciously cooked food was sitting on the floor in front of him: rice, beans, cooked meat, candy, cold water and fruit juice, a Sunday dinner fit for a preacher. The God of Elijah had visited him.

Where'd this food come from? Cebien thought to himself. *The people here don't cook food like this. They are too poor.*

A week later he learned a family in the next town had brought it. Public transportation was non-existent. During the week, a truck went by and would carry passengers for a fee. The truck did not run on Sundays, but on this particular Sunday, for some reason, it ran. The people down the road had prepared the food, brought it to Cebien's house, laid it down quietly, and left secretly.

With renewed strength, Cebien preached with vigor that night on Philippians 4:19: "And my God shall supply all your need through His riches in glory by Christ Jesus." During the next week another seven people came to know Christ because they learned that God can provide.

Starting an army

During college and Bible college, Cebien had started several churches and turned them over to existing denominations to assimilate. When he visited the churches later he found most of them were without a pastor, and the members had dwindled away to a handful.

Why should I plant churches if no one cares for them? Cebien thought. *How can I encourage them?*

Finally he decided he needed to be not just a roving evangelist and church planter; he must continue to care for the churches he planted. He must find and appoint pastors to care for them. He would have to start his own organization.

As he read the gospels, he saw that Jesus and His disciples were like an army. All these disciples carried were the Word and their cloak—like the "infantrymen" who carried only a rifle and a bedroll. Whenever the call for help came from a different quarter, they would pick up and move to the next place.

So Cebien decided to call his ministry "Army of Christ." His purpose was to go anywhere to do anything to help anyone as God led and provided. His goal was to have churches planted all over Haiti before the Lord returned.

Happy moment

During his childhood the family that lived next door had a daughter, Gertrude, about Cebien's age. The father was a tailor and also sold hats. Gertrude went to the same Bible school that Cebien did and was one year behind him. While there, their feelings for each other increased. Now, with his recent prosperity giving him growing confidence, he wrote Gertrude in 1972 that he was coming to Port-au-Prince to marry her in August. She wrote back that she would be ready.

By faith Cebien went to Port-au-Prince on July 27th. When the local pharmacist learned that Cebien was in town, he immediately asked Cebien to fill in for him while he went to the States. Cebien worked 15 days and earned the whopping sum of $450. With that largess he went out and bought himself a Volkswagen Beetle.

The happy moment came when Cebien married Gertrude du Varne on August 12, 1972. The couple moved up north to Garde Cognac, about an hour's commute from Morne Rouge by tap-tap (Haitian minbus) that stopped in front of their house. Cebien would take the tap-tap to Morne Rouge daily to operate his medical clinic and to Ile Adam on Sundays and other times to pastor the church. After a few months they moved into a stick-and-mud house with sheet metal roof in Ile Adam. At least the rent was cheap—$34 per year!

Disillusionment

Soon after this, Cebien met a representative of a church-planting mission from Pennsylvania.

"We'll be glad to help you," the man said, "but if you receive our help you should not receive support from your own people, too."

It seemed strange to Cebien that his own people were prohibited from supporting him.

"You have to sell your car, too," they told him. "Our donors will think you are rich if you have a car."

The organization gave him $125 per month: $85 to care for seven orphan children he had begun to provide schooling for and $40 for himself. Then they asked him to sign a document saying he had received $6,000. They also said he could only preach in Baptist churches; all others were out of bounds.

To Cebien's way of thinking, these people had good intentions but also lots of restrictions. The little help the organization provided was irregular, and after a few months Cebien left it.

Soon the church in Ile Adam was in full swing, so in 1974 Cebien found another man to take over the church and moved to a rented house in Morne Rouge, though he continued to visit the church in Ile Adam regularly. He decided to make Morne Rouge his headquarters and bought land totaling 2.3 acres.

Nearly poisoned

Cebien began his winsome evangelistic program, and the people of Morne Rouge responded. The church began to grow—30, 40, 60.

Near the church lived a witch doctor. He didn't like the intrusion of all this evangelism into his territory. So one day in 1975 he sent the Alexis family a jar of honey.

Cebien stuck his finger in the honey.

"Mmmmm, that's good honey," Cebien exclaimed as he licked his fingers.

Gertrude was suspicious. *Why would a witch doctor send them a gift?* She gave the dog a sample. The dog ate it and immediately died.

"That's it," Gertrude exclaimed. "I'm not staying here anymore. I'm going to live with Mamma."

By this time the church in Morne Rouge had over 100 members. Cebien found a pastor from Garde Cognac to take over leadership of the flock so he and Gertrude could move to Port-au-Prince. There they rented a house for about a dollar a week in a poor section of town.

Snatched from the witch doctor

One day in a town near Port-au-Prince Cebien and several co-workers were walking down the street when they met an old woman. The woman told them her sister was under the care of a witch doctor, and she was going to visit her. They felt the Lord was telling them to go with her, so they went with her to the witch doctor's house.

When they got to the house they knocked on the door.

"We all want to come in to visit my sister," the woman said.

"Well, you can come in," the witch doctor said to the woman, "but those fellows have to stay outside."

"But we have come to give the sister some riches," Cebien spoke up.

"Well, if you've come to give her some riches, then you may come in," the witch doctor said, obviously thinking he might get some benefit himself.

Then they began talking to the woman about the riches of Christ and actually led her to pray the sinner's prayer right there in the witch doctor's house.

"You need to get out," the witch doctor said, somewhat disturbed.

"We will not go without the sister," Cebien answered.

"She can't leave," the witch doctor said. "She's sick and needs treatment. She's been here for two months."

"She's been here for two months and she isn't any better," Cebien retorted. "God can heal her in two minutes."

"All right, take her! Let's see what your God can do!"

As soon as they escorted the woman outside she fell down dead. The voodoo people gathered around and began to chant and celebrate.

Cebien began to pray in earnest. "God, I know You're the One who brought me here. You won't let the witch doctor have victory over me." His prayers became tears as he continued to intercede for half an hour with his eyes tightly closed.

Then he sensed a voice saying, "Call her up."

Cebien called her name three times. The third time she answered.

"Stand up," he said.

She stood and immediately began to testify what the Lord Jesus Christ had done for her. The voodoo people went silent and slunk away.

Like the Gadarene demoniac, the woman became a vibrant witness for Jesus for the next 25 years.

From rags to riches...and back again

Cebien and his family had lived in Port-au-Prince about a year when a U.S. pastor heard about it and offered to provide funds so they could move to a better section of town so his children could attend a better school.

His North American friends insisted he live in a house that cost about $700 a year to rent. Cebien would never have chosen so expensive a house, but it was nice. It had electricity and piped-in water, and was near a good school. Cebien started a church in his living room.

The U.S. pastor paid the rent for a year, but after that did not renew his support. Cebien could not afford the rent and moved back to Morne Rouge. Without leadership, the fledgling church dissipated.

Time to regroup

While attending Carl McIntyre's International Council of Christian Churches' conference in Cape May in 1973, Cebien met some Filipino missionaries who introduced him to Dr. Bob Finley. Cebien liked Finley's approach to missions: helping indigenous missions, and not telling them how to run their ministry, just asking for proper accountability and reporting.

However, not much came as a result of the meeting. Cebien wasn't much of a letter writer. The only time he had for writing letters was at night, and the electricity usually didn't work. With no information coming in, Christian Aid was handicapped in gaining support for his work. Consequently, very little help flowed from Christian Aid to Cebien in the next few years.

Cebien visited Christian Aid headquarters in 1978 and gained a better understanding of how to work with it. Christian Aid found sponsors for some of the gospel workers and for some of the children in the orphanage.

Progress

The connection with Christian Aid made a difference. When Cebien first met Dr. Finley, he had only five pastors and 11 lay workers caring for about 50 mission stations. He was also providing for seven children at the Morne Rouge orphange.

By 1977 Cebien had 78 churches under his leadership. These were manned by 25 pastors. In nine of the

Item	1977	1987	1997	2003
Total churches planted	78	89	97	138
Additional outstations	0	42	35	552
Number of believers	15,000	20,000	35,000	60,000
Pastors	25	30	45	80
Lay workers	16	31	302	1,240
Day schools	10	21	51	70
Children in orphanage	27	68	72	73
Children in day schools	1,200	5,200	6,300	7,200

churches he operated Christian day schools for 1,200 children. In those days the children sat on logs for benches. By this time the number of children in the Morne Rouge orphanage had grown to 27.

After 1978, the ministry progressed more rapidly, as the chart on the previous page shows.

The orphanage program

In 1977 something else happened that proved a great boost to Cebien's ministry. Two young ladies, Alice Gouker and Kathy Wise from Pennsylvania, came to help. These self-effacing young women submitted to Cebien's leadership and used most of their personal missionary support to care for the children, spending little on themselves. They also taught in the Bible school and managed the summer camp program.

Once Cebien took children in, he took care of them until they completed their high school and sometimes college education. Like a father, he wants to make sure his children know a trade, have a job, and are able to make their way in life before he turns them loose.

Today the younger children are taught in the School of Tomorrow curriculum that enables them to proceed at their own pace. Some of the children are already doing fifth-grade level work, even though they have been in the system only two or three years. The older youths complete high school or professional or vocational training in Cap-Haitien.

Secret building plan

Cebien's diplomatic approach helps him start new churches. When he goes to a place to start a church, he doesn't announce what he is doing. He first buys a small lot for about $300. The people think he might be going to put up a business or something there. They don't know it is for a church.

If he were to announce he was going to build a church there, they would ask ten times the amount for the lot. Or, the Roman Catholic Church would come and buy it at a slightly higher price.

After obtaining the plot, Cebien starts holding meetings. When the congregation increases to 100, the members often put up a thatch shelter supported by poles. Sometimes they hang blankets round the sides. Cebien calls this a "blanket" church.

If the congregation continues to grow, Cebien helps them put up a building about 42 by 90 feet, large enough to hold 150 to 200 people. Cement is expensive, but he saves some money by choosing sites that have sand. The people make their own concrete blocks on site.

Training workers

Meanwhile, others who had joined him planted still more churches, increasing the need for workers. So in 1980 Cebien started a Bible school in Champin. He got several pastors in the area who were Bible school graduates to teach the classes and began with 10 students.

Cebien patterned the curriculum after that at Moody, teaching traditional Bible school subjects covering the Bible, hermeneutics, homiletics, sociology, psychology and pastoral ethics as well as law, evangelism and Christian education.

From the beginning, the school ran a four-year curriculum, but in 1997 Cebien reduced it to two years due to inability of the students to pay. About 100 students have graduated from it. Most of them serve with Army of Christ, though some have emigrated to the U.S.

Ironically, many who can afford to pay the $30 per month do not have a missionary call on their lives. Most of these end up as pastors in the U.S. On the other hand, those with a genuine call to the bush areas typically don't have funds to pay. Since Cebien wants new workers for pioneer areas, he trains them, anyway.

Doctor and entrepreneur

To help keep the ministry going, Cebien relies on his mechanical and engineering skill, as well as on God.

"I know the Lord will provide," he says, "but I have to do *something.*"

Sometimes he buys an old junk car for around $300. He and his older students and co-workers fix it up and then sell it for around $1,000.

One time he had an old school bus with a gasoline engine that wouldn't run. Then he bought another old school bus with a diesel engine, but the body was bad. Cebien cut the two buses in half and welded the two good halves together.

But Cebien makes most of his earnings through his medical clinic. He goes to the medical clinic in Morne Rouge nearly every day. He keeps typical Haitian hours—4 a.m. to mid-afternoon. From 100 to 200 people will be waiting to see him every day. He calls his waiting room his preaching room. He preaches the gospel to everyone before he sees any of them.

He charges 40 cents for an office visit. If they can't pay, he treats them anyway. He utilizes his training in medicine as well as phytotherapy, though most of his prescriptions are natural remedies. "They work a lot faster than the stuff you buy in the store," Cebien says.

Witch doctors' banquet

Though witch doctors are a challenge, Cebien has a heart to reach out to them with the gospel of salvation. His diplomatic and persuasive skills really come to life in his outreach to witch doctors.

Several times a year he will hand write invitations and have his workers take them around to all the witch doctors in the area. Each card will say, "We know that you exist, but we have not had opportunity to meet you. God loves you, but hates sin. We invite you and your family to a special banquet we are preparing for members of your profession. Please come and join us on such-and-such a date."

The witch doctors arrive on the appointed date. Cebien and his crew have prepared sandwiches and Coca-Cola for 50 people, but 62 show up.

"No problem," Cebien tells his co-workers. "Just add a little water to the Coca-Cola. And lots of ice. Witch doctors love ice. They usually cannot afford it."

While some workers are "stretching" the Coke, others run up town to buy more bread to make more sandwiches.

Then as the witch doctors enjoy their snacks, Cebien preaches to them:

"Good evening, my brothers," Cebien intones. "Good evening, my friends."

An AOC student planted in the crowd asks, "What's the difference between 'brothers' and 'friends'?"

"I'm sorry to answer your question," Cebien answers. "These men are my friends, but they are not my brothers. Those who are saved are my brothers; those who are not yet saved, I call 'friends.'

"We all have two destinies," Cebien continues, "heaven or hell. We are either a child of God or a child of the Devil."

He shows them John 1:12 and 8:44, and waits while co-workers and students show the witch doctors the passages in Bibles he has made available to them.

"What does Satan do for you?" Cebien challenges. He dare not push them too far, too fast.

"I would venture to say that Satan never gives you anything," Cebien continues. "Satan takes what you have, but never gives you anything back.

"On the other hand, God takes you as you are and gives you more. He gives you things you never had before.

"Now tell me, if you had to choose whom to serve, whom would you choose?"

The answer is obvious.

Outfoxing the Witch Doctors

"God calls you His child," Cebien continues. "Satan calls you a *cheval* (horse or four-footed animal). Tell me: Do you have four feet?"

He waits until they answer, "No."

"Do you have long hair? Do you have a long tail?"

"No! No! No!" they chorus after each question. Cebien now has them eating out of his hand.

"Why does Satan call you that? Because he has no respect for you. He despises you.

"But God calls you His child. He says, 'As many as received him, to them gave he power to become the children of God.'

"Now tell me: When it comes time for you to leave this earth, how will you do it? Will you go as a child of God or as a *cheval* of the Devil?"

The witch doctors are now deep in thought. Then Cebien catches their interest afresh.

The wise become foolish

"I tell you, many people will go to hell—not because of what they do, but because of what they don't do."

"What don't they do?" a cry comes from the audience.

"I'll give someone $2 if he can give the right answer," Cebien offers.

Now he really has their attention. Two dollars would be a day's wage in their culture. In rapid fire they offer first one thing then another, all wrong, of course.

"No, that's not the answer," Cebien says. He is amused that these witch doctors, who think they always have the answer, suddenly realize they don't.

"One thing you don't do," Cebien continued. "You don't accept the Lord." He emphasizes the point.

"Do you know there are four things God doesn't know?" he again challenges.

"We thought God knew everything," some of them answer.

"First of all, God doesn't know a sinner that He doesn't love." Cebien expounds John 3:16 for a while.

"Secondly, God doesn't know a sinner he cannot save.

"Thirdly, He doesn't know another *way* to save a sinner. Jesus said, 'I am the Way and the Truth and the Life. No man cometh unto the Father but by Me.'

"Finally, God doesn't know another *time* to save the sinner. 'Today is the day of salvation.'

"If you don't get saved, it's not because God doesn't want to save you," Cebien chides. "He doesn't care if you're a witch doctor or if you've been bad all your life. He says, 'Whosoever calls upon the name of the Lord Jesus Christ shall be saved.' It's up to you. If you want to accept Him, you can do so now."

The presentation has been pleasant, engaging and respectful of these men who think they are somebody.

Then the music begins. Several soloists and ensembles present special gospel songs. While these are singing, Cebien and his co-workers go one by one through the crowd and pray with those who want to accept Christ as Savior.

This time, workers pray with five witch doctors to receive Christ. Each will be followed up. They will not immediately be told they must leave the Roman Catholic Church. He just teaches them out of the Bible. Eventually he comes to, "Come out from among them and be ye separate" (2 Corinthians 6:17) and, "Let everyone that nameth the name of Christ depart from iniquity" (1 Timothy 2:19).

"I don't tell them what to do," Cebien says. "I let God tell them."

Expansion

When other pastors and churches see the good work being done by AOC, some of them want to join. Others simply want to come under an umbrella organization that would give them recognition before the government as well as training and fellowship opportunities.

One day one of the pastors came to Cebien and complained, "I don't have any mission board to help me. Which mission board should I join?"

"You don't need a mission board," Cebien replied. "Where in the Bible does it say, 'Join a mission board?'"

So Cebien organized the Council of Independent Churches of Haiti (CEIH from the French, *Conseil des églises indépendantes d'Haïti*). With over 4,500 churches, it is the largest fellowship of churches in Haiti.

Before joining, any pastor must pass certain criteria. He must believe in standard evangelical doctrines and must not be involved in politics or practice any form of witchcraft. He also must not be the one handling the church funds, and if he buys property for the church, it must be in the church's name, not in his.

Most of the pastors have little education. So Cebien, CEIH President, conducts regional worker conferences for up to 200 pastors nearly every month. He also holds a week-long convention at his headquarters. In each instance he provides one or two meals a day (depending on his resources at the time) and conducts workshops from 8 a.m. to 7 p.m.

Each convention focuses on one book of the Bible. At the end of the week, the pastors are given a test. Those who pass the test are given a certificate signifying their accomplishment. This means a lot to these pastors who have few other credentials.

If any of them has a problem with another, CEIH has its own arbitration system, so pastors don't have to go to secular courts. Cebien and several of the nine other senior pastors selected by the officers pray over each need and render their judgment based on Biblical principles and their knowledge of the situation. The pastors accept that.

Bicycles needed

Cebien has a heart for the many pastors who often serve without pay in the rural churches. Many travel wide circuits to preach among several villages.

Pastor Meuis, for example, walks 75 miles a week. So do Pastor Leo and Pastor Pierre.

Pastor Joseph walks 90 miles a week.

Each of a dozen or more pastors could use a bicycle, which costs about $115 each. But local sources do not provide for this "luxury."

Building churches

Many congregations don't have the resources to construct a building without outside help. The pastor of such a church goes to Cebien, as head of CEIH.

Cebien and his CEIH colleagues pray over the matter. If they feel the Lord leading, they will go and purchase a site in the area. Cebien's experienced eye looks for a site where sand or gravel is available. Then he will draw up a plan for the church. (Actually he has a "one plan fits all" design that he merely expands when needed.) He arranges for the gathering of materials and acts as general contractor to see the building erected. With everything finished except the exterior waterproof painting or plastering, Cebien leaves. It's up to the church members to finish the job. If they don't, that church will get no more help from Cebien.

It costs approximately $5,000 to construct a church building after the land is obtained. It takes $1,000 to put a corrugated metal roof on one.

Poverty conditions

Cebien does all of this without pay. They can't pay him; they have no money. The average Haitian lives in a wood or bamboo house on stilts (to keep animals from entering and devouring any food supply), or in an adobe house on ground level with a secure door. Most have rusted corrugated metal roofs.

The rural dweller earns very little cash. It used to be if a man grew extra tomatoes, he shared them with his neighbor. Now he tries to sell them. Non-professional city dwellers may earn $20 per month.

Most houses have no running water or electricity. If they are wired, the electricity probably doesn't work most of the time. The toilet is outside. If one wishes to take a bath, he must go stand in the creek or river and splash water on himself, or fill a bucket or two with water and carry it home a mile or more. Water used for drinking is usually impure, containing worms or parasites.

Cooking is usually done over an open fire under a makeshift roof out back. If the family owns land, they might have one or more banana trees, some pineapples, mangoes, grapefruit or coconuts. Rice and dried peas are staples, if one has money to buy them. The price of rice went from 15 cents a pound before the embargo in 1993 to more than ten times that afterward. The family that grows chickens is truly blessed, for it has both eggs and, once or twice a year, meat.

Some families are so poor they can't feed their children and encourage them to run away. They figure their children might fare better fending for themselves.

Reaching street children

Haiti has tens of thousands of street children. They wander the streets looking for food. Sometimes they steal or kill to satisfy their hunger. The worst part is that they get no education. Without that, they can never improve themselves.

The government recognized this problem and licensed Cebien to conduct his ADSED program. ADSED stands for *Association pour le developpement social & educatif des demunis*, which means Association for the Social Development and Education of *Demunis* (Creole word meaning "street children").

As part of this program, the government issues special cards. A child possessing one of these cards can be taught in a non-public school. Whoever conducts these schools must pay the teachers and provide books and materials themselves. Cebien has obtained permission from the government to conduct such schools.

One day Cebien passed an alley and saw six or seven children sleeping in a large cardboard carton.

"You want to go to school?" he asked.

"We'd like to, but we don't have a mother or father to send us," they said.

"I know," Cebien responds, "but I think there is a way.

"We want you to become educated so you can become a doctor or teacher or somebody good. You come with me, and I will show you how you can go to school.

"I will give you one of these cards. We will put the official government stamp on it, and it will let you go to one of our schools.

"I will pay for your books and supplies. The government has given me a special license to do this.

"But you must do well. If you don't do well, you will have to quit. If you do well, we will give you a new card, and you can go again next year."

Cebien has started dozens of schools like this in communities where there is none. They meet in existing church buildings, but running the program is terribly expensive. Cebien hopes that churches in the U.S. will take to the idea of sponsoring a whole school for $500 per month. Each such sponsorship would gather and educate 400 children from off the streets.

Faith Christian University

Giving children a basic education, as essential and wonderful as that is, is not the end of Cebien's vision for youths. For years he has dreamed of providing children of pastors and church members a university education. College opportunities in Haiti are mainly for the rich. He believes Christians, above all, should be educated to provide future leadership for the country. But with pastors receiving such minimal support, sending their children to college has been but a dream—until now.

Funded mainly by missionary-minded medical friends in America, Cebien broke ground for Faith Christian University in the fall of 2002. Located on about 15 acres of land near his headquarters, it already consists of four buildings: a classroom and lecture hall, an administration building, a cafeteria and kitchen, and a library. It also hosted 64 first-year students.

The curriculum includes theological education and training in other fields, such as medicine (with an emphasis on phytotherapy), political science, computer and agriculture. It is hoped that student fees and tuition will keep the university running once it is fully built—construction funds are still being sought. Students can work off some of their fees in the school's agricultural projects, such as growing corn, beets, tomatoes and potatoes, and raising pigs. Growing the crops provides food for the students and operational funds for the school.

Christ's ambassador

Overseeing and obtaining funds for all these projects taxes Cebien's diplomatic skills. His gift of diplomacy did not go unrecognized in worldly circles, either. In 1995, after the change in government, Cebien was approached to be Haiti's ambassador to Germany.

"I was afraid to get into the political realm," Cebien confessed. "Besides, why should I serve man when I can serve the King of kings?"

Chapter 9

The Goldfish and the Whale

The story of Paul Pang and the Schools for Christ in Hong Kong

This chapter was adapted from Dr. Paul Pang's autobiography, Twenty Years in Christian Education, *published by Schools For Christ Foundation, 1989.*

While many residents of Hong Kong worried about China's takeover of the British Crown Colony in 1997, Dr. Paul Pang actually anticipated the event. While tens of thousands fled Hong Kong every year thinking life as they knew it would end, this Christian educator began preparing for a new future.

Many thought the whale of China would swallow the Hong Kong goldfish so completely that the city-state's economy and influence would be eroded. On the other hand, Dr. Pang considered that if the whale of China opened its mouth, the Hong Kong goldfish just might have a new opportunity to go where until now it had been restricted. If so, Pang would do all he could to make sure the little goldfish was packing a mighty powerful suitcase. The contents? Trained Christian educators.

With two master's degrees and two earned doctor's degrees, he might just be the man for the job. After all, he had already initiated four educational ventures: two Christian high schools, a foundation for motivating and training Christian teachers, and a graduate school of Christian education to train Christian teachers in their profession.

All of these endeavors are intended to help teachers influence their pupils to live for Christ in a secular society—even if that society is Communist China.

But arriving at his present level of involvement was no snap. He almost didn't make it.

An idea is born

Paul had become a Christian in high school. He agreed with the apostle Paul that the one compelling reason for living on earth rather than going immediately to heaven was the blessing and obligation of spreading the gospel (Philippians 1:22-24).

After completing one year of teacher training at Grantham Training College in 1958, he began teaching in a Hong Kong elementary school. He felt it was an excellent opportunity to influence young lives for Christ. Suddenly, in his second year, the principal stopped him short.

"Mr. Pang, the government has not hired you to preach the gospel," he declared.

Though Hong Kong had no law against teachers sharing religious feelings with students, the young teacher did not know how to answer the headmaster's prohibition.

If I could start a Christian school, no one could tell me I couldn't share the gospel, Paul thought.

He shared his dream with fellow Christian teachers, church members and members of his family. All thought it was a good idea. While elementary schools were provided by the government, high school education was a private matter. Consequently, only 32 percent of Hong Kong's young people went on to high school.

They questioned only one thing. Could common folk like them start a Christian school? They determined to pray regularly about it.

Two years later, Paul Pang and his friend, Benjamin Chan, committed themselves to further studies to gain the credentials necessary to establish a Christian school. Their friends formed a committee to found the school and gave it a name, New Life School. That took faith and patience, because it would take Paul and Benjamin seven long years to become qualified.

Journey to America

On August 22, 1962, Paul and Benjamin started their long journey to Houghton College in New York. They went by ship so they could carry more luggage. The ship stopped at Tokyo and Hawaii. Enthusiastically, Paul and Ben disembarked in Hawaii to see the island paradise. Not having money to take the sightseeing tour, they contented themselves with walking up and down Waikiki beach.

After 20 days at sea, they arrived in San Francisco and took a train to Los Angeles. There they were welcomed by a Chinese friend who gave them free haircuts.

Haircuts were terribly expensive in the U.S., compared with Hong Kong, and the young men could not have afforded them otherwise.

Their friend then packed lots of sandwiches for their train trip to Chicago. There Rev. Philip Loh met them and took them to a small prayer meeting in a poor section of China Town. Paul began to realize that among all the riches of America were miserable people who needed both spiritual and material help.

Then they boarded the train again, this time for Houghton, New York. Finally, Paul and Benjamin arrived at the college.

Houghton is located in the rolling countryside of western New York State, about 50 miles southeast of Buffalo. In the 1960s, it was a remote area devoid of distractions. There was no shopping mall, no movie theater, not even a grocery store. Compared with the shoulder-to-shoulder high rises of Hong Kong, these were wide-open spaces. Without a car, Paul and Ben could do nothing but concentrate on their purpose for coming there—study.

This was Paul's first encounter with a school which put Christ at the center of its education. All the professsors were Christians and demonstrated their love for the Lord. Spiritual life as well as academic excellence was emphasized. The professors had complete liberty to honor Christ in their classrooms. This whetted Paul's desire to found a school in Hong Kong that would provide the same quality of Christian education.

Paul and Ben lived and studied together. Paul's specialty was mathematics, so his English was not very good. He really struggled with subjects like American history and English literature. He slept only five or six hours a night; almost all his waking hours were spent studying.

His diligence paid off. Paul earned his bachelor's degree in only two years. One leg of the journey was complete. Next, Paul tackled his master's degree and was granted an assistantship in mathematics from the graduate school of the State University of New York (SUNY) at Buffalo.

Crash stop

By this time, Paul had been able to obtain a small, well-used car. It was nothing glorious, but it provided transportation. Saturday evening, August 21, 1965, Paul told Ben he would pick him up for church the next morning. But he never made it.

That evening as Paul was driving home, a large car came crashing into his. The impact broke all but one of Paul's ribs, and crushed both lungs.

"We need to perform a tracheotomy immediately," the doctor in charge determined.

He stuck a form in front of Paul's face. Barely conscious, Paul made an X on the dotted line to give authorization. He was too weak to sign his name.

Ben arrived as soon as he heard about the accident. One look at Paul and he immediately phoned several Buffalo churches for special prayer. Members of the Kensington Alliance Church began a 24-hour prayer chain.

When he regained consciousness, Paul felt pain all over. He couldn't talk or move.

"If my arms or legs are broken, I can still carry on my ministry," Paul thought, "but if my brain is damaged, I'll be useless."

He decided to test his brain by attempting some calculus problems in his head.

"My brain works!" he concluded.

At first, the doctors gave him 48 hours to live. Then they extended the prognosis to 72 hours. At the end of that time, instead of dying, the tracheotomy was removed and Paul was taken off the critical list.

One day, Dr. Tibbit, the physician in charge of his case, took him to a doctor's conference to explain his case to them. He gave Paul an opportunity to speak.

"I thank the doctors for their excellent skill and the nurses for their tender care," Paul said. "But most of all,

I thank God without whose blessing I would not have recovered. He has saved my life for a purpose, and I plan to start a Christian school when I return to Hong Kong."

A few days later, the head of the nursing school invited Paul to share his testimony with the student nurses.

On October 8, Paul was released.

Missionary bride

A few weeks before the accident, Paul had met Marjorie Dunbar at church. The Sunday before the accident the young lady took Paul home after the evening service, and he invited her in for a cup of Chinese tea.

Marjorie had already studied at Houghton from 1958 to 1960. She then studied physical therapy at McGill University and then at SUNY. It was while she was at Buffalo that Paul met her.

After Paul left the hospital, the friendship flourished—for a short while. A month later Marjorie accepted a position in a hospital in Edmonton, Alberta, and left.

Paul and Marjorie kept up a warm friendship by correspondence until she returned the next August to visit her parents, vacationing at Lake Ozonia. There, on a big rock near the lake, Paul asked her to pray about being his wife.

When she returned the next April, Paul offered her an engagement ring. She accepted both it and the call to the mission field. On October 7, 1967, Paul and Marjorie became husband and wife at the Kensington Alliance Church in Buffalo. The words sung at the wedding carried special meaning for Marjorie: "Whither thou goest, I will go; and where thou lodgest, I will lodge: thy people shall be my people, and thy God my God" (Ruth 1:16).

But it would be two more years before either set foot on Hong Kong.

Higher degrees

Paul obtained his Master of Education Degree in February, 1966 and he immediately embarked on a doctoral program.

After one year of course work, he began researching his dissertation. He worked on his proposal for eight months. Then it was rejected and he had to start all over. Finally, in February 1969, Paul received his Doctor of Education Degree from SUNY.

Dr. Bob Finley, founder and chairman of International Students, Inc. (ISI) learned of Paul's plan to start a Christian high school in Hong Kong and offered to provide official receipts for financial gifts for his ministry. The next year, the foreign outreach of ISI became a separate organization known as Christian Aid Mission and has been supportive of Paul's ministry over the years.

The Tempter speaks

Not everyone was thrilled with Paul's plan, however.

"You're too qualified for just a high school position in Hong Kong," one of his friends told him.

"You've already had two years' teaching at SUNY. You could get a good position here. With Marjorie working as a physical therapist, you could have a very comfortable life. Aren't there others who could start the school in Hong Kong?"

It seemed like the Tempter was speaking.

"How will you ever be able to provide a college education for your children?" someone else asked. Of course, Paul and Marjorie didn't have any children, yet, but they expected to have some.

All Paul's friends had good intentions. Were they voicing the will of God? Or should Paul say, "Get thee behind me Satan?"

"Lord, how much should we trust You, and how much should we trust our own calculations? How much should we forfeit the present to worry about the future?" Paul and Marjorie prayed.

As they searched their hearts and placed their lives in the hands of God, Paul felt no release from his original plan. He and Marjorie were one in the Lord. In August 1969, they packed their belongings and drove cross-country with Marjorie's parents to Los Angeles. After seven long years, Paul was heading home.

Marjorie was entering the strange and unknown.

Marjorie's new world

About a month after Neil W. Armstrong took "one giant leap for mankind" by setting foot on the moon, Marjorie first stepped onto the anthill called Hong Kong.

Paul and Marjorie arrived about midnight. Paul's brother met them at the airport and drove them the ten miles to his parents' house in Tsuen Wan. As they walked past the fish market to the apartment building, the hot, humid air reeked of dead fish and seaweed. For Paul, the sights, sounds and smells had a nostalgic familiarity. For Marjorie, they were quite foreign. "Why did you come here?" her senses protested.

They carried their baggage up the dark, narrow stairway to the third-floor apartment. When they opened the door, Mom and Dad Pang greeted them. They dropped their bags to the floor, sending cockroaches and lizards scurrying. After brief but warm introductions, Paul and Marjorie crawled into bed. Everybody was tired. Catching up on seven years would come later.

Home at last, Paul breathed a sigh of relief.

Life here isn't going to be easy, Marjorie thought anxiously, wondering what the future held.

At least Paul and Marjorie were one in the Lord. "It will all work out," they agreed.

The Goldfish and the Whale

Hong Kong's smallest high school

And work out it did. Paul had braced Marjorie for Hong Kong living before they left America. "Due to the high cost of housing, we won't be able to afford a very nice apartment," he had warned.

To their surprise, a spacious apartment was leased to them at a very reasonable rate. It became their home for the next 13 years. Grace was born there in 1970, and Susan in 1972. When the Pangs returned to the U.S. in later years, subletting their apartment helped pay their airfare. Surely, the Lord is good.

After seven years of prayer and study, Paul and his friends were ready to start their first New Life School. Paul would be principal and instructor and Ben would be volunteer superintendent. Mr. Clement Man was the only other full-time teacher. Finances didn't allow another salaried person.

"Mr. Man, why do you want to teach here?" Paul asked the recent graduate of Hong Kong Chinese University's School of Education.

"I just believe that's where God wants me to teach," the young scholar replied.

Seeing such a demonstration of faith filled Paul with joy. Few others could see any future for the fledgling school.

"Where's the school?" one of the student applicants asked.

Paul hesitated to tell the young man that he was standing on the premises.

With only 32 students (and some of them didn't even know the alphabet), New Life School was the smallest high school in Hong Kong when it opened in September, 1969. Paul and Ben prayed that the students wouldn't leave out of disappointment.

Some of the NLS board members suggested they might close the school in order to let Paul gain valuable experience by teaching in a well-established school. Paul and Clement prayed. Suddenly, they realized the blessing of the school's size. Its smallness would enable the innovators to try various methods and ideas. If experiments didn't work, they wouldn't cause a major setback. With renewed enthusiasm, the educators began.

About this time, Hong Kong University, the most prestigious institute of higher education in the colony, needed a mathematics lecturer. Paul, with a doctor's degree in mathematics, was their first choice. NLS students then boasted that they were taught by a faculty member of HKU. Perhaps Paul wasn't over qualified for work in Hong Kong, after all. Paul continued his part-time involvement in HKU until 1974.

Almost all of the NLS students accepted the Lord that first year. They got excited over their new dimension in life. Paul and Ben, as well as neighbors and family members, observed changes in their behavior. Their attempt at Christian education was making a difference. The students' testimonies of their enriched education helped raise student enrollment to 104 the next year, and to more than 200 the third year.

The school continued to thrive. After ten years, it had grown to 11 classes with 439 students and 20 Christian teachers and staff. More than 1,000 students made professions of faith in Christ during those first ten years. Some of them went on to serve the Lord. One member of NLS's first graduating class went on to Alliance Seminary and then returned as NLS's chaplain.

A new school building accommodating over 1,000 students was completed and dedicated in 1985 and the school was renamed the Lui Kwok Pat Fong Secondary School. Clement became the founding principal of a new Christian high school in the area, using NLS as a model.

For some, the objective would have been reached. But for Paul Pang, it was only the beginning.

New Life Schools

In the spring of 1973, Paul was visited by two mission leaders: the Rev. Grant Nealis of OMS International and the Rev. Wesley Mack of the Free Methodist Mission.

"We want to expand our elementary school into a Christian high school," they said, "and our respective groups have already raised considerable funds for this purpose. But they're not sure we could provide quality education with our limited leadership. So they're hesitant to release the funds. We believe you could provide the kind of leadership we need and seek."

Mack's pastor father had heard Paul testify years before in Buffalo and had referred his son to him. Paul thought this was an opportunity ordained of God. One thing stood in the way.

These two men represented two organizations. They wanted Paul as a full third partner, not just as a headmaster under their employ. Yet it did not seem right that the third party should be an individual. The other men suggested that Paul form an organization. But Paul didn't want to form a new organization just to allow him to join the other two groups in forming a Christian high school. He sought a higher motive.

As Paul and his friends prayed about the proposal, the plight of the more than 400 Christian schools in Hong Kong came to their awareness. They all seemed to have the right goal in mind, but their results were being compromised by worldly methods. Many were hiring Christian teachers and then placing humanistic textbooks into their hands. The purposes for which many Christians gave sacrificially were being frustrated.

"If only we could help some of them become more efficient, our evangelistic vision would be realized at a much faster pace," Paul and Clement concluded. So in 1974 Schools For Christ was formed. Through it, Paul joined OMS and the Free Methodist Mission to start the new high school, called United Christian College, and became its first principal.

In search of a Christian curriculum

In the spring of 1976, Paul set aside two weeks to learn how others were defining and structuring Christian education. He selected nine Christian colleges along the U.S. West Coast and made appointments to interview the chairmen of their departments of education.

What he wanted to know was: How did they train their students to teach from the Christian perspective? What written materials, what textbooks, did they employ with such an approach? Did they have a bibliography for Christian teacher training?

To his surprise and disappointment, most of these Christian colleges could not satisfy his quest for specifically Christian structure, content and method of education. None could give him any written materials. None supplied a bibliography.

Then he learned of the Western Association of Christian Schools, now known as Association of Christian Schools, International (ACSI). Soon to leave for Hong Kong, he went straight to their office in Whittier, California.

The executive director, Dr. Paul Kienel, was on his way to another meeting but took time to show Paul ACSI's operation. He also gave him several books, including *The Philosophy of Christian School Education* and *The Christian Teacher's Handbook*.

Paul thanked Dr. Kienel and made a study of them as soon as he got back to Hong Kong. From the books, he was able to compile a bibliography of helpful literature. But how to obtain the books on their limited budget seemed impossible.

About that time, Paul was invited to speak to a group of Christian tourists led by Dr. C. Dorr Demaray, then president of Seattle Pacific University. Hearing

Paul mention the need for a Christian education resource library, Dr. Demaray asked his guests to give an offering. They gave $1,000. The books were purchased and Schools For Christ was off on a solid footing.

Research Institute for Christian Education

Through SFC, Paul and his associates began holding fellowship luncheons for Christian school principals and held several teachers' conferences each year. After several years, they realized that the weaknesses in Christian school education were more than superficial. There was no doubt the teachers were Christians in their convictions and personal lives, but their training had come from so many schools and sources, there was no consistency. In short, the foundations were weak. Research and reeducation were needed. To meet this need, Paul and his associates founded Research Institute for Christian Education (RICE) in 1984.

RICE was to be a graduate level institution of research and learning. Those associated with it had to be more than consecrated volunteers. They also had to have the credentials appropriate to a graduate school endeavor.

Paul was the obvious choice to head the institute. By this time he had added a Master of Education in Administration Degree from the University of Toronto and a Doctor of Education Degree from SUNY to his previous attainments. The challenge drew Paul like a magnet, but the tremendous financial need of founding a graduate school of education made him wonder if it wouldn't swallow him like some black hole from which he would never emerge.

Even so, Paul and Marjorie accepted this as the Lord's call. Paul resigned his position as principal of United Christian College, and cast himself on the mercy of the Lord for support.

Immediately, his home churches in Hong Kong, as well as the SFC board members, pledged financial help.

The church of Marjorie's parents and a church Paul was associated with while in Houghton placed them in their missionary budgets. Other churches and individuals supported their effort as a legitimate missionary work.

Professor Derek Chung of Wheaton College helped introduce RICE to the Christian Colleges Coalition, which accepted the new institute into its membership in April, 1984. Through that contact, Biola University took an interest in the project. Professor Chung also arranged for 4,000 books to be donated to RICE's library. Everything was ready for the opening of the graduate institute in September 1985.

But you can't have a school without students. One month before the school was scheduled to open, RICE had enrolled but one student. Paul and his associates plunged themselves into prayer and self-examination. Were they fully obedient to God? They reminded the Lord that they had embarked upon this ministry at His bidding.

By the time the school opened, 30 students were enrolled. Biola University made the school a special project and sent two professors to conduct courses every summer. All students taking those courses earned Biola credits.

Ten-story building

The need for RICE to have its own facilities was apparent from the beginning. Yet how could RICE ever hope to own its own building in a city where real estate was the most expensive on earth? Land was priced not by the acre, but by the square foot.

As Paul was thinking about this one day, he remembered the 2,000-square-foot property lying between the OMS offices and United Christian College. OMS International had purchased the land 20 years earlier and had never used it. It was now very valuable. Would they allow him to construct a building on it for Christian education?

Graciously, OMS released the land for the construction of a ten-story building for Christian education purposes. The building would be a joint project of OMS, UCC and Schools For Christ.

The cost of constructing and finishing the SFC portion of the building was about 3 million Hong Kong dollars (approximately U.S. $130,000). How could SFC ever raise that amount of money, especially since British authorities had just signed an agreement with the People's Republic of China that Hong Kong would revert to Chinese rule in 1997?

Paul and his friends did what they knew how to do best. They got on their knees. As they prayed, the Lord drew people's attention to their need.

First, the general manager of a paint factory offered to provide all the paint, besides making a sizable cash donation. Others followed. Hundreds of teachers pledged HK$100 (U.S. $13) monthly for a year.

Friends overseas also responded. ACSI and Technical Support Mission made timely gifts. Biola University pledged to set up a Hong Kong branch campus at the institute. Construction started.

As 1989 dawned, completion drew near. Paul and his friends had raised HK $2.5 million, only HK $500,000 (US $65,000) short of the goal. Then came the student movement in Beijing that June, and people began thinking of emigrating rather than building and giving. Would they meet their goal?

One day Paul paid a visit to a close friend, Mr. K.M. Lu, and met his brother, who was chairman of the Lui Ming Choi Foundation.

"Would you consider our project?" Paul asked after explaining the venture.

"I'll be very glad to consider your worthy project," Mr. Lu answered.

All Paul had done was make a verbal presentation. Yet a few days later, the foundation agreed to meet the remaining need.

With the new facility, RICE began training at least 100 teachers per year. These teachers are serving the Lord in both Hong Kong and Mainland China. In the years to come, thousands of them will be reaching their own countrymen for Christ. In fact, the goal for the first ten years of the 21st century is to reach 15,000 non-Christian teachers with the gospel and to train 4,700 Christian teachers with communication methods and principles.

Some may think the whale has already swallowed the goldfish. It doesn't seem to matter to Paul, because he helped pack the goldfish's suitcase.

This is a spiritual battle and prayer support is greatly needed. Paul's ministry can be followed at the Schools For Christ website, www.sfchk.com, and he can be emailed at sfc@sfchk.com.

Chapter 10

The Sadhu's Legacy

The story of P.J. Thomas and Sharon Fellowship in India

Many people turned out to hear Sadhu Sundar Singh. This former Sikh-turned-Christian was turning traditional missionary methods upside down.

"You have offered us Christianity in a Western cup, and we have rejected it," the sadhu said. "Give us Christianity in an Eastern bowl, and we will drink from it."

Hundreds—perhaps thousands—gathered that day in 1922 to hear the sadhu who had traveled barefoot to Tibet to share the gospel of Jesus Christ. Many parents brought their children to be blessed by the man who carried an unusual anointing from God.

Among those present was Iyapillai Painummoottil and his wife, Sosamma. As Iyapillai lifted up his six-year-old son, the sadhu took his child into his arms.

"God, make this child one of your messengers to carry the gospel throughout India." Sadhu Sundar Singh must have prayed words to this effect, for the boy was destined to carry the sadhu's legacy. But Iyapillai would not have gone to hear the sadhu if he first had not heard Daoud Khan.

The Muslim from Calcutta

Daoud Khan was a Muslim from Calcutta. While in college, he attended a Bible class conducted by a missionary from Australia. The lady missionary soon returned to Australia, but left behind a Christian magazine published in Anderson, Indiana. Khan read the magazine and later came to the United States to have closer contact with the group publishing it. The Christians in Anderson led him to a firm commitment to the Lord, and the new "John" D. Khan returned to India to preach the gospel in 1910.

One of the men who went to hear him preach was Iyapillai Painummoottil, from a high-caste Hindu family in Kerala, a tropical state in southwestern India. He went because another traveling evangelist had earlier told the young Iyapillai to memorize John 3:16. Iyapillai did, but then forgot about it.

Some years later, Iyapillai was waiting in a train station when suddenly the words of John 3:16 pressed compellingly upon his consciousness. The recall was so forceful, he blurted out in a loud voice, "For God so loved the world, He gave His only begotten Son, that whosoever believeth in Him, should not perish, but have everlasting life."

Every one turned to see the young man who was practically shouting the Scripture. Iyapillai was embarrassed. Thankfully, the train came. He got on and continued his journey. He could not understand why this verse learned in childhood should suddenly pop into his consciousness. Perhaps he should find out more about Christianity.

So that is how Iyapillai found himself listening to John Dauod Khan. As Khan spoke, the words seemed to burn into Iyapillai's heart. Conviction gripped his soul. Iyapillai studied the Scriptures to see if these things were so. Finally, he committed his life to the Lord Jesus Christ and was baptized, taking the Christian name of John.

He and Sosamma were married soon thereafter. John was employed as a clerk in the court, and made a good wage. Evenings and weekends he conducted Bible studies as a layman in the Mar Thoma Church to which his wife belonged.

Indian tradition says that the apostle Thomas landed on the shores of Kerala in A.D. 52, preached the gospel and established a number of congregations. These churches later formed what came to be known as the Mar Thoma (Saint Thomas) Church. Indian tradition says that the apostle Thomas later went to Madras and there was martyred.

Soon after John and Sosamma were married, a son was born. They named him Daniel. Three years later, another son was born. They named him John Thomas after his father and the apostle. Later, Jacob and Leelamma arrived. Sosamma had all the children baptized as infants according to the tradition of the Mar Thoma church.

Later, as the revival of the early 1900s spread around the world, John left the Mar Thoma Church and established an independent congregation outside Tiruvalla in Kerala. From that time on he was known as Pastor John. And when Sadhu Sundar Singh came to town, Pastor John took his family to the meeting where he asked the sadhu to bless his son, John Thomas.

Exploits of Pastor John

Being outside the institutional church, Pastor John became more dependent upon the Holy Spirit. One night he was awakened about three o'clock in the morning. The Lord appeared to him and told him to immediately go out of the house and he would know what to do. John put on his clothes, went out the door, and started walking. He walked for a couple of hours.

Then he saw a man walking ahead of him. When the man saw Pastor John, he discarded a piece of rope and broke into tears. When the pastor reached him, he recognized him as a young man he had led to the Lord a couple of years previously. The man had backslidden, became a drunkard, severely beat his wife, and recently even tried to kill her. Overcome with shame and despair, he was now going to hang himself. Pastor John led him in a prayer of repentance and restoration. The man subsequently became a fervent gospel preacher.

As Pastor John recounted this and other stories to young John Thomas, the reality of God's supernatural working impressed his son's mind. Pastor John also had John Thomas read the Scriptures in a loud voice as he sat in the courtyard of their home. That way anyone passing by on the other side of the wall could hear the Word of God. Throughout his lifetime, John Thomas continued the practice of reading everything, even the newspaper, out loud.

One night John Thomas attended a routine overnight prayer meeting led by his father. Pastor John asked everyone to pray, but Thomas couldn't. The religion of his parents had not yet quickened his heart. Suddenly, he broke down and wept, confessed his sins, and received assurance of a cleansed heart. A short time later he was baptized in front of other school boys.

Baptism, especially in India, is an outward sign to the world that the believer has turned from his former ways and has decided to follow Jesus Christ. Conducting the baptisms publicly—members of the church and the candidates often parade to the baptism site—helps ensure that the candidate has seriously committed his life the Lord and will not turn back.

For John Thomas, there was no turning back. From that day on he began to proclaim Christ. While he was in high school and continuing into his college days, he would walk from place to place preaching the gospel wherever he could and to whomever would listen. Somehow, the life of Sadhu Sundar Singh had become his model.

Developing preacher

John Thomas studied two years at St. Berchman's College in Kerala, and then went to Serampore University, founded by William Carey in Calcutta. After that, he did further theological studies at United Theological College in Bangalore. Upon completing those studies, the young man Thomas again struck out across the countryside, preaching to whoever would listen.

In 1944, Thomas met and married Aleyamma Kurien. About this time, some Christian leaders saw great potential in the idealistic young preacher with a broad grin and advised him to further his education in the West. If he did that, he would have a great future, they assured him. They gave him letters of recommendation and sent him off to Australia for further study.

While crossing the sea, during a time when others on the ship were engaged in frivolity, Thomas began to reflect on the Lord's will for his life. He remembered that Sadhu Sundar Singh had forsaken his entire inheritance in order to follow the Lord. Thomas went to his cabin, took the letters of recommendation and diplomas (all except the one from Carey's school), tore them into little pieces, and tossed them overboard. He would not rely on human devices. If the Lord promoted him, he would accept that. Later on, he imprinted on his name card, "Crossing the sea does not make one a missionary; seeing the cross does."

After completing studies at Sydney Bible Training Institute, John Thomas came to the United States in 1948. He spoke in several churches, and went to Wheaton College in 1951 to inquire about the revival going on there at that time. Dr. V. Raymond Edman, president of the college, was impressed with the young man and offered him a teaching fellowship in comparative religion while he earned his M.A. in Christian education.

Feeling that he had prepared long enough, he returned in 1952 to his native Kerala to open the Bible school which was to become the focus of his life's work. His friends in Wheaton promised to remember him in their prayers and help him with missionary gifts, as the Lord would direct.

"Sermon on the Mount" Bible school

With a little help from his friends in the U.S., Thomas purchased an old house in the center of Tiruvalla. The house sat on low-lying land, partly covered with water lilies. It reminded Thomas and his first nine students of the Rose of Sharon in the Bible, a name for Jesus. So they called the new school Sharon Bible Institute.

"I didn't realize till later that Sharon was a girl's name," Thomas later confessed.

While Thomas taught the men, his wife, Aleyamma, privately taught the women.

This would be no conventional Bible school. There would be no prerequisites, no tuition, no fixed curriculum, no graduations, and no degrees offered. Students could come and go as circumstances dictated. To this day, many of the school's alumni are not officially ordained and have no degree. Yet they provide a key element in the evangelization of India's masses.

"I got the idea from the Sermon on the Mount," Thomas confided. "As Jesus taught over a period of several days, people would come and go, according to their need or availability. The Pharisees came by; so did the Sadducees, the scribes, the priests, and the Levites. The tax collectors looked on; Greeks and Romans stopped and listened. Likewise, mothers, fathers, children—the common people—came and went as they could. I wanted a school that would meet the needs of the people and would be available to them whenever they could attend."

"Not everyone is born at the same time of year, physically or spiritually," Thomas continued. "So why should they be expected to enter the ministry, or begin preparing for it, at the same time? Why not leave the school when they feel they are ready, or when they've had enough teaching for a while? Let them go out and practice what they've learned."

Soon, there were 20 students at the school. But Thomas's cash ran out, and there was no food in the pantry. The students declared a fast and began to pray.

The students regularly got up at 5 a.m. for their morning devotions. The Scripture for their devotions that morning was Exodus 16—manna from heaven. In faith, the students thanked the Lord for meeting their needs.

Afterward, some of them wandered out into the backyard. Suddenly they began to shout, "Pastor Thomas! Pastor Thomas! Come here, look! God has given us food from heaven!"

When Pastor Thomas walked out into the backyard, he laughed and rejoiced at the Lord's innovative ways. Overnight, the Lord had caused mushrooms to sprout up all over the yard. The students gathered them into bushel baskets and prepared a feast. There was enough to last three days. On the third day, Thomas received word that a check had arrived in the bank at Kottyam.

Never again did mushrooms appear at the school so profusely.

An army of common people

In 1954 Thomas built a 20' x 40' hall for the local church to meet in. Later, it was lengthened to 100', since it was also used as a student dormitory.

The students slept on grass mats during the night, then rolled them up at dawn and dragged in benches for day classes. For Sunday worship and mid-week prayer meetings, they completely rearranged the meager furnishings.

Following his "Sermon on the Mount" agenda, many students came and left at will. Though not earning a formal degree, they became an army of trained laypeople.

"They are not ordained ministers, but they are soul winners," Thomas said. "During Hindu festival days, when hundreds of thousands of Hindus go barefoot to the temples to bow down before images, these barefoot believers stand outside the temples, and during a one-week *mela* or festival, these lay witnesses hand out millions of gospel tracts printed on a crude press.

"Sometimes they stand under bamboo and mango trees. They set up a picture of the crucifixion and preach about Jesus.

"As a result, we get many letters from Hindus wanting to know more about the Lord Jesus. They don't understand how one man can take away the sin of so many people. Then we send some of our Bible school alumni to explain the gospel to them. They are effective witnesses and can explain the faith in the context of our culture."

Comprehensive training

As the school grew, the men's Bible institute developed a more systematic agenda. While still maintaining its "no prerequisites, no tuition, free room and board" policy, it began to offer a structured course of instruction:

The first year curriculum examines all the books of the Bible and emphasizes personal prayer and soul winning, gospel tract distribution and open-air preaching.

Students continuing a second year get basic theology courses.

Third-year students study comparative religions, church history and missions. Persons completing three years get a diploma.

Students who complete a fourth year and successfully pass a final exam administered by a branch of Serampore University in Trivandrum are awarded a Bachelor of Theology Degree.

In the last 40 years, more than 3,000 young people have passed through Sharon Bible Institute. Most of these are actively serving the Lord today with various ministries throughout India.

Practically every Christian ministry in India has one or more Sharon-trained ministers in its service. Nearly 800 Sharon alumni serve the Lord full time as pastors and missionaries with Sharon Fellowship.

"Let the children come to Me"

Though the Bible school work was satisfying and proceeding well, something Thomas had seen in his early years kept haunting him. India is a land of sacred cows. As Thomas had walked the dusty roads preaching the gospel in the manner of a sadhu, he had often seen little children following these cows or walking behind ox carts, picking up the manure to take back to their mothers, who would dry the dung and use it for fuel in their cooking fires. Sometimes the smaller children would run home crying when an older child would steal their treasure from them.

There's no litter in India. If something is burnable, it's gathered for fuel.

With family planning unavailable or unpracticed by the majority of poor folk, India teems with millions of small children wandering the streets.

For them, getting the next meal can be a life-and-death struggle. Often, a child has to fight off other children to keep his treasure of gathered manure. One hungry little child crept into a farmer's garden and ate a sweet potato. The farmer caught him and broke his fingers. Thomas took him in.

Thomas's heart ached for these poor waifs. To those who came to his door, he gave a little food. The Bible students, both men and women, held story times for these children. As God provided, they would give each of the children an egg.

The typical American family might cook it and eat it. But these Indian children carefully took their egg home and protected it until, aided by the tropical climate, it hatched. Then they had a chicken.

Sometimes, as God provided, Thomas gave a hen to each child who memorized certain Bible verses and proved faithful in Sunday school. The hen would produce an egg a day for the child's family. On Sunday, the child would return one egg as an offering to the Lord. The eggs were given to still other poor children. Thus the gifts literally multiplied.

Through this "Chickens for Children" program, Thomas dreamed he could reach millions of children in his state, though funds on so grand a scale never materialized.

To chickens, Thomas added goats. "Kids for Kids," he called them. The child gave the first kid the goat bore to another child or to the orphanage.

Sometimes Thomas gave a heifer.

"Give a child a living animal, and the child will have a pet. The pet will provide for the child, even as the child takes care of the pet," Thomas said.

But chickens were always his favorite. "You don't need to feed a chicken," Thomas explained. "They can scratch for themselves."

Help—with sticky fingers

Eventually the work came to the notice of a worldwide missionary organization in Texas. It provided funds to build an orphanage where 100 children were cared for. It also supplemented the Bible school. Thomas breathed easier. God had noticed. The work was advancing.

Then one day Thomas got a letter from the sponsoring organization. "We can no longer continue to help your work as an independent organization," the letter said in effect, "but we will continue funding the work if it becomes part of our organization. Sign all your property over into our name, and we will continue to support your work."

Thomas was aghast. He gathered his pastors, missionaries and Bible teachers and shared the sorry news. What should they do?

They prayed. Such agony of soul. Such crying out to God. They had learned to depend on help from abroad. How could they get along without it? Would the Bible school close? Would the orphans be sent away hungry? And where would they go?

Hours passed, until their hearts were unburdened, their souls laid bare, every sin confessed. Finally, they arrived at unanimous agreement, as on the day of Pentecost. This was God's work, not man's, and they would not turn it over to a man. They would rather starve first. They didn't know how, but somehow God would provide. The year was 1972.

Thomas decided to take another trip to America.

Introduction to Christian Aid

A year earlier Thomas had met Dr. Bob Finley in Washington, D.C. At that time, Dr. Finley had just separated from International Students, Inc., which he had begun to win foreign students to Christ, to make Christian Aid an independent faith mission specializing in helping indigenous missions. The organization then consisted only of two or three staff and had a gross income of about $100,000. At that time, Finley had just received a $40 donation from an individual, so he gave Thomas half of it for the support of one missionary with Sharon Fellowship.

Now Thomas looked up Dr. Finley at Christian Aid headquarters and told him what recently had happened. Finley, never a man to turn a brother away empty, said, "We'll see what we can do." Finley sent out a letter outlining Sharon's plight to friends Thomas had known in the U.S. and a few donations started coming in. From that humble beginning, Christian Aid stood behind Sharon Fellowship and continued to help as gifts made it possible.

Train women, too

Shortly after this, Aleyamma came to her husband and said, "John, you know that half the people in India are women. Men can't minister to women [especially true in Asian culture]. Up until now I have been teaching a few women privately. If we start a women's Bible institute, I can manage it and we will be able to train women for ministry, too."

So in 1972, with help from Christian Aid, Thomas began Sharon Bible Institute for Women.

All this time, the students were meeting in the church hall beside the Thomas residence, which doubled as an office and dining hall. One day, Thomas received notice from the local officials that he could no longer use the church hall as a dormitory. It did not meet code.

So Thomas, the dreamer, had a large, masonry school building drawn up. It would have multiple floors with plenty of space for library, classrooms, teachers' and administrative offices, guest rooms for missionaries who came to give reports from the field, and dormitory space for both men and women.

It took a long time to finalize the plans. Then there were few funds for construction. Finally the building permit expired.

Hesitatingly, Thomas approached the authorities for an extension.

"You can build your school if you tear down your house," they said. Thomas's property was located in the center of town, and he knew the authorities viewed his site as an ideal location for a taxi stand and supermarket.

Somehow, startup funds were supplied, the permit was renewed, and the building was begun. Many of John Thomas's supporters in the U.S. rallied behind the project and sent gifts for the school to Christian Aid, which sent the funds to Thomas as progress reports were received.

Thomas did not have to tear down the 100-year-old house at that time, though later it was razed after a tree fell across the roof rendering it impractical to repair. A new building was then constructed right behind the place where the old house stood.

Tropical fruit

Someone may ask: Is it worth all the trouble? What fruit results from all this effort? A typical report from Sharon Fellowship reads as follows:

"Last month revival meetings were held in Mallapally, Mylapra, Valanjavattom, Thowhukkal, Kunnathukal, Kottamam and Poovathoor. As a result, 37 persons trusted in Christ and 28 new converts were baptized. At Kadavakonam, a girl who had been stricken with polio was healed and walked. At Valanjavattom, a movie actor received Christ as his Savior. His nature is changed since he came to know a new master."

Probably the greatest fruit is seen in the lives of the Bible school students.

Five-year-old Pappan had an incurable carbuncle on his foot. His constant crying irritated his stepmother, who took him to a hospital and never returned for him. A Christian nurse in the hospital brought him to Sharon headquarters, where Mrs. Thomas took him in.

The Thomases gave him food, clothing, hygiene, and loved him along with their own two sons, John and Kurien. Within three years, his sores were permanently healed.

The Thomases taught Pappan to read and write, and then sent him to the local school. While staying at Sharon Fellowship, Pappan accepted the Lord and was baptized. He joined the young people testifying in church meetings and preaching on the streets.

After high school, he enrolled in the Bible school and completed three years of study. The Thomases helped him find a bride, and now Pappan and his wife serve the Lord together.

"Pappan has become an ardent gospel preacher," Thomas said. "He goes out early in the morning distributing gospel tracts, preaches on the street corner, conducts church meetings, shows kindness to needy children, and prays long hours."

If this is what one child raised by Sharon Fellowship does, think what hundreds have done—and are doing.

Tropical rose

Thankamma came to Sharon Fellowship in 1953 as a teenager to study the Bible. Her parents were sickly and could not provide for her. After completing two years of Bible study, Thankamma decided to stay at the mission and devote herself to the Lord's work.

She helped prepare food for the many poor who visited the mission. She also actively shared her faith in door-to-door visitation and tract distribution.

After a few years, Mrs. Thomas knew the time was right to find Thankamma a husband. One of Sharon's pastors, Pastor Mathaichan who was interested in finding a bride for his son, Varghese. The son had completed Bible college training in Madras and had proved his courage on the mission field in northern India.

Once while Varghese was preaching in the northern regions, a group of radical Hindus accosted him. The fanatics ripped off his clothing, lashed him cruelly, and tied him to a tree, demanding that he renounce his faith in Jesus Christ. Varghese firmly refused.

Then they poured kerosene over his body and lit some matches to set him on fire. Varghese prayed, expecting to be martyred like Stephen of old.

Just then the leader of the Hindu zealots came running from a nearby village.

"Don't light the fire!" he yelled. "Let him go!"

They released Varghese, gave him back his clothing, and warned him not to return to that place again.

Shortly after this, Varghese and Thankamma were married. Now they supervise an orphanage in Kerala caring for 130 children.

The sadhu's legacy

Almost every child cared for, almost every student trained at Sharon Bible Institute, has a similar testimony. They carry the message of Christ throughout India, and sometimes abroad. Though only a fraction of them work as Sharon Fellowship ministers, the number of persons brought to Christ through their efforts easily exceeds 300,000. About 80,000 believers gather in the 800 churches that are part of Sharon Fellowship.

The ministry of Sharon Fellowship continues today under indigenous leadership. T.P. Koshy, long-time vice president of the organization, oversees the daily operation of the churches and missionaries. Thomas's son, John Thomas Jr., oversees the operation of the Bible school and orphanage, while daily operations are carried out by capable men and women trained in the ministry.

In his latter years, John Thomas Sr. spent much time in the U.S. seeking financial support for his beloved dream and institutions. During the last years of his life, he was afflicted with a terrible psoriasis that covered his entire body, and he returned to spend his last days at his beloved Sharon Fellowship. He finally came down with sugar diabetes and went to be with the Lord in 1998. Not all his dreams were fulfilled, but it can be safely said the sadhu's prayer was answered. Or perhaps it would be better to say the effects of that prayer continue to ripple across the subcontinent of India. As James said, "The earnest prayer of a righteous person has great power and wonderful results" (James 1:16 NLT).

Chapter 11

Church Planter Extraordinaire

The story of Rizzy Montes and Living Rock Ministries in the Philippines

The engine throbbed as the waves splish-splashed against the bow of the ferryboat. The sunshine and sea breeze on that Saturday afternoon in April stimulated Risalino Montes's memory of the crusade he had just concluded in San Jose on the northern tip of Samar—the Philippines' third largest island. There was no direct overland route from San Jose to Calbayog City, where he needed to catch the boat to Mindanao. So Rizzy, as he preferred to be called, decided to take the ferry.

Slowly he watched the city appear in the distance as the boat drew nearer.

"I will make you a witness in this place."

Rizzy's reverie was suddenly interrupted by what seemed to be an inward, audible voice.

"No, Lord," Rizzy answered. "You know I am pastoring the church in Cagayan de Oro City in Mindanao."

The year was 1975. Rizzy was a veteran missionary, having already planted 18 churches in northern Mindanao Island. First of all, he started three churches in Babak, Davao del Norte between 1963 and 1966. Then he planted 14 more in Mati, Davao Oriental from 1967 to 1969. Finally, when he learned that the church in Cagayan de Oro City had been abandoned, he and his wife moved there to reopen it. Now it was a thriving congregation of 240 people.

"The people there need me," Rizzy argued.

"These people here need you more," the Lord persisted.

"Well, Lord, if there is no church in Calbayog City, I will be willing to start one."

That was a safe response, Rizzy thought. Calbayog was a city of over 100,000. There would certainly be at least one evangelical church there.

After disembarking in Calbayog City, Rizzy learned that the next ship to Mindanao left on Monday.

So Sunday morning he thought he'd go to church. He hailed a tricycle taxi.

"Please take me to a church," he told the driver.

The driver took Rizzy to a big Roman Catholic church.

"Is there no evangelical church?" Rizzy asked the driver.

The driver knew of none. Further inquiries disclosed none. The promise he had made to the Lord suddenly streaked through his mind.

When Rizzy arrived home, he told his wife, "Rose, get ready to pack your bags. We will be going to Calbayog City."

Of course, it didn't happen that quickly. Rizzy wanted to make sure the Lord was leading him there. He always sought to confirm the Lord's leading. So at the annual convention of the churches he had started in Mindanao, Rizzy announced a city-wide crusade in Calbayog City that June.

"We will see what happens," Rizzy thought. He felt that few could afford to give much, but many might be able to give a little. If God provided the finances, that would be a green light.

No one responded.

"That's it," Rizzy thought. "I guess I misunderstood God."

Shortly before sunset one of the conference speakers sought him out and pressed the equivalent of $200 into his hands.

"This is for the crusade in Calbayog City," he said. It was enough to rent the facilities.

Rizzy couldn't back out of it now.

Unplanned success

The crusade showed Rizzy what he long knew happened when God ordained his steps. The financial gift, though minimal, was evidence of God's endorsement. Volunteers stepped forward to act as ushers, counselors, choir, and to help with physical arrangements. Even the weather was perfect.

Rizzy knew from experience that the Roman Catholic masses tended to look upon any other form of religion as of the devil, and opposed gospel crusades vehemently. On previous occasions, they had attempted to sabotage evangelistic meetings with loud shouting, cursing, disorderly conduct, even rock throwing. But this time, the expected opposition was silent.

Instead, the spiritual vacuum of the place seemed to create a greater hunger in the hearts of the people to receive the Word than Rizzy had ever known before. The plaza where the crusade was held was jammed with an eager throng welcoming the evangelist. As he preached the simple gospel, the Word of Truth displaced rooted superstitions. Literally hundreds came forward to confess their sins and invite the Lord into their hearts.

Burdened hearts were washed clean by the blood of Christ. Many testified of the work of grace in their hearts. Some with various sicknesses experienced instantaneous healing.

The crusade's success posed one dilemma. Where would the new congregation meet? Rizzy hadn't planned that far in advance!

The only place immediately available was the school grandstand, which they rented every Sunday morning for the next six months. By the following March, the new congregation was able to rent indoor facilities. The next year, they obtained a permanent meeting place. A house and lot was purchased for Rizzy and Rose and their seven children. Rizzy and his co-workers at first called the new work Faith Tabernacle Ministries in Samar, but later changed it to Living Rock Ministries.

The work multiplies

Meanwhile, Rizzy, members of his family and lay people continued the evangelistic wave set in motion by the crusade. Preaching points and house meetings were started in several places, and several new congregations organized. Again, success posed a problem. Who would teach and pastor these new works?

Rizzy leaped into a new dimension of faith by starting Faith School of the Bible in his backyard. Though the program later went to two years, that first year, 1978, he trained and sent out six young men. All of them began missionary work in places where there was no church. The church in Calbayog City became the mother church and chief supporter of these zealous, Filipino missionaries.

Within eight years of beginning in Calbayog, Rizzy and his fellow missionaries had established 23 new churches, not counting preaching points and home-group meetings. The ministry was organized, spiritual, and growing. Missionaries labored in harmony and unity. The newly established churches fully participated in the outreach. Apart from some stomach pains Rizzy experienced from time to time, everything was going smoothly.

"Thank you, Lord," he whispered.

Hydrocephalus!

These stomach pains became more than distracting, and over-the-counter stomach medicine failed to help. Reluctantly, Rizzy let his wife take him to the hospital.

The diagnosis was scary.

"Hydrocephalus," the doctors said.

Rizzy was rushed into surgery. Three times the surgeon attempted to insert the needle into the brain to relieve the pressure, but failed. The traumatized brain began to malfunction. Family members feared he wouldn't survive. When he came to, he was paralyzed in his legs and had lost his ability to speak clearly. Even his memory and mental processes were affected.

Friends urged him to sue the doctor. But Rizzy didn't want revenge; he simply wanted healing.

Desperately, he besought the Lord.

"Why is this happening to me, Lord?"

His seeking turned inward.

"Did I sin, Lord? Have I brought this on myself?"

As he searched his soul, he discerned things he should have done differently, but no unconfessed sin. In fact, his search caused him to recite the many things he had done for the Lord.

"Lord, I have done my best for You. I have established over 40 churches. I have preached in the streets, held crusades, passed out tracts, witnessed door to door. I have taken care of the flock of God. I have even gone to the mountains to proclaim your name. What have I done to deserve this?"

The Lord never said he deserved it, but turned him to James 1:3, "The trying of your faith worketh patience."

Next, in 1 Peter 1:7, Rizzy learned the purpose of the trial. "The trial of your faith, being much more precious than of gold that perisheth, though it be tried with fire, might be found unto praise and honor and glory at the appearing of Jesus Christ."

Well, if this is my trial, then let God do His good work, thought Rizzy. He remembered that Job, going through a similar experience, had said, "But He knoweth the way that I take; when he hath tried me, I shall come forth as gold" (Job 23:10).

Rizzy observed, too, that despite the crushing plagues on Job's life, God still was in control (Job 2:6).

"If you are a child of God, don't become hysterical. Whatever circumstances come to your life, God is in control," Rizzy concluded.

Overcoming doubts

Coming to the intellectual conclusion was a matter of logic; living it out became a struggle. He feared he had come to the end of his ministry.

Remembering that the Lord Himself had gone through a period of trial in the wilderness, he read again how Jesus answered Satan. "Man shall not live by bread alone, but by every word that proceedeth out of the mouth of God" (Matthew 4:4).

Rizzy reaffirmed God's Word. Every morning at five he awoke to pray and meditate. But it seemed like his prayers were a rubber ball bouncing back lifeless from the ceiling. As he reflected on past crusades where he had seen the mute speak, the paralyzed walk, and the sick instantaneously healed, it seemed that the devil was mocking him. He who had healed others could not heal himself.

Was he doing everything he could to help himself? he wondered.

He went to therapists and diligently practiced his exercises. He practiced talking, and read the Bible out loud.

The fact that he could barely understand what he said did not stop him. *God is still working within me and can still use me,* he believed.

Suddenly he was afraid of dying.

I know that if I die I will go to heaven, he reminded himself.

But he still couldn't shake this strange dread of death. And he was a preacher!

"God has left you. There is no use in serving Him now," the devil taunted.

But the old soldier of the cross was not ignorant of Satan's devices. The more doubts assailed him, the more he confessed God's Word.

"Even if God does not heal me, I know He has healed others," Rizzy affirmed, "and I know He is still God. My life is in His hands."

Slowly Rizzy refocused his attention away from himself and more on God. Like the gradually brightening sky before sunrise, faith began to dawn in him that he was going to come out of this depression whether he received physical healing or not.

"God is my life. Without Him I am nothing," he kept telling himself. Satan's taunts no longer carried their sting.

Just about the time he was overcoming the hurdle of depression, another trial almost wiped him out. When his oldest son filled the pulpit of the headquarters church, some members became dissatisfied and split. Resentment toward the members who left surfaced in Rizzy's soul.

Some time later he went to a seminar also attended by some of the folk who had left the church.

"Ask them to forgive you," the Lord spoke to his heart.

"But Lord, I am not at fault," Rizzy protested. "They are! "They should ask me to forgive them."

The Lord didn't say anything further, and Rizzy knew the command stood. So he approached them and humbly asked them to forgive him for the resentment he had toward them. When he did so, it was as though thorns of bitterness fell from his heart.

At least he had obtained a spiritual healing.

Gradually, he regained some of his mobility and faculty of speech. By 1986, he had recovered sufficiently to preach again.

Accelerated growth

While Rizzy was preoccupied with his personal struggle, instead of stagnating, his ministry began to flourish.

His eight children, raised in a godly home, all attended Bible school. With their father sidelined, one by one they began to heed the call of God to the ministry.

Herly filled the pulpit in his father's absence, and later went to Catbalogan to pastor the growing church there.

Danny went to Catarman.

Paul preached in Barras.

And Jonathan eventually took over where Herly had left off at Calbayog City.

His daughters similarly took a healthy interest in the ministry. Ruth became a registrar and teacher in Faith School of the Bible. Ninfa took two years of Bible training and returned to Samar to help the ministry. Loida studied physical therapy so she could personally help her father. Joey studied computer to assist with the correspondence and administration of the ministry.

His family became a battalion of missionaries. Instead of slowing down, the work accelerated. With the new impetus sparked by Montes' sons and daughters, God gave them another 23 churches—this time in only six years.

But that's still not the end of the story.

With 46 churches and hundreds of towns and villages to reach, Rizzy and his co-workers prayed earnestly for a jeepney—a popular Filipino vehicle which originated from a stretched WW II American jeep. It was ideal for use on the Philippines' bumpy rural roads and could carry 30 passengers, besides musical instruments and equipment. They also needed a small motorized canoe to take them to more than 50 nearby islets.

The Lord gave them the canoe through the gifts of friends in America. But a jeepney cost at least ten times more, and so for a time, this need went unanswered.

Then in August 1989, Rizzy met an American doctor at the Lausanne II Conference in Manila and shared with him this need. Impressed with the Monteses' track record, the doctor commented, "You are indeed missionaries for whom there is no one else."

Before the conference was over, the doctor gave enough to enable Rizzy to go out and buy a brand new jeepney.

Using the jeepney to transport workers, musical instruments and other crusade equipment to public meetings, Rizzy's co-workers were able to organize another 24 churches—this time in only 10 months! As a result, hundreds of souls have been brought to the Lord.

When asked the secret of their success, son Herly replied, "We just get ready. When God says 'Go,' we go where He leads. It's easy when God does the work; we are just His instruments."

Facing persecution

It sounds easy, but resistance by the people they preach to is actually the norm. When Rizzy and his wife went to Malaga in 1979, the neighborhood captain refused to let them preach. When they attempted to press the issue, the captain got really mad and tried to hit Rose on the head with a rod.

Rose just smiled and said, "Thank you."

They left, but continued praying for the place. When they learned that a new neighborhood captain had taken office several years later, they returned. The new captain said he would allow them to visit the homes one at a time if they would not attempt to preach publicly.

Rizzy and Rose, along with the Bible school students and some full-time workers, began to canvass the town and found many people willing to listen. Others, however, were antagonistic and criticized the neighborhood captain for letting the despised Protestants into their town. Wanting to avoid trouble, the captain told the Montes company not to visit any more houses.

"Then may we just continue to visit those who have already welcomed us?" Rose asked.

The captain consented.

But those opposed to the gospel didn't like it one bit and began throwing rocks at the house where the Bible school students were conducting a Bible study. The next night, angry townsfolk stormed the house and chased the students out of the house.

On Sunday, Rizzy conducted the first Protestant service in a rented house. The anti-gospel people stormed the meeting throwing rocks, and even killed one of the persons attending. But Rizzy and his Bible school students didn't give up.

"If we gave up every time we experienced persecution like this, we would never have established any churches in Samar," Rizzy says.

In fact, the ordeals Rizzy and his co-workers face regularly would discourage the fainthearted. Rizzy described the circumstances facing their ministry two days before Christmas, 1988:

"The Lord has been with us and has kept us in His hands in spite of what has been happening in this part of our country. Successive typhoons visited us and even though many houses and our church buildings were destroyed, no member of God's family was lost. Most of those who died were not Christians. It challenges us to bring more of them to Christ.

"There was an earthquake last month. If it had lasted longer, many would have died.

"The New People's [Communist] Army was planning to attack the military in our city, but their plot was discovered. Otherwise, there would have been killings before Christmas.

"Because of all of that has been happening, we feel challenged to work harder for Christ."

Such is "evangelism as usual" on Samar Island.

Reaching the rebels

Working harder sometimes means going to the more dangerous rebel-infested areas.

Danny married an LRM Bible school graduate in 1981 and went to preach the gospel to the villages in northern Samar. The NPA rebels were strong in that area and could offer deadly resistance.

While conducting a gospel meeting on the second floor of a house, he heard a noise on the floor below, and looking down, he saw a man holding a .45 caliber pistol. Danny feared for his life, but dared not tell anyone that the meeting had been infiltrated by the NPA. Suddenly the Lord brought to his mind the words spoken to Paul in Acts 18:9-10, "Do not be afraid, but speak, and do not keep silent; for I am with you, and no one will attack you to hurt you; for I have many people in this city."

The words quelled Danny's fears and he preached with boldness. After the service the very same man came upstairs and asked Danny to pray for healing in his body. Then he left.

"Who was that guy?" Danny asked.

"He is a member of the NPA," someone answered.

About a month later, the man returned and told Danny he received healing from the Lord, and Danny prayed with him to accept Christ.

After this Danny continued ministry in that area and established several churches. By 1993, the rebel threat in that region had subsided and he began a new work in Catarman, a major town in northern Samar. It grew to 300 members by 1994, and then Danny went to Ormoc City in northern Leyte.

Rizzy's oldest son, Herly, was preaching in a town one night and noticed four armed men standing behind the stage. Fear gripped the young preacher as he thought of his young wife and three small children.

Sensing his fear, the men looked up and said, "Don't be afraid. Somebody sent us here to guard you."

That night many received eternal life.

Rebel becomes missionary

One of Living Rock Ministries' missionaries is a former rebel named Roding Holgansa. His father had been a witch doctor, who often beat his wife and children in fits of drunkenness. Roding hated his father, and when Communist rebels preached their false doctrine of shared wealth and happiness, Roding was a ready recruit.

He returned home one day and brutally beat up his father with his rebel rifle.

"I did not notice his bloodied nose," Roding said. "I ignored his cries for mercy. I just wanted to avenge my mother and brothers and sisters of all the abuse they had suffered from that man."

When one of LRM's missionaries was sent to Roding's hamlet, Roding was assigned to spy on him. When the little flock the missionary had gathered began growing, the rebels decided it was time to force the missionary out. Roding stood with a squad of rebels outside the chapel one Sunday morning, waiting to deliver their final warning.

Roding overheard the missionary speaking about Jesus' love for the Father, and the Father's love for Him. Roding had never known that kind of love. Suddenly, he broke into tears. Excusing himself from his squad, he ran toward home. When he found his father, he threw his arms around the startled man.

"Father, forgive me," he begged. His shocked father finally consented, "Yes, I forgive you, son."

Roding then went back to the chapel, and asked the preacher to lead him to Christ.

Under the missionary's tutelage, Roding became an ardent soul winner. He led his mother and father and brothers and sisters to the Lord, and two of them became missionaries. Two of the five rebels in his squad became Christians. Roding eventually left the rebel movement and became a full-time missionary.

His wife accompanied him in his endeavor. After she died giving birth to their fourth child, Roding decided to concentrate his work among the mountain villages where the rebels live.

"It's dangerous to go there," Rizzy warned.

But Roding would not be deterred. With a local child guiding the way, he walked up into the mountains without a weapon or a companion.

Arriving at a mountain village, the local official searched him for weapons. All he found was a Bible.

Opening it to Psalm 23:4, Roding read, "Yea, though I walk through the valley of the shadow of death, I will fear no evil, for thou art with me; thy rod and thy staff they comfort me."

The official gave Roding permission to preach.

As the once-hardened rebel, now tenderized with the compassion of Christ, preached about a Savior who died for them, the people began to cry. He asked them to surrender themselves to Christ, and they did. He continued preaching unmolested for five days.

The message of the gospel penetrated the ranks of the Communist rebels. No less than 20 young men—most of them former rebels—dedicated themselves to the Lord's work, and half of those went on to Bible school.

The vision continues

The ripples of Rizzy Montes's church planting efforts continue to spread across the Philippines. On October

27, 1998, 8000 evangelicals gathered in Pasig City to recognize the hundredth anniversary of the entrance of the gospel into their country. In recognition of his church-planting efforts, the Centennial Mission Congress presented a plaque to Rizalino Montes "for his distinguished contribution to the spread of Biblical Christianity in the Philippines."

Only he was not there to receive it. His sickness flared up again, preventing him from attending, and continued troubling him for the next several years. On August 18, 2001, he came down with a high fever and went to be with the Lord three days later.

He left behind a band of four daughters and four sons who are diligently serving the Lord, plus a small army of about 250 pastors and missionaries spiritually birthed and trained in his ministry. Together they look after 81 established churches while they continue to man missionary outposts and plant more churches

His son, Herly, had left the church in Catbalogan in 1990 to begin pioneering new churches back on Mindanao, and had planted 11 churches there by 2003.

"There are still 13 unreached people groups in Mindanao," he said in April, 2003, "and we desire that our ministry will contribute to reaching them before the Lord returns

Also, by 2001 Danny had built up a nice-sized congregation in a middle-class neighborhood in Ormoc City and could have continued ministering there comfort-ably. But he became burdened to carry on his father's ministry and returned to Calbayog City to pastor the church there and make sure the needs of the workers in all mission posts and churches were met.

"I revived the vision of my father to plant churches in every barangay and reopened the Bible school to train the Waray-Waray people for ministry," he said.

A new generation has heard the missionary call. It's time to plant more churches.

Chapter 12

He Danced With Angels

The story of Subhang Sodemba and Himalaya Crusade of India

Hamal Singh Limbu beat the big nagara drum. Boom-boom, boom-boom, boom-boom.

Again and again he pounded out the message on the huge cylinder. Then he waited.

Gradually the Sodemba clan, a subset of the Limbu tribe, began gathering outside his house. From all over Terthum in eastern Nepal, they came to their chief.

When the chief was satisfied, he stepped forward.

"Tomorrow I leave Terthum," he announced. "I will no longer be your chief. You must choose a new chief."

The people stared in disbelief.

"I hereby turn over to you all my land, my house, my territorial rights. From now on a new chief will rule in my place."

The people were stunned, but did not challenge their chief.

The next day, Hamal Singh Limbu left on a ten-day trek through the Himalaya Mountain range to Kalimpong, the trading center in the plains of Darjeeling District in India.

Little did he realize how big a break he was making with his past—or what dramatic consequences it would bode for the future. For in severing ties with his tribal community and going to a new city, he would eventually give up his Brahmin Hindu religion and adopt a new one—that of faith in the Lord Jesus Christ.

From Brahmin to Christian

It was in the mid-1800s and Kalimpong was the crossroads of the Himalayas. From Tibet wool merchants would drive their 100-mule trains laden with bags of raw wool through Sikkim to Kalimpong. Then the wool would be transported overland to Bombay where it would be shipped to the woolen mills in England. When it returned as woven woolen goods, the people would pay a dear price for it.

The English had established their East India Company in 1600. William Carey came in 1743. Scottish missionaries followed in the wake of the ensuing economic development and set up their mission headquarters at Kalimpong. Hamal Singh, away from home and open to new ideas, accepted Jesus Christ as his Savior and Lord as preached by these Presbyterian missionaries. He rose to prominence and eventually became chief tax collector for the whole city.

His tribespeople back in Terthum cared little for his economic advancement. When they heard he had adopted a foreign religion, they sacrificed and ate a buffalo to mourn the loss of one member of their tribe.

Hamal Singh had three sons. Two maintained the ancestral Hindu religion. The youngest, Nirmal, born in the latter half of the 19th century, was educated in the

He Danced With Angels

Scottish missionary schools and became a teaching elder in Dolapchan and Pudung villages. Then he had a remarkable new birth experience in 1905 and submitted to baptism by immersion.

"You can't do that. That's 'rebaptism,'" the Scottish missionaries argued.

But Nirmal paid them no heed. He resigned from his teaching position and started traveling all over India preaching the good news of personal salvation. He first trekked across northern India into Kashmir preaching the gospel. Then he went down the west coast past Bombay all the way to Ceylon (present-day Sri Lanka). Finally, he went back up the east coast past Kalimpong into Terthum, his ancestral home.

The Sodembas in Terthum were not interested in Nirmal's Jesus and told him to go back to Kalimpong. Despite the initial rejection, Nirmal visited his ancestral home many times to preach the gospel, although there is no record that any church was ever established by him among the Sodemba people.

Taking up residence in Darjeeling, Nirmal pastored two churches in the villages where he had formerly taught. Besides his native Nepali, Nirmal wrote and spoke Hindi and authored two schoolbooks in the Limbu language. He also practiced homeopathic medicine and was gifted in visions.

Nirmal had nine sons and five daughters. The second son, Kewal Singh was born to him in 1890. He was a building contractor by trade. Though a nominal Christian, his heart was not given to spiritual things. To him in 1926 little Subhang was born. Subhang means "good king." He was followed two years later by his sister, Mika.

Subhang's mother died about three years after he was born. Kewal was away most of the time in his construction business, so little Subhang and Mika were raised by their grandparents and their father's two sisters. Grandfather Nirmal made sure his grandchildren went to Sunday school and church every Sunday. In 1931, Grandfather Nirmal went to be with the Lord, leaving the spiritual burden on Subhang's grandmother, who encouraged him in the things of God until she went to be with the Lord in 1950.

His grandmother inherited Nirmal's "trucking" business, consisting of 11 pairs of oxen. She would send the carts to Siliguri, a six-day journey, and transport goods back to Kalimpong for the merchants. In this way, she and Subhang's aunts sustained themselves and their wards.

Subhang grew in knowledge of God and did well in his studies. He was conscientious, alert, pleasant to his schoolmates. Then something happened to change his life forever.

Divine visitation

Sadhu Sundar Singh visited Kalimpong on his way to and from Tibet in the 1930s and met with the Christians there. What he shared made many of the believers at MacFarlane Church, founded by the Scottish missionaries, believe there was more to Christianity than the traditions they had experienced.

They were not satisfied with just head knowledge and church attendance. They wanted to see changed hearts and attitudes. They longed to see the spirits of men yielded to the Spirit of God. They earnestly coveted those "best gifts" of faith, hope, and forgiveness. They were so desirous of seeing God move in wondrous ways that after the Sunday morning church services some of the more mature among them retired into the jungle to pray. They continued this practice for several years.

Then about 1940, Kamal Prasad Tewari, a high-caste Brahmin convert, arrived in Kalimpong. When he accepted Christ, his Hindu father tried to kill him—once by poisoning the food he ate, and a second time by ordering a domesticated elephant to walk over him.

Kamal miraculously survived both attempts, was filled with the Holy Spirit and began preaching about the power of Christ. It was under this anointing that he came to MacFarlane Church in Kalimpong.

For ten days the MacFarlane Church was packed with people, and some even stood outside hungering for more of God. Young Subhang attended those meetings, felt the presence of God, and saw people instantly healed. Some, brought to the meeting on stretchers for prayer, went home walking without assistance. The whole town was stirred.

About a year later, a Nepalese Christian sadhu by the name of Dhanbahadur Tamang returned to Kalimpong to hold meetings. Originally from Kalimpong, he had traveled all over India preaching Christ.

During those days strange manifestations became commonplace. One time the people looked up and saw Sadhu Tamang moving about the platform with his feet not touching the floor. Another time, a teenager by the name of John Gurung told how an angel awakened him in the night and escorted him through the night sky over Kalimpong.

Equally impressive to Subhang were the processionals to the church each night, people winding through the narrow streets from different directions, torches in hands, singing gospel songs.

"It seemed like we could hear the angels singing with them," Subhang remarked later.

In the meetings, the sins of the people were exposed, evil spirits were cast out and non-believers converted. The presence of God became so heavy that new people entering the room suddenly fell on their faces and began repenting of their sins.

These meetings began at six in the evening and lasted long into the night—sometimes until daybreak. Thirteen-year-old Subhang and his sister attended these meetings and when they returned home in the wee hours of the morning they often found the house locked. Their father and stepmother were not sympathetic to the things of God as their grandfather had been. They often had to sleep with the chickens or the goats.

Caught up in the Spirit

One night while these meetings were going on, Subhang's friend, John Gurung, came to the Sodemba home. The boys were praying in Subhang's bedroom when he heard John say, "You sinner, get up from here." Subhang thought John was speaking to him, so he went immediately to the living room, and began to pray that God would have mercy on him and forgive him of his sins. As long as he could remember, he had believed in God, but now a compelling conviction gripped his soul that he was a sinner in need of the Savior.

Suddenly the room filled with light and he saw two angels with bright faces standing on either side of him. As Subhang looked up, he saw a ladder descend from heaven. The angels took him by the hands and in an instant they ascended the ladder and were standing in heaven. He was surrounded by such beauty, he could not describe it in human words.

"Where's God?" Subhang finally asked.

In an instant they were transported in front of a huge throne. Subhang saw a figure sitting upon it but could not discern His face because it shone with such a bright light.

"Where's the Father, Son and Holy Spirit?" he asked.

"Right there on the throne," the angels told him.

Suddenly angels seemed to come from all over heaven and formed a large circle around Subhang and the two other angels. Such happiness overcame him that he began to dance with his two personal angels. They danced and danced and danced. Subhang was so happy—he wished he could just stay there forever.

Suddenly Subhang was conscious that he was dancing on his bed. How he had gotten there he did not know.

People were in the room and standing outside the room watching him. As Subhang stepped down off his bed, he perceived the sins in the hearts of everyone in the room.

With his eyes still closed, he turned to the person next to him and said, "Your heart is full of sins. Repent, and God will forgive you."

When he opened his eyes, he saw it was his own father. Immediately Kewal dropped to his knees and asked the Lord to forgive him. One by one, everyone in the room dropped to their knees and repented of their sins.

This was the first effect of his visit with the angels. It would not be the last.

Teenage preachers

Subhang had heard the missionaries preaching that Jesus was coming soon. Inflamed with passion for the lost and with heightened spiritual sensitivity, Subhang and John Gurung left home with a knapsack and began preaching the gospel from village to village. Everywhere they went people were astonished at the sincerity and innocence of these boy preachers.

The boys preached in the street, ate what food was given them, and slept wherever they found room—sometimes in a home, often outdoors. They kept up the fervent pace for six months. Many people, mostly elderly folks, repented at their preaching. After that the boys reassessed their situation.

"We've been preaching that Jesus is coming soon, and He has not come," they observed. "Maybe He won't come just yet."

The youths decided to stop their preaching and go back to school. They never knew how many turned to the Lord, but they felt exceedingly happy.

Teenage soldier

Subhang did well in school and the revival continued up through 1944. At the same time, World War II was reaching its climax and a patriotic fever was gripping everyone. So in 1945, Subhang left school with some of his companions and enlisted in the Indian Army using Sodemba, his clan name, as his family name.

The army discipline was beneficial but Sodemba fell in with worldly fellows and often spent the evenings drinking, sometimes up to seven glasses of rum a night. Staggering back drunk, Sodemba would kneel beside his bed and pray, "Lord Jesus, please forgive me. I know I am drunk, but I do not want to forsake You." Then he would sing his prayer:

> "Jesus, keep me near the cross,
>   There a precious fountain,
> Free to all, a healing stream,
>   Flows from Calvary's mountain."

The Lord listened to the prayer of His sodden saint. While home on extended leave in 1948, the Lord gave him another vision. While meditating quietly in his room, he seemed to hear God speak to him. "You will return here to look after widows and orphans," the voice said. For two hours the episode continued, giving instruction. When it was all over, Sodemba looked around the room to find a piece of paper on which to record this visitation. There lay his grandfather's diary. He picked it up and carefully wrote two pages of notes. He had no idea how this vision would be fulfilled 20 years later.

Sodemba's tour of duty took him to Kashmir, Abottabad, Lahore, and finally to Dehra Dun. It was at Dehra Dun that he met Ruth, the daughter of a military officer. They fell in love and looked forward to the day they could get married.

In a move to reduce its forces, the army discharged thousands of its men in 1953. Sodemba was among those receiving an honorable discharge. He and Ruth immediately traveled to Kalimpong and were married in the church. Sodemba's parents despised him because he could not provide for his bride. In disgust, they locked them both out of the house.

Subhang and Ruth found a shed as a temporary shelter, though the roof leaked when it rained. After about six months, Sodemba was offered a job as bookkeeper for the St. Andrew Colonial Mission run by the Scottish missionaries. It had been started by the Rev. J.A. Graham and was fondly called the Graham Home.

Children's home steward

This was no small mission. It contained 20 cottages that housed 600 children. Subhang Sodemba was in charge of accounts for all supplies. Like Daniel of old, an excellent spirit dwelt in him and he was meticulous in his accounts. He allowed no pandering. Every penny was accounted for.

"Your founder worked very hard to establish this home and arrange for the money to be sent for its operation," he told his Scottish superiors. "Every penny should be spent on behalf of the children."

For his strictness, many despised him. He wouldn't let them get away with anything.

Perhaps his uprightness was a result of his prayer life. The first thing Sodemba did upon arriving in his office every morning was to pray over the day's business. It only took him about five minutes to ask the Lord's guidance, and he considered it indispensable. One day the superintendent of the home walked in and found him praying.

"What are you doing?" he asked sternly.

"I'm praying over my work," Sodemba politely replied.

"Do that at home, not at the office," the man retorted.

"I pray at home," Sodemba responded, "but I must pray about my work after I arrive here in the office."

"Well if you don't quit, you'll be out of here. We don't pay you to pray; we pay you to work."

With that the superintendent left in a huff.

The very next day the Scotsman and his wife were returning from a road trip when the car they were in went off the road and down a mountainside. The man broke his leg and his wife fractured her collar bone. Both were shipped back to Scotland before the week was out.

Sodemba continued his work, and his prayers.

Part-time evangelist

Employed by the mission by day, Sodemba went out preaching on the streets every evening. He preached in the market every Saturday, and his son, Abner, born in 1956, helped him hand out tracts. The call to preach became stronger and stronger.

After coming to the mission Sodemba had put aside his drinking. He had become secretary of the Kalimpong church and preached on occasion. In 1962 he was recognized as an elder in the church and in 1964 he was elected pastor—a non-paying position, since he was salaried by the Graham school.

But his employment at the mission barely met his needs—it gave him nothing extra for preaching trips.

So Ruth bought a cow and sold the milk to finance short preaching trips to the Darjeeling hills for her husband. He was allowed 30 days leave per year from the mission, and he used all of them preaching the gospel on trips into the surrounding Himalayan mountainside.

In 1967, a visitor from America prophesied in one of his meetings, "You must go full time for the Lord or He will take away your wife." Over a year later, a crisis pushed him out by faith.

Birth of a mission

In October of 1968 Kalimpong was hit by severe floods. Many children lost their homes and some their parents. Moved with compassion, Sodemba determined in his heart to help some of them. Remembering the testimony of George Mueller's orphanage in England, he gave away his well-built house to friends and then resigned his job as accountant for the foreign mission society. He somehow felt that in order to care for these orphans, he himself must also become like them. He was determined to live by faith and let God prove Himself. So with only 365 rupees (about $20) in his pocket, he set out to devote himself full time to care for these hapless youngsters.

A Roman Catholic lady offered to sell him a 100-year-old two-story mud house on very reasonable terms. Sodemba signed the contract by faith and on April 2, 1969, dedicated the new Children's Faith Home. Somehow money came in to make the monthly payments, but he had no money for food.

The way this need was met tested their faith. His former employer donated a truckload of bird feed! So for the next 30 days the Sodembas and their 30 children cooked and ate the bird feed. When the bird feed ran out, a sympathetic Roman Catholic priest gave them a truckload of wheat flour. By the time that was used up, local people began giving them small envelopes with donations inside with which to buy food.

In 1970, while still pastoring the Kalimpong church, he organized his evangelistic and church-planting efforts as Himalaya Crusade. Other men of like vision and passion joined the work. An evangelistic association in America offered to support eight of his native preachers and soon eight new churches were planted.

Sodemba suggested to the Kalimpong congregation that since he was no longer employed by the Scottish mission, they could start giving him some support. They ignored his suggestion, despite the fact that from 1964 to 1973 the church tripled in size. In 1973 Sodemba led the church in constructing a new meeting hall that would hold 500 people.

Also in 1973, Christians in Sweden sent him money to construct a new dormitory for 60 children. Just when it looked like the whole operation was going to be successful, Sodemba nearly died.

Raised from a death bed

In the spring of 1973 while workmen were constructing the new dormitory, Sodemba grew very faint from preaching in the tropical heat and humidity and went into a semi-comatose state. His hands and feet were atrophied and he could neither stand nor walk. He could barely whisper as he lay paralyzed on his bed for days on end. Finally, he was unable to eat. His wife wept quietly as she saw the bones show through his gaunt form.

A letter arrived from Christians in Meghalaya requesting him to speak at their annual convention. An American woman missionary had married a Khasi tribal convert, and he had become a very powerful preacher. Through the ensuing revival, 150 churches were established. Now they wanted Sodemba to come and speak to their annual gathering.

Ruth immediately replied, "We are so sorry to inform you that Pastor Sodemba will be unable to honor your request. He is too sick to come."

The Meghalayans would not take "no" for an answer. "The announcements have been made and the pamphlets have been printed. Pastor Sodemba must come," they insisted.

"Pack my bags," Sodemba whispered. "If God wants me there, He will give me strength to preach."

Two days before he was scheduled to leave for Meghalaya, two believers from the Kalimpong congregation came to pray for him. While they were in the middle of their prayer, Sodemba felt himself lifted up from his bed. The instant they said "Amen," he came back down on his bed. He put his legs over the side of the bed and sat up. Finally, he stood.

Everyone in the room was weeping and crying out to God with joy at seeing this manifestation of God's power. The laborers who were constructing the children's dormitory heard the commotion and thought Sodemba had died. When they looked in the window, they saw him walking around the room!

Though he was still too weak to walk any distance or stand for any length of time, two days later his associates carried him on a stretcher to the train station. Ruth had arranged a special compartment on the train for him. When he arrived in Meghalaya, people took him in a special car to the site of the convention.

"Lord, you have brought me here. Now you must give me strength to preach," Sodemba prayed as he stood behind the pulpit. When he finished his prayer—weak in voice but strong in faith—he opened his mouth and preached in a strong voice to a crowd of 8,000. At the close of the meeting 600 hungry hearts came forward to surrender to Christ.

Open door to the Lepcha Buddhists

Though located in West Bengal, Sodemba has sought to preach the gospel throughout the surrounding Himalayan areas. In 1973, he made plans to go and preach the gospel in the Buddhist kingdom of Sikkim before it was an integral state with India. Christians who were part of nominal churches which were offshoots of foreign denominations didn't want Sodemba to come and preach there. "He's a Pentecostal," they objected and referred the matter to the king.

"Who is this man? What is his message? Is it good for our people? Check him out," the monarch instructed the head of his Central Intelligence Department, equivalent to the FBI. This man had taken advanced studies in London, and while there had attended one of William Branham's meetings. There he saw the blind see and the lame walk. In response to the king's inquiry of Sodemba, he sent word: "This man is not violent; he is preaching the gospel and praying for the sick. His work will be good for our country."

From that time forward Sodemba was free to preach the gospel to the Lepcha Buddhists in Sikkim. Today there are 35 Himalaya Crusade churches in Sikkim.

Evangelism in Assam

Later that same year, while Sodemba was talking with some friends in his house, he felt God was commanding him to go and preach in Assam, a state in the extreme northeast extension of India. Sodemba made arrangements and went by bus to Dingdingha. That was as far as his guidance led him.

When he got off the bus, a man walked up to him and asked, "Are you a Christian?"

Sodemba affirmed he was.

"Then come with me," the man said, and led him to his house.

"Can you preach?" the man asked.

"I've had some experience at it," Sodemba modestly affirmed.

"Then you must preach tonight," the man said matter-of-factly.

That night as Sodemba stood up to preach, he noticed that most of the women were wearing the red spot in the middle of the forehead common to Hindu women. So he began to preach against the red spot.

"If you are a Christian woman, how can you wear that red spot?" he asked.

As he pressed his point home, suddenly two of the women got up and left the meeting. Then all the rest got up and left.

"Oh, me, what have I done?" Sodemba thought. "I have made them angry with me."

Soon all the women came back into the meeting with their faces freshly washed.

That was the beginning of a real move of God in that area, and many Hindus came to the Lord and were baptized. At the end of several days, Sodemba had established not just one but two congregations—one among the Bengali tribe, and another among the Senthali tribe.

Attacked by the Bodos

But members of the animist Bodo tribe were incensed at this Christian incursion into their territory and came to the house in which he was staying armed with hatchets.

"Send that preacher out so we can kill him," they shouted.

Sodemba's host made sure the door was tightly bolted.

"If you don't send him out, we will come in and take him," they threatened.

Whack! Crash! They attacked the house with clubs and hatchets. They broke out the front window, but couldn't climb through it. They battered at the door, but the lock held. Finally, after many shouts and coarse insults, they left.

Perhaps we should leave, Sodemba thought. *The Bodo people don't like us.*

But the local believers encouraged him to continue preaching. So Sodemba went to the market in Sapkata, a small village on the outskirts of Dingdingha, and preached in the open market.

Bodo tribals stood in the shadows by the jungle waiting to shoot him with their bows and arrows. Others held large slingshots. As the meeting continued, he was so surrounded by people that he never became a clear target. Eventually, the Bodos just left.

One day during the hot July rainy season, Sodemba and some companions were walking through the rice paddies to a place called Alinagar, a town inhabited by Brahmin Hindus of Nepali ancestry. Suddenly Sodemba fell sick of malaria. The people put him in a bullock cart and took him to the next village where they put him on a bus to the next town. There he was put on a truck and driven back to Siliguri in Darjeeling. Friends from

Kalimpong came and took him back home by hired car. The sickness he contracted in Assam lasted six months, but while he was there he had established 20 churches.

Defying the dragon

About the most difficult place in the Himalayas to preach the gospel was Bhutan. Religion in this "Land of the Dragon" lies firmly within the grip of the *Je Khempo* or head Buddhist lama. And Bhutanese Buddhism is of the most rigid kind, brought in from Tibet during the 12th century. Monasteries dot each hilltop and host nearly 4,000 monks—one-and-a-half times the number of teachers in the country's whole school system.

In 1974, Sodemba went to Thimphu, the capital of Bhutan. During his journey he visited the grounds of the old king's palace now abandoned in favor of a new palace. As he strolled through the old rose garden, he looked toward heaven and prayed.

"Father God, this Land of the Dragon does not know You nor recognize You. It does not accept Your Bible or Your church. I request of You, please let me plant the gospel in Bhutan."

A peacock danced before him. As soon as he said "Amen," the peacock stopped dancing and walked away.

Since that time Sodemba has preached several times in Bhutan to believers meeting in secret. Other Bhutanese cross the border at Jaigon and attend meetings at the Himalaya Crusade church there. Rejoicing in their new salvation, they return and spread the gospel to whoever will listen.

Some Buddhist lamas received the Bible and read it in their monasteries by kerosene lamplight at night. They found the Bible very interesting, containing revelation superior to their own writings.

But they have to be careful. Some believers have been arrested and tortured, even imprisoned, and several meeting places have been torn down by officials.

So believers meet in homes. Some of the younger men in government service have studied in Christian schools and are sympathetic to the gospel. House churches in Thimphu now count over 500 believers. Altogether, at least 13 congregations meet in southern Bhutan.

The growing evangelistic outreach of Himalaya Crusade demanded more and more of Sodemba's attention. His success as church planter and preacher drew him away from the Kalimpong church more and more. This frustrated the congregation, which insisted that he preach more to them. So in 1977 Sodemba resigned as pastor of the Kalimpong church.

Preaching at knife point

One of the boys in Children's Faith Home was from the village of Namchi in Darjeeling District. The boy, Milan Rai, had accepted the Lord and underwent a remarkable change in his life. As a result, Sodemba received an invitation from Rai's home village to come and preach the gospel there. So in August 1977 Sodemba struck out with car and driver for Namchi. However, when they came to the Rangit River, seasonal monsoon rains had washed away the bridge.

"You still want to cross the river?" the driver said.

"Yes, I do," Sodemba replied.

"Then take my hand," the driver said.

Together they waded into the strong current. Sodemba felt the rocks bumping against his legs as the water rose to his chin. With one hand Sodemba held the driver's hand and with the other he vainly tried to hold his Bible out of the water. After what seemed a mile of such treacherous walking they both reached the other side. Sodemba turned to thank his courageous leader, but couldn't find him. Silently and without a trace, he had disappeared.

After that, Sodemba walked six or seven miles through the mountains to Namchi village. There he preached to about a dozen people huddled in a little house. None of them were believers, but the testimony of the boys from that village he was caring for had prepared their hearts. At the close of the meeting, several prayed to receive Christ. During the next few days, Sodemba visited several homes, leading the family members to Christ. By the time he left, one of them had donated land for a church meeting hall.

Another time he felt led to go to the Pashok tea plantation in Darjeeling District to preach the gospel. The estate had fallen into hard times. Production was down, workers were not paid, and many had left. Those who remained were surviving by eating roots. When Sodemba heard about it, he decided to go there with some medics and preach the gospel to those who remained.

As he was preaching to about 300 people at an open-air meeting that evening, several young Buddhists came up to him and put their Nepali knives on four sides of his neck.

"Stop your preaching immediately," they demanded.

Instead, the Lord gave Sodemba even greater boldness. The men withdrew their weapons and disappeared. After the meeting, Sodemba looked for them but could not find them. The next day he baptized 18 people in the stream, establishing a small congregation of believers.

Jeep wreck

Though Sodemba by now supervised more than 135 workers and churches, he had no vehicle. Every time he went somewhere, he had to hire a jeep and driver. So when he was asked to officiate at a wedding at the Pashok tea plantation, he hired a car and driver and went with his wife and some friends. While they were at the wedding, the driver went somewhere and got drunk.

On the way back down the mountain, the brakes failed on the jeep and the driver bailed out! Everyone in the car screamed and covered their faces as it seemed inevitable that the jeep would either strike the oncoming car head on or go over the edge.

"Lord save us!" they screamed.

The jeep's hostages apparently blanked out, but about 200 tea workers picking tea from the shrubs lining the road saw what happened. As though pushed by some power, the jeep veered to the inside, struck the bank of the mountain and overturned like a toy.

Sodemba came to underneath the upside-down jeep. Some passengers were screaming; others, including his wife, appeared to be not breathing. He heard a voice say, "Look out!" He looked, and with Samson-like strength, lifted his wife out and set her down on the road. He then extricated two or three other persons in similar fashion. The rest got out by themselves. Only one woman had a slightly wrenched back.

"Your God has saved you all," the tea workers shouted as they rushed up to the wrecked vehicle. "We've seen many accidents in this place, but we've never seen anyone saved like you were."

Accused by the brethren

Though opposition from non-believers was expected, trouble from those who called themselves Christians hurt even more. As the work prospered, some Christian leaders in India became jealous. One of them wrote to Sweden:

"Sodemba and his family have pocketed the money and have become very rich."

Soon two gentlemen from Sweden showed up at his doorstep. "That is a false accusation," Sodemba told them.

So they went to the chairman of Children's Faith Home and read him the letter accusing Sodemba of pilferage.

"In a word, it's jealousy," the chairman said. "When Sodemba started Children's Faith Home, there was no one in Kalimpong who would help him. He was hungry; he was poor. No one else could undertake this faith work."

After the interview, the Swedish brother opened his briefcase and took out the blueprint of the boys' dormitory Sodemba had sent to the Swedish Christians earlier. It was three stories tall and 135 feet long.

"I know this is a false accusation," the man from Sweden said, "and I recognize the integrity of Brother Sodemba and his ministry. I hereby give my approval for him to begin construction of this new building, and we will send him the funds." He initialed the document.

"One thing we know," Sodemba says. "If God is with us, we are not going to be afraid of any man. We have to be very sincere before God in whatever we do. We are stewards of all funds coming to us. We do not personally handle the funds sent to us for the children's home. All of our accounts are audited by the government auditors, and a copy of the auditor's statement goes to New Delhi. And the auditors in New Delhi will notice every single dime, because all the money that comes in from outside the country must go through the Reserve Bank of India."

Tricksters at work

During this time, an evangelistic association in America was supporting a number of Sodemba's evangelistic workers. The leader of another indigenous Christian work in India learned about it and inquired of some of them.

"How much are you getting?"

"250 rupees per month."

"You should be getting 300 rupees per month," the leader misinformed him. "This Sodemba is not treating you right. He is putting some of your support into his own pocket."

The leader dutifully informed the evangelistic association in America that Sodemba was keeping back some of the funds for his private use. Without investigating, the Americans promptly cut off Sodemba's funds. Some of his workers had no recourse but to switch their allegiance to the leader in Calcutta.

Some time later, Sodemba saw one of the workers who had left.

"How much are you getting now?" Sodemba asked.

"250 rupees per month," the worker answered.

"Isn't that what I was giving you?" Sodemba asked. "Didn't the other brother promise you more?"

"Well, that is all we are getting," came the reply.

Sweet reward

Sodemba and Ruth remained sweet through all they suffered. They know that Christian workers rarely receive reward for their labors in this life and look forward to the mercies of a just God. Yet, when they were totally crushed by the mistrust of Christians in a foreign country and the subsequent cutting off of ministry funds in 1992, God smiled on them in two ways.

First of all, Dr. D.L. Browning, president of Kingsway Fellowship, International in Des Moines, Iowa, conferred upon Sodemba a Doctor of Theology Degree in recognition of his life's work and doctoral thesis.

That same year God sent a delegation of 35 people from Sweden all the way to Kalimpong to award both of them a Medal for Meritorious Service.

"We have also given similar medals to Mother Theresa and the President of Argentina," they said as they pinned the medals on their chests.

This act of appreciation lifted the sorrows of Ruth and Subhang's hearts and sweet tears of happiness flowed down their cheeks

Apostle to Nepal

Sodemba's heart's desire was to reach his ancestral homeland and clan with the gospel. With Nepali as his mother tongue, he had no problem communicating with the people. He set a goal of establishing 200 churches throughout Nepal and began making treks into the mountainous country. After several rugged trips, he and his co-workers had established 28 churches.

He visited Terthum again in 1997, but was not able to meet any of his relatives. The next year, Amos and Joseph, his two youngest sons, began making visits to Terthum District and sharing the gospel. By 2000 ten new believers from the Sodemba clan were ready for baptism, and Sodemba returned to do the honors. In February, 2001, he returned to baptize more. Now one of the Sodemba converts pastors a church in that area.

Then on Sunday, May 6, Sodemba told his central congregation in Kalimpong he was celebrating the Lord's Supper with them for the last time. On May 10, Subhang Sodemba had a heart attack and went to be with the Lord he loved.

Widow's might

Himalaya Crusade today has about 230 churches, with over 300 church-planting missionaries serving in West Bengal, Nepal, Bhutan and neighboring regions. In addition, it also operates Faith Children's Home for 115 orphaned, semi-orphaned and destitute children and three elementary schools enrolling more than 600 students.

Though missing the presence of her beloved husband and leader, Ruth Sodemba carries on the work with the help of her children and co-workers. One son and his wife run the academic school and oversee the work in Sikkim. The youngest son and his wife oversee the Children's Faith Home in Kalimpong. The eldest daughter and her husband direct the school in Jaigon and disciple believers and guide workers in Bhutan. The youngest daughter and her husband run the Mount Carmel School in Kalimpong. Workers have requested that new schools be opened in three additional places. Ruth awaits funding for the projects. Despite her age, she is proving to be just as much a pioneer missionary as her husband was.

Though Subhang has gone to his eternal reward, Ruth is determined to carry on the vision. Even when her time comes to join the angels in heaven, the work, founded on faith and steeped in prayer, will continue. Those who follow in their steps are going to make sure those angels have plenty of reason to dance.

Chapter 13

Undoing Goliath

The story of Vasily Boyechko and the Good Samaritan Mission in Ukraine and the former Soviet Union

Most Americans think Russia opened to the gospel when the Soviet Union collapsed in 1990. Actually, the preaching of heroic native Christians in the 1980s triggered the end of the Communist era.

"Boyechko! Denounce God now, and you can continue your education. "Refuse, and you will be expelled from the school."

Seventeen-year-old Vasily Boyechko stood before the Communist review board. Many times he had stood for faith in God before these atheistic Communists. They had already expelled from school three times for refusing to compromise his faith. The first time was in 1950 when he was 13. The second time came in 1952.

It was not merely a matter of godliness vs. atheism. In those days, the Ukrainian underground was resisting control from Soviet Russia. Shortly after Vasily's second expulsion from school in 1952, five armed Ukrainian soldiers hid in the Boyechko house. Thirty armed Soviet soldiers were looking for them.

"Go see where they are," the Ukrainian soldiers said. The Boyechkos had no window facing the street. So Vasily went out and scouted the neighborhood. He returned, opened the door cautiously and came face to face with the Ukrainian soldiers aiming their weapons at him. They did not know who was coming through the door.

The third time Vasily was expelled from the institute was in 1954. At that time he heard the Lord tell him, "I have plans for you." Vasily thought it might be through scientific or technological achievements and naively appealed the decision to a higher authority. That nearly cost his preacher father exile to Siberia.

Vasily had escaped the wrath of the KGB long enough to graduate from high school and had now completed three years at L'viv Forest Technical Institute.[1] He needed only one more year to graduate. But his active preaching as a youth evangelist flagged the KGB's attention once more. They kept a dossier on him and studied the matter gravely. So in May of 1958 they decided to give him one final chance.

---

[1] The contemporary Ukrainian spellings of L'viv and Rivne are used instead of the now-disdained Russian spellings of L'vov and Rovno.

The meeting convened in the second-floor office of Volodymir Demidenko, Secretary of the Ukraine Communist Party. Yury Tretyak, rector of the institute, chaired the meeting attended by 15 institute professors, party officials, and General Millerov, head of the ROTC.

After an hour-long interchange and harangue, Tretyak stated the terms of surrender: "Boyechko, this is all you have to do: renounce your faith publicly on radio, TV and in the newspapers. Then you will have an open door to pursue your brilliant career."

Tretyak cleared his throat and moved in for the kill.

"If you don't, you will be expelled from every institution in the land. This rejection will carry such a stigma on you that you will not be able to free yourself from it for the rest of your life. You won't even be able to obtain a decent job. You will be persecuted without any rights. This is your last chance. There will be no more appeals."

There was a moment of silence as all waited to watch the young Christian capitulate.

"I will never do that," Vasily said firmly. "I love learning and education, but I love God above all. I will never deny my God."

"That's it then," Tretyak said loudly. "Vasily Boyechko is hereby expelled from the L'viv Forest Technical Institute and barred from every educational institution."

General Millerov stood to his feet, pointed a finger at Vasily, and said with passionate hate, "I will do everything I can to see that your bones *r-r-rot* in prison!"

Destined to reach the nations

Vasily left the old brick building, not realizing he would return there years later to proclaim the very faith for which he was expelled.

Outside, he wondered what his fate would be. It seemed the Communists had everybody in their vice-like grip and controlled them like a taunting Goliath. What would he do?

Inwardly, he felt God speak to him, "I have great plans for you." This time he paid closer attention as the voice added, "You will bring the gospel to many nations."

Immediately, Vasily began preaching Christ throughout the unregistered churches in Ukraine. His vibrant preaching again attracted the ire of the KGB, and they decided to silence this preacher forever.

Within six months, he was recruited by the army and sent to the Urals. While there, false charges were levied against him. If convicted, he would spend the next seven years in prison. Perhaps General Millerov's curse would come true.

Suddenly orders came to send him to work on a large nuclear reactor. The assignment would rob him of any freedom and could be a death sentence. He wrote what he thought might be his farewell letter to his family:

> *Dear Mom and Dad, Brothers and Sisters,*
>
> *They are now sending me to a place from which I may never return alive. Once I am there, contact with the outside world is forbidden—not even by letters.*
>
> *I want you to know in advance that I submit myself to God's will. With the Holy Spirit as my Helper, I pledge to remain true to Jesus Christ in the most difficult situations. I expect to see you all in heaven.*

Instead of hindering his missionary activities, Vasily's first tour of duty turned out to be his first year of missionary service. He witnessed to his fellow recruits; they couldn't get away from him.

With little to do for recreation, and not interested in the vodka-drinking and womanizing of typical soldiers, Vasily spent much time in prayer for the people of the Soviet Union.

After two years, he fell seriously ill. The military chiefs thought he would die of the disease. So they gave him 750 rubles for his back pay—the equivalence of a wage earner's monthly pay—and discharged him.

Upon returning home, Vasily learned that six months after issuing his curse on him, General Millerov suffered a heart attack while drinking vodka at a party celebrating the Communists' October Revolution and died on the way to the hospital. A few months later, Yury Tretyak died in a similar fashion. But Vasily recovered.

Go East, young man

Vasily now seemed to hear God speaking to him: "Go to the Far East—to Siberia, and I will show you My boundless field for your spiritual work." So Vasily headed east.

In those days, the central government heavily subsidized all means of travel. It cost only 40 rubles to purchase a train ticket to Omsk, the western-most town in Siberia. Vasily preached to the Christians there. Then they purchased his train ticket to the next stop. Vasily used his military pay to meet his personal needs along the way. It took him a month to go from Omsk to Khabarosk on the border with China.

At Khabarosk, he learned that Vladivostok was closed to travelers, since it was on the coast. The only way one could enter would be by producing a passport or evidence that one lived there.

Vasily prayed, "Lord, how am I going to visit the brethren in Vladivostok?"

"Wait until the train is ready to leave and then tell the ticket clerk, 'I want a ticket to Vladivostok, but I don't have my documents with me,'" came the answer.

Vasily waited until it was time for the train to leave, and then stepped to the ticket window.

"I want to purchase a ticket to Vladivostok, but..."

"You better hurry," the clerk interrupted him. "The train is leaving *now*."

The clerk took his money, gave him the ticket, and Vasily was on his way to Vladivostok unhindered.

Unbeknown to him, the Lord had been dealing with the believers at Vladivostok at the same time. While praying, the pastor saw a clock in a vision, and the hands pointed to 9 p.m. *Vasily must leave no later than 9 p.m.*, he concluded. As soon as Vasily arrived, the pastor told him about the vision.

That night the presence of the Lord seemed especially precious. Vasily was ministering in the Spirit and was in no hurry to leave, since he knew the last train left at 11 p.m.

Suddenly, just before 9 p.m., two church members came up, one on his left and one on his right, and kindly and firmly said, "You must leave *now!*" Immediately they pulled him off the platform and pushed him out the door.

Vasily was out the door with the two companions and about 100 yards from the church when he looked back and saw a police car and a motorcycle cop arrive in haste from the other direction. He looked down at his watch. It was exactly 9 p.m.

Stalin's missionaries

Back in Khabarosk, Christians told him that the gospel had been brought to Chukotka in the far north-eastern tip of Siberia by Christian brothers who had been arrested and sent there under Stalin's regime. Many of them planted the seed of the Word of God among people of the frozen tundra before they died in the inhumane conditions of sub-zero labor camps. Their example pricked Vasily's conscience. *They came involuntarily*, he thought. *Shouldn't we be going to this place voluntarily as missionaries?*

The thought fanned the evangelistic embers that always glowed in his heart. Again, he was faced with the choice of kowtowing to the Communists who forbade preaching the gospel or obeying Christ who said, "Go ye into all the world and preach the gospel to every creature" (Mark 16:15).

One thing more disturbed him. He saw that even the preachers in this otherwise God-forsaken land did not have Bibles. Before evangelism and church planting could begin in earnest, he knew Bibles and Christian literature must be supplied. Yet to publish Christian literature in the Soviet Union was nearly impossible.

Domestic life

Vasily returned to his native Ukraine considering all these things, and got a job working in the Kinescope factory making patterns as a lathe operator for the manufacture of TV tubes. In his available free time he worked alongside his father. The gospel had been brought to western Ukraine in 1916 by a peasant preacher. Vasily's parents had given their hearts to Christ in 1934. By 1936, his father, Michael, was a fiery itinerant preacher. The Communists persecuted him, and once sent him to prison, but never to Siberia.

About this time Vasily noticed a Christian girl in the church. For four years, he watched Galina grow into a sincere and faithful believer. He became convinced that God was giving her to him as a spiritual co-worker for the rest of his life. On February 11, 1962, Vasily and Galina were married in the church his father pastored.

It was a happy marriage that immediately bore fruit. Jaraslov was born in 1962. Olexander came in 1965. They were followed by Olga in 1970, Tanya in 1975, Luba in 1978, and Yura in 1982. All the children accepted their parents' faith. In fact, the more they were persecuted, the more firmly the children clung to it.

Mysterious visitors

Occasionally, someone from the West would sneak into the Soviet Union carrying Bibles or Christian literature. If they were caught, they would suffer arrest, mocking, confiscation of their cars and properties, and imprisonment or expulsion. The KGB seemed to have everyone under surveillance.

One day in 1965 a knock came on Vasily's door.

"I am Paul and this is my wife, Marcela," said a handsome man with his wife standing beside him. "We are from Argentina."

Vasily invited them in and learned they were the first known foreign missionaries to Communist Ukraine. The next day they returned. As they were getting ready to leave, Paul said, "God told me to give you something," and he pressed into Vasily's hand 25 rubles—enough for his family to live on for a week.

Vasily did not know how this man and his wife had been able to walk to his house from the hotel undetected by the ever-present KGB.

A few months later, two young men from the Slavic Mission in Stockholm came to his house. Vasily shared with them how God had burdened his heart to start a mission that would send missionaries to the farthest reaches of the Soviet Union. The men said they would carry his burden and share it with their brethren back home.

In 1967 Vasily's father went to be with the Lord, followed six months later by his mother. Vasily began inviting other preachers and pastors to his home for prayer and fellowship. They came two, three, four at a time.

The Communists' strategy was to keep each pastor ignorant, isolated, and in fear that the man in the next church might be a spy. Slowly, the Holy Spirit overcame this fear and mistrust and bonded their hearts together in brotherly love. The circle of contacts spread outside Ukraine to the regions beyond.

Through these meetings Vasily also made contact with Christian pastors in Czechoslovakia. Up until then he had no idea that Christians in Western Europe, Canada and America were operating publishing houses and Bible institutes, heard God's Word freely and were praying without ceasing for the persecuted believers behind the iron curtain.

Bible smuggler

About this time, Richard Wurmbrand was released from 13 years of imprisonment in Romania. In 1968, before the Soviet army occupied Czechoslovakia, Vasily traveled to Czechoslovakia where he met Wurmbrand's assistant. She told him Wurmbrand was committed to help supply Christian literature for believers in Ukraine and other parts of the Soviet Union. In two years, tens of thousands of books were delivered.

Two others who helped transport thousands of copies of Bibles, New Testaments and gospel literature during those days were Valdemar Sardachuk and Hans Ollesh from the international mission, Nehemiah, in Germany. Ironically, Vasily met none of these men face to face until years later.

In addition, God used many unsung heroes to carry His Word. In some places, Czech children tied New Testaments under the wings of geese and then shooed them across the Tissa River by throwing stones at them. Ukrainian children on the other side removed the Bibles. The geese then paddled back to their Czech home ready for another escapade of Bible smuggling.

Vasily's ever-widening contacts helped transport those precious books throughout the Soviet Union. They began funneling information about people groups, languages, alphabets to their friends in Stockholm. At great risk, Slavic Mission personnel entered the USSR to make contact with these equally courageous pastors. Once two mission representatives were arrested by the KGB while traveling from Brest to Odesa and were imprisoned for six months. Two other friends from Slovakia were caught carrying literature and were put in prison. In addition, the father and son of the Slovakian Yuhashchik family spent six months in a Slovak prison.

Still, Bibles and Christian books continued to enter through Hungary, Poland, Romania, Finland and

Sweden. Each book became a hammer blow that together wrought the first cracks in the iron curtain. Then, in 1971, a bigger hammer blow landed.

Several missionaries from the Slavic Mission in Stockholm secretly visited Vasily. Their primary strategy had been to beam gospel messages across the entire Slavic world from powerful broadcasting stations located in Korea, Portugal, Malta, the Philippines and elsewhere. Their broadcasts covered virtually the entire Soviet bloc with the gospel in Russian.

They brought Vasily maps and documentation about 104 ethnic groups in the Soviet Union showing where each people group lived, how many they were, and to what degree they were evangelized. Their statistics showed that only about 40 percent of the Soviet peoples could read any part of the Bible in their national language. The remaining 60 percent represented more than 100 million ethnic peoples without any access to the Word of God.

"We cannot reach these people with the Word of God because many of them do not speak Russian," the Swedish Christians explained. "You must find missionaries from among your own people who can take the gospel to them."

Twelve-year prayer meeting

That clandestine meeting prompted Vasily to call together the brethren from far and wide. Ministers from various areas gathered and prayed for missions to the unreached peoples. Then they went home and began a series of secret prayer meetings in their churches. Each pastor then encouraged his church members to pray one hour daily for the preparation of gospel workers and for an increase of God's power.

They prayed an hour every morning. Sometimes they fasted and prayed for seven days. Sometimes they prayed all night. This strategy continued for 12 years. It would culminate in the sending out of the first full-time missionaries to the far reaches of the Soviet Union.

A breakthrough came in one of those prayer meetings in the rural village of Bukhariv near Rivne. A woman named Zhenya Polischuk had contracted some undiagnosed disease. Then about 40, she had suffered four years and seven months. It had paralyzed her arms and legs, but she could still speak and spent her days praying and praising the Lord.

Late one afternoon she was visited by a preacher. He asked if he could pray for her, and she said, "Yes," and he began to pray.

Suddenly Zhenya leaped out of bed with such force she broke the bed. She began walking around the room praising God in a loud voice. It was about supper time and peasants were returning home from their fields. They heard Zhenya shouting praises to God and came to her door, wanting to see what was happening. When they saw her prancing around the room glorifying God, they immediately began going down the street telling everyone they met.

Her testimony inflamed the believers to further prayer and intercession. Everything was saturated in prayer. Young people boarded city buses and trains and filled the streets and town squares preaching about Jesus. They were arrested, fined, and ridiculed by the radio and press, but nothing deterred them. The prayers of the saints sustained them.

Then, just as Stalin had spread the Word by sending Christian prisoners to Siberia in an earlier era, economic necessity now pressed these young people to go to the Far East in search of work. They carried with them their Bibles and zeal for the Lord.

Secret mission society

In 1974, at the very height of anti-Christian persecution by the Soviet Communists, Vasily thought the time had come to organize a secret mission society. He called the brethren together and shared his burden with them. They wanted to assist families of Christian prisoners, to distribute Christian literature (and secretly publish it, if possible), and to train young people for future missionary service. They called their work Good Samaritan Mission. Vasily wrote a set of bylaws on about ten pages of tissue paper and hid it in one of his books.

Soviet law forbade such missionary deeds and acts of mercy. It would not even allow the pastor of one registered church to preach in another registered church. Parents could not legally take their children to church. They weren't even supposed to explain points of religion to them at home. In this context, a missionary, even one originating on Soviet soil, was considered the enemy of the people and an anti-Soviet spy.

"God wants us to begin our missionary movement now, at this most difficult hour, so that if we pass this test, the rest of the work will be easier," Vasily told his fellow pastors.

The courage of Richard Wurmbrand of Romania and Valdemar Sardachuk and Hans Ollesh from Nehemiah Mission in Germany encouraged them. In addition, Christians from the West—Swedes, Czechs, Slovaks, Finns, Hungarians—hundreds, perhaps thousands, had braved godless Soviet soldiers to bring Bibles and Christian literature across the borders.

Many of them were young women. Some told how the soldiers had loosed dogs that were trained to tear into pregnant women.

"If these young people can stand so bravely for their faith and risk their lives to carry the gospel to people they don't know in a foreign country, how can we keep silent in our own homeland?" Vasily challenged.

The Ukrainian Christians came to another conclusion: The Soviet system's resorting to such cruel methods meant it must be on the brink of demise. Only those doomed to death could marshal such inhumane measures. They remembered the Scripture, "Evil shall slay the wicked; and they that hate the righteous shall be desolate" (Psalms 34:21). They took courage. While the rest of the world still feared the Soviet Behemoth, with their spiritual eyes they clearly saw the brightness of the triumph of Christ over dark atheism.

For the next ten years, the work proceeded quietly underground.

The plan revealed

In the spring of 1984, Vasily felt the Lord telling him, "Hurry up! Do My work! Don't miss this moment!" This was before Gorbachev had launched his *perestroika* (restructuring) and *glasnost* (openness).

Vasily called a meeting of the pastors and youth leaders of the unregistered churches to intensify the prayer effort and target specific people groups. The brethren came from all over the Soviet Union, including the Islamic republics where young people had gone seeking work and carrying the gospel. They arrived from different directions and at staggered hours. They came by foot, bicycle, car, bus and train.

About 80 men gathered in two rooms while others stationed themselves at street corners to keep watch. Now for the first time Vasily showed them the maps and documents he had kept hidden all this time. The men learned about each of the 104 ethnic groups in the USSR, some of which were on the brink of extinction. One people group, the Aleuts, had only 600 people left. The pastors were amazed that such detailed information was available.

"I want each church present to choose one or two people groups to be responsible to reach with the gospel in the next two years," Vasily said. Then they spread their hands on the maps and prayed specifically for each people group. A missionary burden fell on them all.

When they rose from prayer, the young people stood with tears in their eyes. "We are ready to take Jesus to any part of the Soviet Union, to any nation, large or small," they declared one by one.

Then each one present took information on one or more people groups to share with his congregation. All agreed to devote the first and 15th days of each month to fasting and prayer on behalf of these unreached peoples.

Slavik Radchuk, 24, selected information about the Caraimy, Ukagiry, Kirgizy and Chukchi people groups of Siberia and shared this with his 400-member congregation in Rivne. On the first and 15th of each month, 200 of these church members crammed into two rooms in his house. Unable to sit, they stood the whole night, praying from about 10 p.m. until sunrise.

Other congregations did similarly. This continued for about a year.

Raided by the KGB

But before that year was up, early in the morning in January 1985, seven KGB agents burst into Vasily's flat led by the public prosecutor, a colonel. For 13 grueling hours they searched his apartment without letup. During this time Vasily was not allowed out of their sight. They even accompanied him to the toilet.

After 11 hours of searching, one of the older KGB agents discovered the bylaws of the Good Samaritan Mission in one of Vasily's books.

"You can quit working now," he shouted with hellish arrogance. He looked at Vasily with steel blue eyes as he held up the tissue-paper document. "This document is enough to put this man in prison for a long time."

But his boasting was premature.

Five KGB agents sat Vasily at the table, laid the bylaws on it, and then began selecting all books they thought would be incriminating and piled them on the table. They picked up each book one by one.

"What is this book?" they asked, and Vasily would tell them.

Beneath the stack of books, Vasily spotted pages of the Good Samaritan by-laws.

"God, you blinded the eyes of the Syrian army in the days of Elisha. Please blind the eyes of these enemies of the gospel," Vasily prayed.

As the interrogation continued, Vasily picked up each book with his right hand, and while he talked about it, he deftly slipped the tissue-paper bylaws one page at a time out from under the stack of books and stuffed it into his socks.

After a while, Vasily said, "Please, may I go to the restroom?"

A KGB agent escorted Vasily to the outhouse, but stayed outside while Vasily went in allegedly to relieve himself. With the door closed, Vasily pulled the incriminating pages out of his socks, quietly tore them into tiny pieces, and then poked them into the sewage.

Vasily thought he had outsmarted the KGB agents, but as he returned to his apartment, he saw still more bylaw pages in the pile of books. Again Vasily successfully repeated his sabotage before the unsuspecting agents. The God of Elisha had answered his prayers.

After 13 hours of grueling interrogation, they took Vasily, weary and hungry, to the police station. There the interrogation process was repeated in the presence of a KGB agent and three public prosecutors. As they dumped the pile of books onto the public prosecutor's desk, Vasily again saw two more pages of the dreaded document.

"Lord, help me to destroy those pages," Vasily prayed silently.

This time he slipped the two remaining pages out from under the books and stuffed them up his sleeve.

After two more hours of heavy interrogation, the prosecutors went to put their prized documents into the safe and, behold, they couldn't find them. They looked everywhere for the document, but could not find it. Without that key document, their allegations lacked substance. In the end, they could do nothing more than warn Vasily and reluctantly released him. Vasily knew his time was short.

The incredible spy mission of 1985

In mid-February 1985, Vasily called the brethren together again in L'viv. About 60 men gathered for prayer. This time they commissioned two brothers to spy out the land for missionary purposes just as Moses had sent Joshua and Caleb (see Numbers 13). Since ten of the 12 had brought back a bad report, Vasily decided to forget about the other ten!

They chose Slavik Radchuk from Rivne and Sergei Sharapa from Minsk to survey the potential response to the gospel. After fervent prayers, they dressed them in warm clothing and put them on a plane for Siberia. Slavik was 25 years old and Sergei was about 28. They had already proven their mettle by preaching in those areas in previous years.

Slavik and Sergei flew to Moscow and from there to points east. Krasnoyarsk became a jumping off point for separate trips to Tura, another to Igarka, and a third to Noril'sk and Khatanga north of the Arctic circle. Then they dipped south of Kyzyl among the Tuva people only 100 miles north of Mongolia.

After that, they left Krasnoyarsk and went east as far as Khabarovsk. Then they swung south to Vladivostok, less than 100 miles from the North Korean border. Next they flew north to Magadan and from there west through Yakutsk, where they made a side trip into Batagay and Verkhoyansk in northern Siberia. Then they returned to Yakutsk and then to Krasnoyarsk, stopping at Mirnyy along the way.

From Krasnoyarsk, the two gospel spies headed southwest through the Islamic republics of Kazakhstan, Tajikistan, Uzbekistan and Turkmenistan. After crossing the Caspian Sea, they continued through Azerbaijan, Armenia, Georgia, and other areas of the

Undoing Goliath

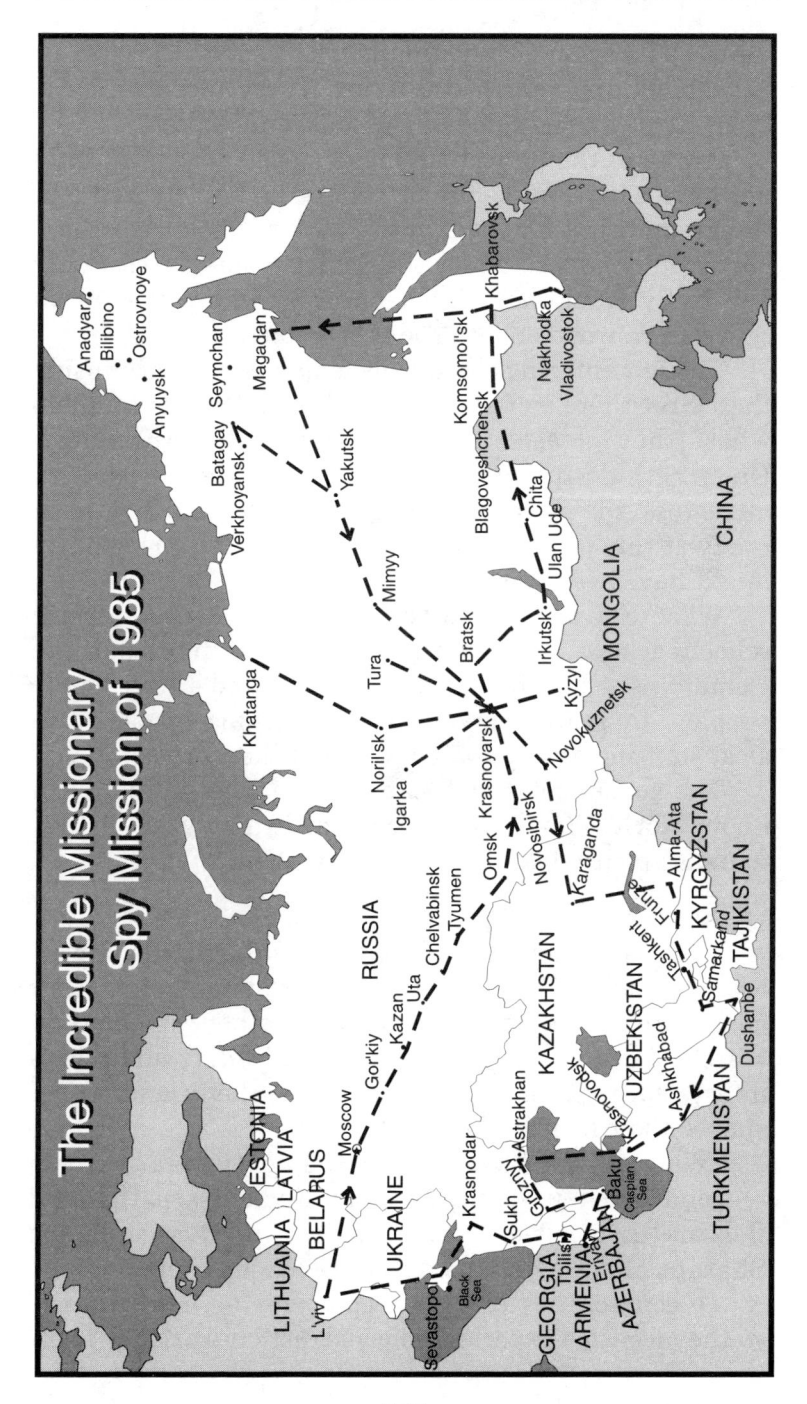

Caucasus region. They finally re-entered Ukraine at Sevastopol and returned to L'viv. These modern Marco Polos had traveled some 30,000 miles in 50 days.

It was in the perfect timing of God, a feat that could not have happened before or since. The Soviets had laid the groundwork for the trip with their subsidized transportation network. Under the Soviet system, it cost only $60 to fly from Kiev to Khabarovsk, where the trans-Siberian railroad ended. Today it would cost $1,000.

Though entering the Soviet Union was tough, inside the USSR there were no border checks; Soviets could go where they pleased. After the breakup of the Soviet Union, ethnic interests again raised national barriers all across the former empire. If Vasily had not been ready at this precise moment in history, the opportunity might have been lost forever.

What Slavik and Sergei saw shocked them. Their schoolteachers had fed them the party line that the Communists had liberated and benefited these ethnic peoples. In reality, many of these ethnic people were sick, starving and cut off from rest of the world.

The gospel spies met some people who did not even know World War II had occurred. In every place they found a spiritual void ready for God to fill.

First missionary team

They returned to L'viv more exhilarated than exhausted and told Vasily all they had seen and heard. After hearing their findings, Vasily called another conference in March. Three hundred pastors, youth leaders and others interested in missions showed up. As Slavik and Sergei shared their hearts, the people wept.

"Who will go?" Vasily asked. Twenty young people responded. They were from L'viv, Rivne, Carpathia and Belarus (then called Byelorussia or White Russia). Sergei Sharapa and Slavik Radchuk were among them.

Of course, they could not go openly as missionaries, so they went as experienced construction workers. Their hands were strong for physical work and their hearts were hot for the gospel.

So in spring of 1985, the first missionary team went to Kyzyl and began to minister to the Tuva people.

Wanting to see how his young, courageous missionaries were doing, Vasily flew to Tuva to visit them that July.

The last night before returning to L'viv, Vasily went with the team by small tractor to a mountain site to celebrate the Lord's Supper by moonlight. Just as Vasily was consecrating the bread, a tick bit him over the right eye.

These Siberian ticks are known for carrying a form of encephalitis that can bring paralysis or death. The team arrived back down the mountain about midnight. There the women missionaries gently pulled the tick, piece by piece, from his swollen eyelid. But the poison had begun to do its work.

By the time Vasily arrived home by plane, his right eye was swollen shut. He dared not seek medical help for his problem. He dared not let anyone know where he had been.

He had anointed many sick people and had seen them recover. So the next morning, he took the very same anointing oil from the drawer, got on his knees, anointed himself and prayed quietly. Two hours later, he left for the airport. He had a very important meeting in the church at Kharkiv.

Disembarking from the two-hour flight, he looked in the mirror and saw that the swelling had completely disappeared. Quietly he praised God.

Letter to Gorbachev

In August, he traveled to Vohynia where he had grown up. There he had cut his gospel teeth and had learned how to preach. There he had been ordained a bishop over the unregistered churches in Western Ukraine. And while there, he took part in the funeral of a dear friend of the family, bishop Ivan Matviychuk.

Mikhail Gorbachev had become General Secretary of the USSR that March and began implementing his *glasnost* and *perestroika* policies. Encouraged by what he heard, Vasily wrote Gorbachev, making seven appeals. Among them, these three were foremost:

- Release Christians who were prisoners of conscience;
- Change the law barring children from attending church meetings;
- Grant pastors and church workers the freedom to preach the gospel without threat of imprisonment.[2]

Vasily passed the letter on to government leaders in L'viv. Later, two pastors of unregistered churches passed it on to Gorbachev's office in Moscow. But Gorbachev never saw it. It was intercepted by a KGB deputy and given to the general public prosecutor of the Soviet Union. Forty-six pastors of unregistered churches had signed the letter. Vasily Boyechko's signature was at the top of the list. It was clear who they would go after.

Final arrest

On September 3, 1985, six KGB agents burst into Vasily's L'viv apartment again. They had maliciously waited until he was the only one home. His wife was at work in the factory; his two older sons also were at work; his three younger daughters had gone to school, and his mother-in-law had just taken his youngest son, three-year-old Yuriy, for a walk.

The agents were determined to arrest him before anyone returned and did not search long. By two o'clock that afternoon, they had collected a bag of Christian

---

[2] A translation of the complete text of the letter is repro-duced in the Appendix, "Letter to Gorbachev."

literature. They led him out of the apartment and took him to a plain white Volga, license plate LVA-20-13.

Vasily was dressed in summer clothing. He could take nothing with him.

They first went to the regional prosecutor's office. There he was interrogated for two hours in front of several women "witnesses." After this, they removed all metal objects from his person, including his eyeglasses. They would have taken his belt and shoelaces, but Vasily wasn't wearing any

"You are under arrest," the interrogator finally said, but didn't mention the charges.

"Please, let me call my wife," Vasily requested.

The request was categorically denied.

He was escorted to a restroom, but had to leave the door open.

"Get back into the car," they told him. This time the white Volga took him to the railway police station (KPZ), where suspects were detained until charges were filed.

There the police routinely treated every suspect in as inhumane way as possible. First, he was stripped naked, and then the police did a cavity search. The process was repeated several times.

Finally, they led him off to cell Number 2, already occupied by two villains, shoved him in and slammed the door behind him.

Vasily greeted his cellmates, then knelt on the dirt floor and immediately began to pray for his wife and children and the work of God.

"Why, Lord?"

"Why, Lord, is this happening to me?" he prayed. "Why, when we have just begun our very important missionary work, do I have to sit helpless in this dirty, iron cage?"

Vasily measured the floor—seven shoe lengths by eight shoe lengths. At one end was a small, wooden platform that served as the only bed. Two boards substituted for pillows. Instead of a blanket was a filthy soldier's greatcoat that inmates took turns using. It was so soiled that Vasily preferred to shiver on the floor rather than use it.

Legally, authorities could detain someone only 72 hours in KPZ without filing charges. Exactly three days later, Saturday, September 6, which happened to be his birthday, they filed the charges and transferred him to the dreaded *Brigidki* central prison where 1,500 prisoners were incarcerated.

The Soviets had converted the old Catholic convent of the St. Brigide Order into one of the worst prisons in eastern Europe. There they tortured thousands of Ukrainian and Polish patriots as "reactionaries." Nikita S. Khrushchev, the chief of the Ukrainian Communist Party, had ordered all prisoners killed before vacating the city in the face of the oncoming Germans in 1941. When the Germans arrived, they found virtually every cell floor covered with a viscous mass from the rotting corpses stacked four or five deep. Would this be Vasily's "end of the line?"

They led him through a maze of 17 steel doors. He was told that each door was locked with a combination lock, the code of which was changed every two hours! As each door clanged shut behind him, Vasily cried out in his spirit, "Lord, how is this fitting into Your plan?"

Ordeal in the Brigidki

Meanwhile Galina searched frantically to learn what happened to her husband. She went to the police station.

"Where is my husband?" she asked.

"I don't know," came the reply.

Then she went to the city magistrate's office, the KGB, the military, the courthouse, the jail, the prison. Everywhere she went she received no answer. There was no record of his arrest. She feared the worst.

Meanwhile, at *Brigidki*, Vasily was plunged into cell number 24, a filthy cell about 10 feet by 13 feet, occupied by seven other men. He could not help but wonder what human corpses had rotted in his cell. There was no heat and the filth bred lice. At night, mice came out in droves and chewed on their clothing. Some nights Vasily and his cellmates caught as many as 15 mice with their hands.

Every day, prison officials took sadistic delight in applying their favorite slogan, "Prison is the place where a man must be tortured." The prisoners nick-named their guard "the godfather" after their sadistic practices.

Prisoners were escorted to the toilet twice daily—once in the morning and once in the evening. Consequently, their cells became cesspools of filth—moral and physical.

Prisoners were provided just enough food to keep them alive. Breakfast was cold barley porridge. It was served with two ounces of black bread—so sour it caused disturbances in the digestive system. They could eat everything then, or save some of the bread for later.

Lunch was a hot watery soup with a piece of dirty potato in it—no meat—and some cold porridge. Supper was about the same as lunch, sometimes with a few small slices of salted fish. Their drink was boiled water. They were rationed to 9 grams (less than two teaspoons) of sugar per day. The whole daily allotment of food equaled about half the cheapest lunch Vasily could buy in the canteen of the factory where he worked.

Prisoners awaiting trial could receive 5 kilograms (11 pounds) of food per month from their families. Since Vasily's family didn't know where he was, he got nothing, and the other prisoners shared precious little. Neither could he write to his family. He went seven months without any information about them.

Prisoners were supposed to get an hour's exercise every day. In actual practice, the men were taken to the roof in groups of 30, herded into a steel cage about 12 feet by 15 feet, and told to "walk." Their outing usually lasted only 15 to 20 minutes.

The hardest thing for a Christian, however, was to be put into the same cells with foul-mouthed, hardened criminals. During Stalin's day, there had been a separation between political prisoners and hardened criminals. That was no longer the case.

Prison preacher

Vasily decided he had no choice. He began to preach to these vile outcasts of society. It was certainly different than preaching to his beloved L'viv congregation. Soon, every one of his cellmates trusted in Christ. Some of them were healed in answer to prayer. There wasn't a foul word from any of them for two-and-a-half months. Cell No. 24 was nicknamed "the holy cell."

When prison officials learned that Vasily was conducting "church" in prison, they became incensed. They yanked him out of that cell and shoved him into a cell on the opposite side of the prison with some of the foulest prisoners they could find.

There, Vasily accepted the "call" to his new "congregation" and began sharing the gospel with them. Soon they became Christians and joined him in worship. The enraged guards would then come and transfer him to yet another cell. During the next nine months Vasily was transferred eight times. In every cell, the preacher kept up his patient witness and the hardened criminals caved in to the grace of God.

Every time he was relocated, news of his change of venue would be communicated through the prison's "telephone" system. Prisoners used tin cans as mouth and earpieces and spoke into the sewer pipes. Soon he became known affectionately as "our prison priest."

When he wasn't preaching to prisoners or praying, Vasily was singing.

"What are you singing about?" the prisoners asked.

"About the blood of Jesus," Boyechko answered

"Sing some more."

First, it was his lone baritone voice. Then a few other brave prisoners joined in. Before long antiphonal hymns resounded throughout the iron vault. It nearly drove the guards crazy. They decided to move him to a different part of the prison.

There Vasily resumed his preaching and praying and singing—until the guards there became weary of his religious activity, also. So they move him again. This continued until the entire prison was evangelized.

Aborted trial

In January 1986, Vasily was given four volumes of his "case" to study before his trial. He had already decided the Holy Spirit would be a better defense attorney than any appointed by the court.

He learned that 75 prosecution witnesses from Ukraine and Byelorussia had been subpoenaed. Not one of the 43 Christian witnesses who had come forward would be allowed to testify. This was the Communist version of "right to trial!"

The day for his trial arrived, and Vasily was loaded into the paddy wagon dubbed "the Black Raven" and accompanied by armed guard to the courthouse. Those few seconds getting in and out of the van were the first he had seen the outside world in five months. A huge crowd surrounded the courthouse.

Vasily was quickly ushered into the courtroom. Bright lights and television cameras glared at him. *What's going on here?* he wondered.

The judges, clerks and officials were abuzz. Vasily sat on the prisoner's bench wondering why they didn't start. *He* was the one on trial, but *they* were the ones who seemed anxious.

Finally, the captain of the guard said, "Come with me. The trial has been postponed."

The KGB would not allow the presence of believers in the trial of Christian pastors. Suddenly Vasily realized that the huge crowd outside were his friends.

Despite the prohibition, hundreds of his parishioners, friends and believers from other parishes had turned out *en masse*. Some had come all the way from other Soviet republics.

Moreover, the Communist Party Congress was in session in Moscow, and guardians of Communist "justice" didn't want to risk any public disturbance interrupting the political process.

"C'mon," the angry captain of the guard said. "There's a large crowd out there. We have to run for it."

He shoved Vasily quickly through the crowd. Vasily caught a glimpse of his wife out of the corner of his eye, but had no time to nod before he was shoved back into "the Black Raven" and locked in his three-foot square cage. Within 30 minutes from the time he had left prison, he was slammed back into the *"Brigidki."*

Trial at the factory

The Party Congress concluded on March 9, 1986. So on March 11, Vasily was again driven to trial. This time several hundred believers jammed the halls of the main courthouse. To avoid them, the trial was quickly and secretly transferred to the Kinescope plant where Vasily had worked for 25 years.

L'viv officials had again banned Vasily's parishioners and fellow pastors from attending, and Vasily saw that many pastors in his region were absent from the trial.

"God forgive them," Vasily prayed from his heart.

But the ban had no effect on Christians from outlying areas, and other Soviet republics. The crowd was just as big as the one in January.

Most of them could not enter the hall, and most of the seats were taken by Communist officials. For the first time in seven months, Vasily saw Galina and his children across the courtroom. The judge noticed this and dismissed his sons and daughters.

Based on his letter to Gorbachev, Vasily was charged with disobeying Soviet authorities and making false accusations against the Soviet regime.

Of course, Vasily's letter had been legal. To make the charges stick, the Communists would have to rely on false witnesses. Even though none of Vasily's 43 Christian witnesses were allowed at the trial, he took some comfort in learning that the ten factory co-workers who had been requisitioned by the prosecutor wouldn't be allowed to testify either. In preliminary questioning, they had given only truthful answers upholding Vasily's honor and integrity! Some of them were lathe operators Vasily had trained.

In fact, the factory workers went on a sympathy strike and shut down the whole plant. Now they came, not to work, but to witness the trial. They were locked out of the proceedings, but they watched from the factory windows to show their sympathy and shame the tyrants.

The trial took three days. As expected, Vasily was convicted and sentenced to three years in a concentration camp. If Vasily had not been successful in destroying the pages of the bylaws, he would have gotten at least five years. Still, it took two more months in *Brigidki* before he was transferred.

"Most dangerous" prisoner

The concentration camp VL 315-50, located about 20 miles west of L'viv, was even worse than *Brigidki*. During his first five months there Vasily lived in a deep cellar. The slit of small windows across the top of his cell were three feet below grade. The cold, damp cell ruined his health. He suffered constant pain in his heart and liver. The prayers of fellow believers sustained him. He did not know that March 22 was declared an International Day of Fasting and Prayer for Christian prisoners the world around.

Seeing his godliness, the chief prison official commented, "Vasily is more dangerous to me than any other prisoner." Vasily considered that quite an honor, considering there were 800 prisoners in the camp. *If Satan is so afraid of God's little servant, then his kingdom must be ready to fall,* he thought.

Meanwhile, Ukrainian believers thought that the missionary outreach should not be held up because their leader was in prison. In fact, they felt that sending out more missionaries would honor their brave leader. So in 1986, the churches sent out more missionaries. Some went to Irkutsk by Lake Baykal. Others went on to Komsomolsk, 600 miles north of Vladivostok. Everywhere they went, they planted a church.

Gorbachev's reforms

Emboldened by Vasily's bravery and encouraged by Gorbachev's talk of reform, the Christian pastors retyped Vasily's original seven-page letter to Gorbachev. Slavik Radchuk added his own epilogue. Then a band of courageous pastors went to Moscow and insisted on seeing Gorbachev personally. They weren't going to let their second letter be shunted off to some KGB official. They were not able to see Gorbachev himself, but they placed it into the hands of Gorbachev's personal secretary. The changes that followed astounded the world.[3]

They were also buoyed by the International Day of Prayer for prisoners of conscience in the USSR held on March 22, 1987.

On April 22, Gorbachev, then President of the Supreme Soviet, lifted the ban on Christianity and three days later released all Christian prisoners. At 3 p.m. on April 25, Vasily walked out of the concentration camp a free man. The little preacher had faced the Goliath of the Supreme Soviet, and Goliath had been undone!

---

[3] The Letter to Gorbachev in the Appendix includes the epilogue by Slavik Radchuk.

What made Vasily even more elated was the news that none of his family members, none of his fellow pastors, and none of his Christian friends had bowed to Communist pressure to compromise. The missionaries who had gone out in the spring of 1986 had borne fruit and had not returned empty. They were still on the field faithfully proclaiming God's Word. Churches had been started where there were none and were growing stronger daily.

In 1988 Gorbachev honored a holiday celebrating 1,000 years of Christianity in Russia, dating from the baptism of Vladimir, Prince of Kiev, in 988. Government radio, television, newspapers, even schools suddenly opened to the gospel. It was like a dam had burst and pent-up gospel waters gushed out.

In Ukraine, previously underground groups began registering with the government. Several branches of the Good Samaritan Mission were among them. Slavik Radchuk and his five brothers registered their work in Rivne in 1989. Vasily registered his work in L'viv using the same name. To him, this was no conflict, but honored the underground work carried out during pre-freedom days under that name. Innovative ministries started reaching prisoners, school children, even members of the KGB.

Then came the event that shocked the world: After a failed coup attempt by hard-line Communists in August 1991, the leaders of Belarus, Ukraine and the Russian Federation met in Minsk on December 12 and agreed that the USSR would end on December 31, and that in its place would be the Commonwealth of Independent States.

Foreigners started rushing to Ukraine and other parts of the former Soviet Union to conduct high-profile and well-funded evangelistic crusades. Most of these were conducted in major cities where thousands made decisions to accept and follow Christ. Then they left to tell of their exploits among their supporters, and indigenous churches like those that comprised Good Samaritan Mission did the legwork of following up new believers and discipling them.

Good Samaritan missionaries stepped up their efforts to go to the remotest parts of the former Soviet Union to preach release to those held captive in Satan's bonds. It didn't matter they had little or no support or lacked provision of life's barest necessities. They felt compelled to go, and go they did.

Consolidating forces

Yet even before this date, changes were in the wind. Up until this time, the Pentecostal churches under Soviet repression had been fragmented into two groups: the registered and the unregistered. Each division had two branches. Among the registered churches were (1) those that registered along with Baptists and were included in the Baptist Union, and (2) those that registered separately. The non-registered churches were composed of another two groups: (1) followers of Voronayev, who practiced foot washing, and (2) followers of Gustav Schmidt, who did not practice foot washing.

So in the summer of 1988 the governments of Ukraine and the Soviet Union suggested that these four divisions should form their own Pentecostal Union. They came to Vasily with their proposal.

Vasily felt strongly that unity of the churches was Christ's will. A unified structure would (1) help prevent Bible and eliminate spiritual errors in the leadership, (2) resume publication of a spiritual magazine, which had been suspended for 50 years, (3) provide backing for a school, of which there was none, (4) facilitate the publication of spiritual literature, and (5) open contacts for fellowship among like-minded believers throughout the world.

He went to Moscow and for four years worked as a member of the coordinating council and then a member of the central committee of the newly created fellowship.

While there he resumed publication of the Christian magazine, *Primiritél (Pacifist)*, begun in 1929 by Gustav Schmidt, but suspended under Communist suppression in 1945. To his glad surprise, highly qualified writers and editors from the Academy of Sciences of the Soviet Union assisted him in publishing the first new issue in 1991. Publishing that spiritual magazine gave Vasily as much pleasure as preaching, for now this little publication would reach tens of thousands with spiritual messages from God's Word written by the choicest of His servants.

But it didn't quite turn out that way. Men who gained supremacy in the new Pentecostal Union were those who had served under the political system that had brought repression, imprisonment, suffering and death to many of their fellow believers. So neither the magazine nor the Pentecostal Union was able to attain or maintain the spiritual pinnacle to which Vasily aspired.

After publishing four issues of his precious magazine, he resigned his position, left Moscow, and returned to L'viv in 1992.

Televised gospel

While in Moscow, Vasily had prepared a weekly television program, "Eternal Source." Back in L'viv, he approached L'viv TV and offered to produce the 20-minute program for weekly viewing. By this time, evangelicalism had invaded even the established churches, and the TV officials welcomed the program. So Vasily began broadcasting his "Eternal Source" television program to about 15 million viewers weekly. The cost: about $500 per month.

Vasily didn't want to take over his old church, which was now guided by another pastor. So he formed a new church in L'viv from the viewers who responded. At the same time, he began conducting evangelistic meetings in the Communists' cultural hall.

The new congregation grew quickly. One-third of them came from watching "Eternal Source." In 1994 Vasily added 103 new members to the church, including 66 new converts. Many of these were cultured, educated people who could help him with his work. The congregation grew to 300 by 1996 and purchased an old Roman Catholic church building.

Publishing ventures

Vasily also plunged into editorial work. First, he translated Valdemar Sardachuk's booklet, *To Be a Christian*, from Russian into Ukrainian. Churches and evangelistic teams used at least 30,000 copies to follow-up those who made decisions for Christ.

Next, he worked with David Wilkerson to print 30,000 copies of *The Cross and the Switchblade* in Ukrainian. He also worked with Robert Haskins to translate and publish booklets like *Book of Life* and *The Report of Pilate* for children and youth.

But the work dearest to his heart was the retranslation and publication of the New Testament, Psalms and Proverbs in modern Ukrainian. Foreign missionaries had published a Ukrainian New Testament in earlier years, but that version could not be read and understood by the younger generation. The new translation by P. Kulish in modern Ukrainian can be read and comprehended by all Ukrainians. Some 10,000 copies have been printed.

The Scriptures are often available in overseas languages, but Christians reading them lack the cross references and study helps so prolific in the West. To produce a Ukrainian study Bible, Vasily worked with Life Publishers to translate the study notes of the English *Full Life Study Bible* published by Zondervan into Ukrainian. The *Full Life Study New Testament and Concordance* was completed and the first 17,000 copies came off the press in 1997.

During the Communist persecution, most of the Ukrainian hymnals were destroyed. At the same time, while he was in prison, Vasily composed and sang new songs given to him by the Spirit. So his next dream was to publish new Ukrainian songbooks. At least 24,000 copies of *Psalmospivy* have been published.

In addition, Vasily translated and published several thousand each of *Marriage from Heaven*, *Truth About Charisma*, *The False Teaching of Jehovah Witnesses*, and *Tradition in Light of the Word of God*.

Ministry of Defense

After the formation of Good Samaritan Mission in 1989, high officials of the Ministry of Defense invited Vasily and other spiritual leaders to Moscow. *I wonder what this is all about*, he wondered.

"What will be your spheres of activity?" they asked.

"Well," Vasily began cautiously, "We plan to conduct evangelistic meetings in the parks, visit the elderly, distribute gospel tracts to the school children, visit prisoners in jails..."

"Do you have any plans to preach to the military men?" one official asked abruptly. "Military men need regeneration, too. In fact, don't you think they need it most of all? I think you should revise your bylaws and include an article about preaching to the military."

While they talked, Vasily and the others worked out a paragraph to make sure preaching to the military was part of their mission. So the call to evangelize the armed forces came from the military itself!

Now Vasily had ordered eight tons of paper for printing some of the above-mentioned books, and soon after returning to L'viv began looking for a place to store it until press time. He decided to ask the colonel in charge of the convoy detachment in L'viv if he had a place to store the paper for him.

"Before I say whether or not I will store the paper for you, I want to know this: Do you agree to preach God's Word to our soldiers?" the colonel asked.

Vasily stopped in his tracks. Was this a trick, or an invitation?

"I'm just here on business," Vasily said. "How did you know I was a preacher?"

"I feel in my heart you are a man of God," the colonel answered. "That's why I asked if you would preach to my men. Tell me first if you agree, then I will decide what to do with your paper."

"I believe the military men are giving me a Macedonian call," Vasily responded. "I will preach."

"Good! And I will store your paper," the colonel said.

A short time later, Vasily received an invitation to preach not only to the troops, but to the officers and their wives, as well. The whole affair was televised and broadcast throughout the ebbing Soviet Union.

Ukrainian police

Next, he had a run in with the police. One day Vasily and some of his co-workers were handing out clothing at their storefront mission to some of the poor people who had come in off the street. A police colonel stood near the entrance of the facility and watched intently.

I wonder what he wants, Vasily wondered, remembering his unpleasant memories with the police. Finally, when Vasily left the building to do something, the colonel walked over to him and spoke.

"I am a colonel and leader of L'viv's regional police. I have been watching you work, and I feel God is telling me, if we help you materially, you will help us spiritually. Come to my office tomorrow, and we will talk."

The next day, Vasily went to the police colonel's office. He explained how they had arranged to do spiritual work among the military and suggested he could do the same thing with the police.

Then God opened another door. "Why don't you come and preach to the prisoners, too?" the colonel said. "They need it the worst."

From that moment on Good Samaritan missionaries had open doors in prisons throughout the country. By 2003, they had approximately 200 ministers reaching 5,000 prisoners. In one three-year period, they distributed over 600,000 New Testaments, 80,000 Christian books, and over a million tracts and gospel booklets to the prisoners. The mission even has a fruitful work among what are considered incorrigible offenders.

Visit to the fields

Vasily's heart was thrilled every time he heard reports of work done by his missionaries among the unreached peoples throughout the former Soviet Union, and especially in the far northeast.

Word reached him that the church planted by those early pioneer missionaries in Komsomolsk by 2003 had grown to over 800 believers. Moreover, it had trained and sent out a dozen of its own missionaries who had planted at least 20 other churches in the surrounding area. And they hadn't stopped there. They went on "to the end of the earth" and planted additional churches along the lip of the Arctic Ocean. The Magadan church grew to more than 500 believers and planted five daughter churches.

During Stalin's reign of terror, Magadan, located on the Sea of Okhotsk, regularly received shiploads of convicts sent there by Stalin's satraps. From there they were led by convoy deep into the interior to do hard labor. Many of them never made it to the concentration camps; sometimes whole columns of convicts and their convoys froze to death.

Vasily decided to visit the area himself and see what great things the Lord was doing. In February 1996, Vasily flew to Komsomolsk off the northeast corner of China. Then he traveled north to Magadan, past

Providinnya Bay and the Bering Strait, to Bilibino, Beringovskiy, and other villages along the northern rim. Despite temperatures ranging 80 degrees below zero Fahrenheit, whole villages responded to his messages.

High-risk venture

Most memorable was his visit to the village of Anyuysk, about 80 miles south of the East Siberian Sea on the Kolyma River. Vasily and Pawel Radchuk, Slavik's younger brother, flew to Anadyr, the capital of Chukotka, and from there to Bilibino. From there they rented a truck, filled it with coal for traction, and started out for Anyuysk, a town amid the Eveny nation. They would travel 300 miles over frozen marsh and swampland.[4]

Vasily held his breath and prayed to heaven as the heavily laden truck spun out on one turn after another. In all, he counted 107 life-threatening turns on roads carved out of solid ice in one 40-mile segment.

Upon reaching Anyuysk on the Arctic coast, the preachers were met by Olexandr Ryazanov, the mayor. He had done his best to get the whole town out for the special meetings.

About 400 Evenys lived in the village, and about 300 came to the meeting. That night Vasily preached the gospel of Jesus Christ in the cultural house built by the Communists to promulgate their atheistic propaganda. When he gave the invitation, nearly everyone present responded and give their hearts to Jesus. By the time Vasily left, a church had been planted.

The meeting at Ostronoye produced similar results. There, Yevdikiya Ovchinnikova, head of the village, was first in line.

---

[4] Pawel later moved to a Ukrainian community in Seattle and frequently visited and encouraged the churches in Siberia. He was killed in a private plane crash in Alaska in 2002.

It was physically impossible to preach in all villages of the frozen North, but what he could not do in person, the Lord allowed him to do electronically. Authorities opened up their television station to him and allowed him to preach to the entire Chukotka region via TV.

Next Vasily went to Seymchan, about 600 miles north of Magadan on the frozen marsh that feeds the Kolyma River. In the very area where Stalin had 21 concentration camps, Vasily had the privilege of ordaining the first pastor of a church raised up by young missionary Ivan Trachuk from Ukraine. Ivan had left his fiancée behind, telling her conditions were too harsh for her to come with him; she would have to wait until he had evangelized the Kolyma region.

When Vasily visited him, it was much colder than in Chukotka—no less than 90 degrees below zero Fahrenheit. Yet it was 50 degrees warm inside Ivan's house! In the next two years after Vasily's visit, Ivan and his colleagues planted six new congregations

Everywhere Vasily went he saw the impoverished missionaries from Ukraine never asking anything for themselves, only that they might be used of God to bring the gospel of Jesus Christ to people who had never heard. Perhaps it was the fire in their hearts that kept them warm through the long, dark winters.

Explosive church growth

Churches in the Islamic republics of Uzbekistan, Kazakhstan, Kyrgyzstan, Tajikistan and Turkmenistan planted by the original band of missionaries that went out in 1985 similarly prospered.

In the 90 percent Muslim country of Uzbekistan, one of the Ukrainian missionaries who had immigrated there planted a thriving congregation that by 2003 had 9,000 believers plus 3,000 children meeting in 167 house churches, besides the central assembly. Half of these people came from Muslim backgrounds.

"Why do so many people come to your meetings?" one of the town officials asked the leader.

"Many people have personal problems with their marriages: drugs, alcohol, despair," he answered. "When they turn to the living God, they find answers to their problems and freedom from their addictions."

That satisfied the officials and they gave the brother no more trouble at that time, though restrictions have since been tightened.

Church growth similarly was seen in neighboring Tajikistan, Kyrgyzstan, Kazakhstan and Turkmenistan. For example,

- In Krgyzstan, two main churches—each with 300 believers—help guide 150 house churches and worshipping congregations. They operate a Bible college in Bishkek, the capital, that has 70 students in a two-year program. A Bible institute elsewhere provides short-term training to 30 students at a time.
- Kazakhstan has 80 churches, some with as many as 800 believers.
- At least 15 congregations exist in Tajikistan.

Meanwhile, the congregations in Siberia continue to grow, with some 35 churches in Chukotka and a dozen churches in Irkutsk. This is reflective of the explosive growth of evangelical churches throughout Russia and the former Soviet lands. In 1990 there were 1,652 evangelical churches in the Soviet Union. By 2000 there were 18,009. And just two years later there were 28,000!

Missionary urgency

Vasily knows the season for his Ukrainian missionaries is short. So far, most people in all these republics still know Russian. But there is a new generation emerging that does not know Russian. Each independent republic is schooling its youth in its own culture and language. The time will soon come when each nation can be reached only by native language speakers. By that time, he trusts that missionaries sent out by Good Samaritan Mission will have raised up missionaries among each nation who will evangelize and disciple their own people.

That's quite a fulfillment of what God spoke to Vasily in 1958, "I have great plans for you. You will bring the gospel to many nations."

In July 1996, Vasily was invited to speak to an important conference of intellectuals examining science in the light of the Christian faith. They gathered in the very same building in which atheistic Communists had ended his scholastic career. On the second floor just a few rooms down the hall from the one in which he was cursed by General Millerov, Vasily preached God's Word to professors from all over Ukraine. Not only was Goliath undone, Vasily was preaching from his headstone.

"How unsearchable are His judgments and His ways past finding out!" (Romans 11:33b).

Appendix

Letter to Gorbachev

In May, 1985, a group of pastors of unregistered churches sent this letter to Mikhail Sergeyevich Gorbachev, then General Secretary of the Central Committee of the Communist Party of the Soviet Union, in hopes of gaining some reprieve from the harsh regulations preventing them from freely exercising their faith and rearing their children as believers. The first draft was intercepted and sent to the KGB, followed by the arrest of their chief spokesman, Vasily Boyechko. A second draft was retyped a year later with an addendum questioning the arrest of their bishop as a consequence of writing the original letter and hand carried to Mr. Gorbachev's office. This is the letter that is translated here.

Highlights have been added to distinguish the main points of discussion. The letter was translated by Professor M.Ya. Blokh, Head of the Department of English Grammar at Moscow Pedagogical State University.

To: Cmr. M.S. Gorbachev, General Secretary of the Central Committee of the CPSU

Copy to: Cmr. K.M. Kharchev, Chairman of the Board for Matters of Religion under the Council of Ministers of the USSR

From: the Christians of Evangelical Faith residing in various parts of the USSR (unregistered)

"Wisdom is better than weapons of war, but one sinner destroyeth much good" (Ecclesiastes 9:18).

Dear Mikhail Sergeyevich:

Urged by some vitally important circumstances, we, Christians of Evangelical Faith (C.E.F. Pentecostal adherents) apply to you, as the Supreme Legislative Power in this country, with a request to pay a special and profound attention to the problem of relations between the Evangelical Christians and the Soviet Government.

We will try to present the essence of our petition in a concise form.

On the one hand, being Christian believers, we must devoutly honor and follow unreservedly the commandments of our Lord Jesus Christ. On the other hand, being citizens of this country, we must recognize and abide by the Laws of the State. We do not lay any claims on the laws of our State. Following Jesus Christ's precepts to render unto Caesar the things that are Caesar's and unto God the things that are God's (Matthew 22:21), we honestly fulfill our civil duties not out of fear, as men-pleasers, but from the heart (Ephesians 6:6-8).

With the deepest gratitude we note the fact that at the initial stages of the young Soviet Republic, during the difficult years of the Civil War, with its famine and devastation, the Soviet of the People's Commissars [the then Cabinet of Ministers] headed by V.I. Lenin not only thought of the believer citizens, but wisely resolved this problem by the decree, "Concerning Freedom of

Conscience," of January 23, 1918. This document put an end to the centuries-old conflict in this country between the State Power and the long-suffering Evangelical Christians.

But from the year 1929 on, the question of our religious freedom became more and more complicated through the adoption of a continuous succession of new laws and decrees (on both union and republic levels) referring to religious cults. Likewise, the wording of the article on Freedom of Conscience as part of the successive constitutions of the USSR became more and more restrictive for us Christian believers. It should be especially noted that, while this or that law regarding religious worship was being reformulated, the will and the wishes of the believers were utterly disregarded.

Thus, it is not at all surprising that even the contemporary laws and decrees concerning religious associations and congregations do not take into due consideration the conscience and spiritual needs of the believers. We wish to draw your attention to the most important questions that arouse our bewilderment and act as an obstacle to the registration of the congregations (as our basis of reference we take the "Provisions for the Religious Associations in the Ukrainian SSR" of 1976).

1. *Paragraph 1 of the "Provisions" reads: "Profession or non-profession of a religion does not involve any restriction of rights."*

We will not find enough space in this letter to list the innumerable facts of infringement of the rights of religious believers (such as mentioning the person's relation to religion in his or her record of professional work, non-acceptance of believers as students of universities or vocational schools, expulsion from educational institutions, refusal to permit a believer to visit his or her relative living abroad, etc.). However, all such restrictions being of a purely material nature, we in all honesty do not consider the paragraph in question as a very great annoyance for us, for the Evangelical believers have, throughout centuries, reconciled themselves with their status of people of the second rate. We are not going to refer to V.I. Lenin's statement that the infringement of the rights of believers is inadmissible. You must be acquainted with Lenin's teaching much better than we are.

2. ***Paragraph 10, point B reads: "Believers who have set up a religious association have the right to receive, free of charge, both a house of worship and the corresponding implements of worship in accord with the resolution of the Board for Matters of Religion under the Council of Ministers of the USSR."***

We are surprised at the local administrative bodies ignoring this paragraph: almost everywhere they refuse to let the registered congregations have at their disposal the existing houses of worship; the congregations are allowed to reconstruct or build a house of worship relying on their own resources. But this practice, the same as the practice mentioned in section 1 (see above), does not trouble us very much. As believers we are ready to sacrifice both the last penny and all the remaining strength of the body to our cause. However, we are much troubled by another factor. Namely, after the acceptance of the State Commission, any house of worship becomes the property of the state, and the state may cancel the rent agreement with the congregation under certain conditions such as violations by the congregation of this or that paragraph of the law. Indeed, these "violations," far from being premeditated, may proceed from the essential principles of our faith.

3. ***Paragraph 11, point B, reads: "Religious associations have no right to grant material support to the believers."***

In spite of the numerous and seemingly logical explanations of paragraph 11 by various representatives of the state, we lay a special emphasis on it for the following reasons:

Firstly, material support, as well as mutual contacts, refer to the vital principles of believers set out in the Lord's Commandments (Daniel 4:24; 1 Corinthians 16:1-4; 2 Corinthians 9).

Secondly, according to Jesus Christ's teaching, material support cannot in any case serve as a means of affecting the conscience of people, a means of religious propaganda, or, which is the most abominable, a means of enriching clergymen. Whereas secrecy or ambiguity in these matters may engender the said morbid phenomena.

Thirdly, Christian practice of this kind presupposes care of the genuinely impoverished and suffering people, whose needs cannot be fully satisfied by the State due to various reasons. This practice should be conducted honestly and wisely. If, on the other hand, the funds of the congregation are placed under constant control of the Finance Department of the State, the said practice may become dishonest and sinful, leading the clergymen to certain offenses against God and the State. Paragraph 10, Point D reads: "Religious associations have the right to collect voluntary donations in houses of worship." Why, then, the distribution of these donations motivated by the humane Christian principles should be assessed as a violation of the law? In this connection it would be appropriate to remember V.D. Bonch-Bruyevich's statement on the matter (Collective Works, Vol. I, pp. 244-245), which stands in apparent contradiction with Point B of Paragraph 11. But we will not bother you with this, believing that V.D. Bonch-Bruyevich's works are perfectly familiar to you.

4. *Paragraph 12 of the "Provisions" reads: "A special permission should be obtained of the*

Executive Committee of the district, or town council of people's deputies to hold a general meeting of believers who have set up the religious association to consider questions referring to the management of the association's activities, the use of the implements of worship, the election of the executive and inspection bodies, as well as other organizational matters."

The "Provisions" divide our Evangelical meetings into general, or member meetings, and meetings of worship. According to Paragraph 23, meetings of worship are held without a special notification of the Executive Committee, whereas general meetings require the said notification. Besides, the executive body of the congregation is to inform the Executive Committee not only of the time of the general meeting, but also of the number of those present and the problems discussed. Here we must not only express our bewilderment, but also point out our great difficulty. We allow anybody to attend our meetings (provided their attendance is effected within the bonds of the law and does not disregard the feelings of the believers). But we cannot allow outsiders to interfere in the inner canonical activity of the church. Considered at our general meetings are problems of education, the conformity of each member's activities with the evangelical truths, questions of family life, standards of assessing amoral actions, etc. Nobody has the right to interfere in this sphere of the life of the church; the same as nobody has the right to interfere in the innermost of the human soul or the convictions of any citizen of our State.

5. *Paragraph 13 refers to the election of the executive body of the congregation, which is entrusted with the corresponding work within the congregation and with the outward representation of the congregation. Paragraph*

14 reads: "The Executive Committee of the District and Town Councils of the People's Deputies has the right to expel certain persons elected to the executive bodies of religious associations."

According to the Gospel, the management of the activities of the church (including outer representation) is effected by the presbyter (Acts 20:17-38; 1 Peter 5:1-5; 1 Timothy 3:1-15). To assist the presbyter in these matters deacons are elected (Acts 6:1-7). It follows from this that the functions mentioned in paragraph 13 are performed in the church by deacons. If we take into consideration the fact that persons of absolute honesty and integrity are elected to conduct this kind of service, the question logically arises: Can there be any cause to prevent these people from fulfilling their legitimate mission? Is it necessary at all to elect an executive body in the church in defiance of the Word of God, which states: "If anybody adds anything to the prophecy of this book, then God shall add unto him the plagues that are written in this book" (Revelation 22:18). For all this, we do understand that to prevent a servant of the church from performing his functions should be permitted on the ground of his moral degradation or some antisocial action (immoral conduct in his family, reprehensible behavior in society, involvement in theft, nationalistic propaganda, etc.).

6. *Paragraph 17 reads: "Ministers of cults, religious preachers and tutors perform their activities within the residential area of the members of a religious congregation in which they serve, as well as within the locality of the house of worship."*

Elementary violation of this paragraph is always considered by the authorities as missionary activity, for which clergymen are called to severe administrative or even criminal account. They may even be dismissed from performing their presbyter functions. Paragraph 17 runs counter to the teaching of Jesus Christ (Matthew 28:19; Romans 1:14-17). All physically sound members of the church must be engaged in active work for the good of society, for the good of the family (incidentally, the families of believers are, as a rule, large), and this means that we intrinsically cannot be involved in missionary activity. Why, then, are such innocent meetings with our co-believers, as for example attending a wedding, a funeral, a party celebrating the birth of a child, or marking one's joining the army, etc., often classified as missionary activity entailing severe administrative punishment?

This paragraph is at serious variance not only with the Gospel, but also with the "Concluding Act" of the Helsinki Conference.

7. Paragraph 11 reads: "Religious associations have no right to organize special worship meetings of children, youths, and women."

—We do not understand the rights and obligations of the religious community as regards the presence of children in a house of worship, as well as the extent of their participation in the life of the church. According to Paragraph 3 of the "Provisions," religious congregations are organized by citizens of 18 years of age and upwards. By the Word of God (Matthew 28:19-20), these citizens must be first educated, brought up, and prepared. How can this be done if church has no actual right to conduct educational work with the rising generation?

How should we understand the expression, "special worship meetings of women?"

The Church, as well as our Socialist State, unreservedly proceeds from the principle of developing the healthy and happy family. This can only be achieved by careful Christian education of both men and women, together or separately, as a result of which there are no shameful cases of divorce in the families of believers. How can this inner church activity be classified as a breach of the law?

Finally, we have very serious difficulty connected with paragraphs 25 and 27. We were more than once subjected to severe penalties by the authorities not only in connection with our visiting seriously sick people or attending weddings, but also from attending the funerals of our dearest relatives and members of their families. Why does Paragraph 25 not provide for the fundamental distinction between the ritual services of the Evangelical Church and the Orthodox Christian Church? It should be remembered that the Evangelical Church is based on the social method of service and management, while the Orthodox Church on the clerical method. All our clergymen are workers, employees and farmers as distinct from the Orthodox and other churches. And this fact causes a number of handicaps for the performance of our service, as regards the present wording of Paragraph 25 and 27.

We have presented a brief enumeration of our difficulties connected with the "Law of Religious Cults" as well as their concise analysis.

How can we characterize our status in the country at the present time?

We clergymen of the Evangelical Church have repeatedly drawn the attention of local, regional, and republic authorities and also of the Commissioners of the Board for Matters of Religion, to the aforesaid difficulties and handicaps. And each time we received almost the same answers: We are not the legislative bodies; the existing laws should be unreservedly fulfilled, and those who break them are to be subjected to severe punishment. And the result of it all was as might be expected: Everywhere we came to be characterized as malicious breakers of the law; public opinion was set against us; our peaceful meetings were dispersed. It was not infrequent, especially in the Ukraine, when two or three members of a family were fined (50 rubles each) for taking part in one meeting of worship, the fine being imposed by the district executive committee of the territory in which the service took place. Then the same case was transferred to the executive committee of the district where the fined people were residing. After that, the case was presented to the places where the fined persons worked for social ostracism, which deprived the "offender" of the year's bonus and month's progressive payment. The conesquence of all this was that the honest worker's pay was reduced to a beggarly 200 to 300 rubles. Fancy that the said worker had given his factory and the State 20 to 30 years of his life in continual labor. Can this be called humane? Judge for yourself.

But money is not our primary concern. The problem is much deeper. After the fines like those described, even at present court proceedings are instituted, and our society loses numerous capable and honest workers. True, someone will cynically say, "Even in a labor camp they will produce a return!" It is common knowledge that we work quite painstakingly in those places, also. But let us pose a moral question, if for a monetary consideration: Of what benefit for the state is the said solution of the religious problem? What will our children say about it? There is nothing new here. Our grandparents remember the pictures of cruel persecution of the Evangelical Church by the Czarist autocracy and the governing Synod: It was like an awful nightmare! There are many painful recollections referring to the subsequent years casually mentioned at the beginning of the letter. We are profoundly grateful to God and to our government for the fact that during more than 20 years now almost no cases have occurred in this country resembling the religious persecution of the past.

Letter to Gorbachev

We are convinced that the state has never lost—and will never lose—anything resulting from the understanding and goodwill existing between the believers and the government. Is it possible that we are standing on the threshold of the renewed bitter experiences of the past? We do not wish to believe it! We are convinced that reason, truth and humane principles will be triumphant!

Our conviction becomes ever more firm due to the fact that the present course of the party and government of this country is aimed at the restoration and complete triumph of Lenin's principles in all the spheres of life. This aim is vividly depicted, dear Mikhail Sergeyevich, in your speech at the March plenary session of the Central Committee of the CPSU in connection with your election to the post of General Secretary of the CPSU. We are convinced that this course will not leave neglected the many thousand believers in our country.

Marking the beginning of a businesslike and active dialogue between the Evangelical Church and the Soviet government, our Ukrainian representative, P.Z. (of the Voronoyev and Schmidt congregations), was sent to the Board for Religious Matters under the Council of Ministers of the USSR, acting on behalf of the Evangelical Church of the USSR. On the first days of April 1985, also on behalf of all the Pentecostal adherents of the USSR, our two representatives, N.M. Kaminsky and N.A. Melnik, were sent to the Board for Religious Matters, and they had a detailed talk with Cmrs. Tarasov and Dostovalov.

On March 30, representatives of the Evangelical Church gathered in the town of Kivertzi, Volyn region, for finally agreeing on all the essential questions that should be presented to the Soviet government for the sake of normalizing the status of our church. But this peaceful conference was rudely dispersed by the militia;

the names of all participants were recorded, and they were taken to the militia station for identification.

Dear Mikhail Sergeyevich, dear members of the Presidium of the Supreme Soviet of the USSR: We draw your special attention to the cited fact. If new strict disciplinary measures are taken against the registered evangelical clergymen, it will clearly show that our government does not want peaceful settlement of the problem of the Evangelical Church, which will make our further dialogue with you without purpose. We ask you urgently to exert your direct influence in the solution of this question. Your humane and correct stand in the situation will serve as an incentive to gain our mutual confidence, whereas callousness and indifference can only lead to the contrary.

If you, our Esteemed Government, heed our call and treat us, as regards the problem in question, in accordance with state wisdom that you have been endowed with, then we, the Evangelical clergymen, ask you to take the first step toward the desired solution of the problem. This step should consist in giving an official instruction throughout the country to permit us to legally conduct our Christian services, together with placing at our disposal the necessary premises (or granting us permission to construct or reconstruct them), based on our teaching of the evangelical Christian faith, which we will present to you in a comprehensive exposition.

We understand this as a temporary measure, valid until the whole problem has been completely resolved on a legislative foundation.

Dear Mikhail Sergeyevich, we do hope that either you personally, or those specially authorized by you, will study this letter of ours carefully and impartially, and we will get clear and rational answer to it.

We tried to word our ideas as concisely as possible, yet the letter has turned out rather long. But even shaped as it is, the letter does not fully express the profoundness of our worries about fate of believers in this country. That is why, taking an opportunity of written talk with you, we express our strongest wish that a meeting be arranged of the representatives of the Christian Evangelical Church from all the republics of the country with the members of the Soviet government. This wish was expressed orally during the meeting of our representatives with the members of the Board for Matters of Religion under the Council of Ministers of the USSR at the beginning of April 1985. It is for the government to determine the time and place of the meeting, as well as the number of our representatives, and inform us about that. Since all the clergymen of our church (except for some pensioners) are hired workers and employees, we are faced with difficulties in arranging their travel to Moscow: They cannot obtain the necessary travel documents allowing them to be excused from work. So we would like to know whether the meeting in question could be scheduled for Saturday or Sunday morning. The final decision rests with the government.

May the loving God bless you all, our Esteemed Government. We constantly pray for you. May God give you clear state wisdom necessary for achieving well-being of all the people of this country, both believers and non-believers, for contributing to the peace and prosperity of all the people inhabiting our planet.

    Sincerely respecting you,
    Servants of the Evangelical Church

Addendum to the letter resent to Mr. Gorbachev in 1986:

This [above] is the letter sent in May, 1985 to the Central Committee of the CPSU, the Board for Matters of Religion, the First Vice-Chairman of the Presidium of the Supreme Soviet of the USSR.

The believers throughout all the regions of the country carefully followed the further actions of the government and local administrations. Representatives of the Church were received in the Board for Matters of Religion; Cmrs. Tarasov and Kharchev had a personal talk with them. They were assured that there would be "warming" for believers, and even the dates were given when the change in the "Provision for Religious Cults" would be published. It was suggested that decisions referring to these problems be published in the journal, "The Human and the Law."

But alas! . . The second year is expiring without any positive answer to the questions raised.

The letter written by the believers of Schmidt persuasion was sent from Moscow to city and district committees of people's deputies. Further on, following the proper procedure, it got to the Inspectors of Religious Cults. The inspectors received the clergymen for talks.

In this "Appeal" addresses were given for the prospect that the letter had been received and was being considered. To one of the said addresses a notification did come, and it stated, "Your letter is sent to the Office of Public Prosecutor." So the "appeal" was answered by the arrest of the bishop, Vasily Mikhailovich Boyechko, inhabitant of the city of Lvov, of the Ukrainian SSR. The arrest was carried out on September 3, 1985, while V.M. Boyechko was conducting service.

Vasily Boyechko was born in 1937; he is married, has six children. He was sentenced to three years' imprisonment according to Articles 187-1 and 187-3 of the criminal law. He is serving the sentence in the camp of General Regime VP315-50, the settlement of Zaklad, Nikolayev District, Lvov Region.

We do not propose to describe the personality of V. Boyechko, but from the words of the forced witnesses to his case, it follows that there is nothing but positive traits to characterize him as a human being. His main alleged "crimes" consisted in his taking part in certain services and being one of those who had signed the "Appeal."

At the checkpoint of the factory in which Boyechko worked, the KGB agents declared openly that he was being convicted at court for his refusal to get registered. The believers in the Soviet Union conducting services illegally are not against registration, but they are against those points in the regulations that that run counter to the common sense inherent in evangelical teaching. Are pressures like that on the part of the local authorities to continue for long?

Dear Mikhail Sergeyevich, we have no doubt that the letter addressed to you personally has not been carefully read and studied, otherwise there would not have been a trial of V. Boyechko. It should be taken into account that the state of health of this breadwinner for six children is quite unsatisfactory.

Dear Mikhail Sergeyevich, this second letter is addressed to you by Pentecostal adherents attending services in unregistered churches.

At present, broad public circles, as well as masses of working people in general, accept with satisfaction the course of the Party and government for the *perestroika*—reconstruction of all the spheres of human life and activity. The fundamental trend of the acting government is: liberal policy, democracy, publicity, freedom of speech, freedom of conscience. For the first time in Soviet history the people witness real steps of the powers that be toward the aspirations of humankind.

This may be seen in the fact that many of the differently minded persons have been set at liberty.

We wish to believe that the government will continue considering the problem of releasing the prisoners of conscience from jails and camps. If you, Mikhail Sergeyevich, and the Central Committee of the CPSU, are going to meet the needs of the believers in the Soviet Union, we ask you urgently to carefully consider the fate of our brother prisoners and set them at liberty, to analyze the "Provisions for Religious Cults" using the Word of God and being aware of the spiritual needs of those devoted to God.

The representatives of the Evangelical Church express a wish to meet those in positions of authority, and you personally, Mikhail Sergeyevich, in connection with the problem of believers in the USSR. To achieve this we suggest (do not judge us by preconception) that during a month's time after your receiving the "Appeal," we get the corresponding satisfactory answers to the questions raised.

One of them should consist in notifying us (to the given address) that the "Appeal" has been received and the question is being settled on positive lines.

Another of them concerns the release of prisoners of conscience sentenced on religious grounds:

Vasily Boyechko,
Afanasy Melnik,
Evgeny Gul,
Ivan Fedorchuk,
Vladimir Loboda,

as well as the believers of the village of Chuguyevka (Primorsk Area), and others.

Finally, we are not aware of what you have in mind, Mikhail Sergeyevich, but we cherish a hope that the questions relating to the fate of many thousands of believers in the Soviet Union will be settled positively.

It is worth while to listen to the voice of the Church. For it is only God Almighty acting through His Church on the earth that can save humankind from the pending catastrophe of annihilation, adequately solve the problems of peace, social justice, equality and fraternity of all the people of the world. At the present moment, which is exceptionally perilous, and wanting responsible decisions, the church is in a position to say its Word before God, who hears its prayer and will give the world prosperity and peace.

The address is given below for the Central Committee of the CPSU to send us the requested answer.

About Christian Aid

Christian Aid is a faith-based mission board that sends and supports thousands of missionaries by assisting hundreds of evangelical mission groups based in lands of poverty and persecution.

Most of these ministries were pioneered by men chosen of God from among the nations of the two-thirds world whom God anointed to take the gospel to their own people. A few are offshoots of ministries started by traditional missionaries of previous generations.

Christian Aid assists only those ministries that are Biblical in doctrine, evangelistic in practice and show financial integrity and accountability. Financial help is sent to the headquarters of each mission organization where national leaders direct their mission's goals and ministries and apportion support to each missionary. All such ministries are strongly supported by believers in their own lands.

Bob Finley went as a missionary to China in 1948. After the Communists took over in 1949, he went on to preach to large crowds in Taiwan, Korea and Japan. He returned to the U.S. in 1953 and began International Students, Inc. and Overseas Students Mission in Canada to bring foreign students to Christ and send them back as missionaries to their own people. In 1970 the AID (Assisting Indigenous Developments) division separated from ISI as Christian Aid Mission to focus on equipping and supporting indigenous missionaries on the field. OSM in Canada later changed its name to Christian Aid, also.

Today these combined organizations assist over 700 mission boards of the two-thirds world that have more than 90,000 missionaries on the field. Gifts from believers in North America are used to train and support missionaries, conduct evangelistic campaigns, translate and print the Scriptures, produce Christian literature, disciple new believers, and plant churches. Assisted ministries also help widows and orphans, care for the elderly, aid lepers, and bring relief to victims of natural and manmade disasters. At home contributions also support a skilled missionary staff needed to communicate with thousands of mission groups overseas, assist foreign visitors, produce and send out brochures, newsletters, prayer bulletins, and *Christian Mission* magazine, as well as receipt contributions, send help to overseas groups, and maintain strict financial records.

Contributions to Christian Aid help do all these things, although gifts can be designated for specific ministries such as those described in this book. Gifts may be made via credit card on line or by telephone, or checks may be sent by mail. All gifts are tax deductible.

U.S.A.
Christian Aid
P.O. Box 9037
Charlottesville, VA 22906
Phone 1-800-977-5650
www.christianaid.org
info@christianaid.org

Canada
Christian Aid
201 Stanton Street
Fort Erie, ON L2A 3N8
Phone 1-800-871-0882
www.christianaid.ca
friends@christianaid.ca